AN INTERNET FOR THE PEOPLE

Princeton Studies in Culture and Technology
Tom Boellstorff and Bill Maurer, Series Editors

This series presents innovative work that extends classic ethnographic methods and questions into areas of pressing interest in technology and economics. It explores the varied ways new technologies combine with older technologies and cultural understandings to shape novel forms of subjectivity, embodiment, knowledge, place, and community. By doing so, the series demonstrates the relevance of anthropological inquiry to emerging forms of digital culture in the broadest sense.

An Internet for the People: The Politics and Promise of craigslist by Jessa Lingel

Hacking Diversity: The Politics of Inclusion in Open Technology Cultures by Christina Dunbar-Hester

Hydropolitics: The Itaipú Dam, Sovereignty, and the Engineering of Modern South America by Christine Folch

The Future of Immortality: Remaking Life and Death in Contemporary Russia by Anya Bernstein

Chasing Innovation: Making Entrepreneurial Citizens in Modern India by Lilly Irani

Watch Me Play: Twitch and the Rise of Game Live Streaming by T. L. Taylor

Biomedical Odysseys: Fetal Cell Experiments from Cyberspace to China by Priscilla Song

Disruptive Fixation: School Reform and the Pitfalls of Techno-Idealism by Christo Sims

Everyday Sectarianism in Urban Lebanon: Infrastructures, Public Services, and Power by Joanne Randa Nucho

Democracy's Infrastructure: Techno-Politics and Protest after Apartheid by Antina von Schnitzler

Digital Keywords: A Vocabulary of Information Society and Culture edited by Benjamin Peters

Sounding the Limits of Life: Essays in the Anthropology of Biology and Beyond by Stefan Helmreich with contributions from Sophia Roosth and Michele Friedner

An Internet for the People

The Politics and Promise of craigslist

Jessa Lingel

PRINCETON UNIVERSITY PRESS

PRINCETON AND OXFORD

Copyright © 2020 by Princeton University Press

Published by Princeton University Press
41 William Street, Princeton, New Jersey 08540
6 Oxford Street, Woodstock, Oxfordshire OX20 1TR

press.princeton.edu

All Rights Reserved

ISBN 978-0-691-18890-4
ISBN (e-book) 978-0-691-19988-7

British Library Cataloging-in-Publication Data is available

Editorial: Fred Appel and Jenny Tan
Production Editorial: Jenny Wolkowicki
Jacket design: Layla Mac Rory
Production: Erin Suydam
Publicity: Kate Hensley and Kathryn Stevens
Copyeditor: Maia Vaswani

This book has been composed in Adobe Text Pro and Gotham

Printed on acid-free paper. ∞

Printed in the United States of America

10 9 8 7 6 5 4 3 2 1

CONTENTS

ACKNOWLEDGMENTS

Writing this book was a lot of fun but also a lot of work. Luckily there's no support system like a Lingel support system. For my parents, my siblings, and their partners, the berms and beams of my life, I couldn't be more grateful.

Parts of chapter 7 and the conclusion were published in a 2018 article in *Internet Histories* and parts of the introduction and conclusion were published in a 2019 article in *Surveillance and Society* (Lingel, 2018, 2019).

Like all qualitative work, this project has depended on the kindness of participants. Interviews are a gift of time, energy, and intimacy, and I am always humbled by and profoundly thankful for the openness and generosity of the people who agree to share their experiences with me.

Much of the early work on this project was conducted while I was a digital studies fellow at the Library of Congress' Kluge Center. I am particularly grateful to Travis Hensley, Chelsea Stiebler, Dan Turello, and Ted Widemer for their support and friendship during my nine months in Washington, DC.

I've now been at Penn for four years, a period in which it has become an intellectual home. Annenberg's IT staff, particularly Rich Cardona, John Garber, and Vladimir Gordynskiy, provided crucial help when I needed to scrape Reddit and craigslist's blog. I'm indebted to Jonathan Pace and Matt O'Donnell for analysis of the craigslist help forum, and to Sharon Black for pulling together sources on craigslist in the news. A number of Annenberg graduate students provided help for this project, including Zane Cooper, Kelly Diaz, Betty Ferrari, Eric Forbush, Staci Jones, Muira McCammon, and Chloé Nurik. Aaron Shapiro, Julia Ticona, and Joe Turow read chapters and provided helpful feedback. In less direct but still crucial ways, my work at Annenberg has been supported by Kelly Fernandez, Sandra Gonzalez-Bailon, Marwan Kraidy, Sharrona Pearl, Victor Pickard, Monroe Price, Guobin Yang, and Barbie Zelizer. Michael Delli Carpini and John Jackson have been incredibly supportive as deans, and I consider myself very lucky to have spent my time at Annenberg under their leadership. Elsewhere at Penn, Ezekiel Dixon-Roman, Anne Esacove, Pilar Gonalons-Pons, and Whittney Trettien have been comrades and cheerleaders as this book lumbered toward the finish line. I'm also grateful to the Penn GSE Writing retreat, where I toiled away in very amiable company on this manuscript during the summer of 2018.

Outside of Penn, Jen Ayres collaborated with me on recruiting and interviewing participants for chapter 5, and has been a wonderful Sherpa in figuring out how secondary markets work. Megan Finn and Tarleton Gillespie read chapters and their feedback made my work much better. Devon Powers read the whole manuscript and the book is better for it. Early conversations with Finn Brunton were crucial for thinking that this project might actually be worth doing. danah boyd and Mor Naaman have continued to provide mentorship, advice, and encouragement, way after the formal title of "advisor" had seemingly expired. I'm grateful to Ben Merriman, Germaine Haleguoa, Warren Allen, and Jack Gieseking for their lifelines of pre-tenure support. Michelle Mariano, Emma Johnson, and Cathy Hannabach provided much-needed editing. At Princeton, Fred Appel was an enthusiastic supporter before this book had a chapter (or even a proposal) and his encouragement has been much appreciated. I'm also grateful to the anonymous reviewers for their feedback on this manuscript.

Finally, this project grew out of a genuine affection for craigslist, and I'm grateful to all of the people who have sold me bikes and helmets, coffee tables and coffeemakers, patio furniture and artificial Christmas trees over the years. Thanks to the roommates, landlords, and bosses who wrote and answered ads that led to jobs and places to live. My house, my CV, and my early twenties would all have been a lot duller without you.

Introduction

THE POLITICS AND PROMISE
OF CRAIGSLIST

You can get anything on craigslist. Right now, you can buy a Dolly Parton pinball machine for $750 in San Diego, and in Bend, Oregon, a custom *Star Wars* snowmobile is up for sale or barter. In Philadelphia, someone is selling forty life-size wax figures in Amish attire, ideally as a set. A burgundy Fitbit was reported lost in San Francisco, five days before a Fitbit charger was posted as found, also in San Francisco. You can find things on craigslist, but you can also find jobs and people to hire. In Philadelphia a county library is looking for someone to drive the bookmobile, and in Los Angeles an actor is offering lessons in impersonating Tom Cruise. Used iPhone? A ride to Baltimore? A one-bedroom apartment in Cincinnati? You can find it on craigslist.

In more than seven hundred cities around the globe, thousands of posts are uploaded to craigslist every day.[1] The site is both a map and a time capsule, a snapshot of the informal marketplace and a mixtape of local opinions. Yet craigslist is more than a window to the world's ephemera—this book argues that when it comes to practicing Web 1.0 values of access and democracy, craigslist is an increasingly lonely outpost in a hypercorporate web. With its stripped-down functionality and minimalist design, craigslist speaks to an older ethos of online life that contrasts sharply with the values of today's mainstream internet. In its rejection of venture capitalists, paid advertising, and rapid design changes, craigslist is the internet, ungentrified.

When I call the contemporary internet *gentrified,* I mean the ways that some forms of online behavior have become ingrained as the "right" way to use the web, while other forms of behavior are labeled "backward" or "out of date." The early web was characterized by excitement at connecting with strangers from across the world and trial-and-error experimentation with online personas. As more people came online and new platforms sprouted to meet their needs, norms of use developed and stabilized, with older practices sometimes falling out of favor. The web we have now is dominated by self-promotion, long-winded legal warnings, and sleek design aesthetics that require constant upgrades. Since the transition from Web 1.0 to 2.0, we've moved from an internet of messy serendipity to one of slick commercialism.

I'm painting in broad strokes here—of course there was self-promotion in the early web, and of course DIY hacking is still an important part of online life. While much of the web has come to feel developed, safe, and predictable, there's still a lot of messiness and experimentation to be found. But there's no denying the fact that a very small number of corporations control what online life looks and feels like for a huge number of people. Google answers our questions about pop culture and local news, while Google Maps affects our perceptions of space and landmarks. When Facebook tweaks its News Feed, it alters what we know about current events, our neighborhoods, and our friends and family. Amazon redefines what's normal in the marketplace, shaping our expectations through product reviews and by predicting our next purchases. These companies have normalized some uses of the web over others, and in the process have altered what we think everyday life on the web should look and feel like. Craigslist represents a different kind of everyday online life, one characterized by aesthetic minimalism, anonymity, and serendipity. The platform is a holdout in its appearance, its business model, and its policies. It is a corner of the web that's light on design changes, heavy on user responsibility, and possibly on the brink of obsolescence.

Most people think of craigslist as a simple-looking site with a few basic functions, a way to sell a used couch or find a local handyman. But in terms of the platform's value to digital culture, craigslist is both popular and multifaceted. Craigslist is the nineteenth most visited website in the United States, and hosts tens of thousands of exchanges every day (Alexa, n.d.). Besides for-sale, job, real-estate, and personal ads, craigslist hosts a range of discussion boards, for everything from pets and haiku to web development and "Rants & Raves," a discussion board where users can post random thoughts and musings, like a less-moderated version of Reddit or 4chan. Until March 2018, the site hosted an active personals section, which included subcategories for everything from casual sex to strictly platonic relationships. A "Community" section contains sections for rideshares, adopting pets, and local news, plus "Missed Connections," where people can post ads that attempt to contact someone from a fleeting encounter— a cute girl on the subway, a handsome bartender or barista in the neighborhood. Craigslist is at once a marketplace, a job hub, and a message board.

This book tells a history of digital culture through the lens of craigslist. While a number of sites could offer a starting point to charting how internet norms have changed over the past few decades, I've picked craigslist for a couple of key reasons. The first has to do with its unusual approach to being a tech company. Craigslist has always been on the small side, with fewer than fifty full-time employees. The current CEO, Jim Buckmaster, has been at the helm since 2000, and as he notes on the company's "About" page, he is very likely "the only CEO ever described by the business press as anti-establishment, a communist, and a socialistic anarchist" (craigslist n.d.[c]). Although craigslist is headquartered in the preeminent tech hub of San Francisco, the company's financial model and design values make it feel more like an outsider—or, more appropriately, a throwback. For people who see mainstream tech companies as overly beholden to profit and shareholders, often at the expense of everyday users, craigslist presents a fascinating countercase.

A second reason for studying craigslist is its longevity. Craigslist started out in 1995 as an e-mail list and grew into a website the following year. Almost as soon as internet access was widely available, craigslist was there, ready to help people search and find, buy and sell. For more than two decades, the platform has weathered the internet's boom-and-bust cycle, while countless peers and competitors have come and gone. Craigslist isn't just old, it's also incredibly stable—the site looks more or less the same today as it did in the late 1990s (see figures I.1, I.2, and I.3). It isn't quite accurate to say that the platform hasn't changed at all: categories for ads have come and gone, while features like uploading photos and integrating Google Maps have been added. But on the whole, craigslist has proven profoundly stable. From both a historian's view and an industry view, craigslist is an outlier, giving us a fixed point for considering the current online norm of constant flux and change.

You might think that craigslist's stability would make it feel safe or comforting to use. Instead, craigslist often summons a sense of fear or anxiety. Fear dominates many people's first impressions of craigslist, mostly in the form of worrying about scams and fraud. It wasn't always this way. In the

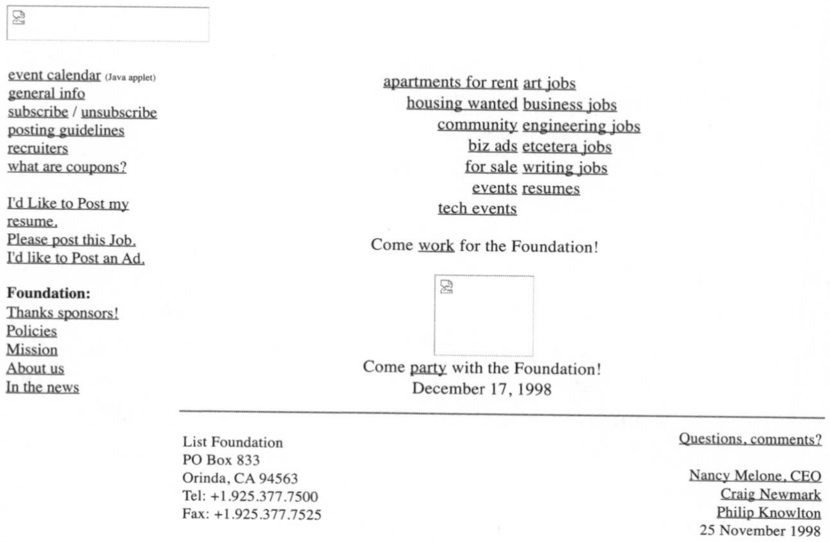

event calendar (Java applet)
general info
subscribe / unsubscribe
posting guidelines
recruiters
what are coupons?

I'd Like to Post my
resume.
Please post this Job.
I'd like to Post an Ad.

Foundation:
Thanks sponsors!
Policies
Mission
About us
In the news

apartments for rent art jobs
housing wanted business jobs
community engineering jobs
biz ads etcetera jobs
for sale writing jobs
events resumes
tech events

Come work for the Foundation!

Come party with the Foundation!
December 17, 1998

List Foundation
PO Box 833
Orinda, CA 94563
Tel: +1.925.377.7500
Fax: +1.925.377.7525

Questions, comments?

Nancy Melone, CEO
Craig Newmark
Philip Knowlton
25 November 1998

FIGURE I.1. This screenshot from December 2, 1998, is the earliest screen capture available from the Internet Archive's Way Back Machine.

early days, before Google and Facebook, craigslist generated a lot of hype and enthusiasm. Here was a classified-ad site that helped people find local information and job opportunities, but also connected strangers with similar interests. As more and more people got online, craigslist helped them to get ordinary things done, from buying and selling used goods to dating to learning about one's neighborhood—but as users became more savvy and sophisticated, so did scammers, crooks, and thieves.

Online platforms have always had to contend with rule breaking. The same tools that could be used to communicate for free could also be used for scams and spam (see Brunton 2012). Platforms originally designed to build a sense of community and play also had to contend with unexpected forms of violence and harassment (Dibbell 1999). On craigslist, harassment and spam are real problems, compounded by a small number of highly publicized violent crimes. These incidents represent a tiny fraction of craigslist interactions, while the overwhelming majority go smoothly. Nevertheless, the actual number of violent crimes on craigslist matter less than perceptions that the site is overrun with bad actors. Thinking about craigslist's transformation from the first stop for online exchange to a punchline for jokes about online sleaze opens up questions of what it means to stigmatize certain platforms and the people who use them. What do our fears and judgments say about our relationship to the internet, about our expectations for safe behaviors?

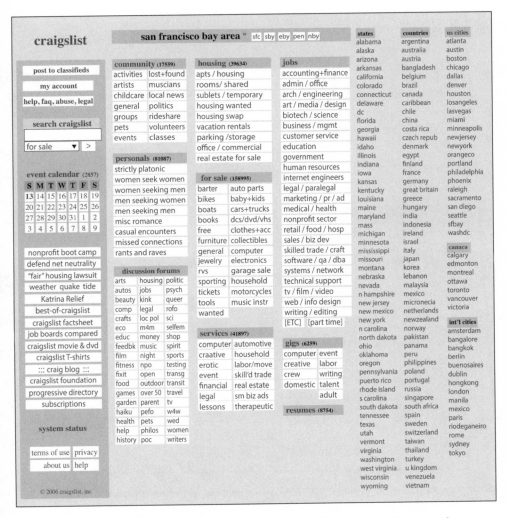

FIGURE I.2. Image from June 30, 2006. By 2006, the site design had expanded without significantly altering its aesthetics, a difference of degree rather than kind.

The many general-interest books about craigslist fall into two broad categories: how to make money, and stories about sex and murder. The first is a collection of entrepreneurial self-help books with tips and tricks for making a profit selling used goods, including advice on how to describe items, when to post, and selling etiquette. The second cluster of books includes sensationalized accounts of real-life crimes connected to the platform, as well as tell-all tales—autobiographical and fictional—of sexual and romantic encounters made via the site's personals section. The two categories make sense as reflections on our assumptions and apprehensions about the internet: an

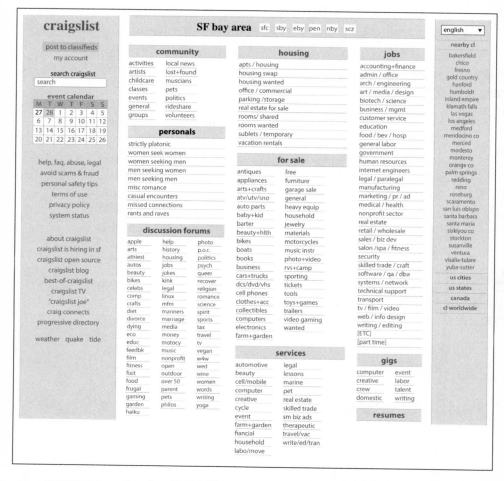

FIGURE I.3. Image from June 15, 2017. Eleven years later, the site had barely changed—in fact becoming more simplified by removing the count of posts per category.

only half-glib assessment might say that the majority of internet use is about either making money or watching porn. Moral panics about the internet tend to concentrate on either fraud or sexual predation—conjuring images of bogeymen roaming the web, trying to swindle people out of money or into sex (see Marwick 2008).

Fears about a technology can paradoxically illuminate our hopes. When it comes to the internet, anxieties about fraud and predation contrast sharply with the initial hype of diversity and tolerance. Early narratives about the internet and techno-optimism have been critiqued by scholars like Wendy Chun (2008) and Megan Sapnar-Ankerson (Ankerson 2018;

Sapnar-Ankerson 2010). People who saw the internet as a powerful tool for social change and education were relying on the problematic assumption that access to technology could level out differences of class and privilege, despite radical differences in geography and background (Burrell 2012; Warschauer and Ames 2010). But access to technology can only mitigate so much when it comes to significant differences in wealth and education. Moreover, while projects like Wikipedia and Linux are very much in line with early web values of collaboration and openness, not everyone is content to cooperate without compensation. Nevertheless, initial aspirations for a technology often linger, sometimes long after early proponents have changed their views. When people describe their anxieties about using craigslist, I hear the echoes of an earlier hope—for an internet that could bring people together to share ideas, solve problems, and build community.

In thinking about how digital culture has (and, in some ways, has not) changed since craigslist first burst onto the scene, a number of elements have to be brought into view, including the social, political, and technological— that is, the *publics* that form online, the *politics* that shape our interactions, and the *platforms* that host our activities and conversations.

"Publics" has become a popular term to refer to groups of people who come together online for a shared activity, whether that means gaming, socializing, or commenting on the news (see Langlois et al. 2009; Papacharissi 2002, 2015; Varnelis 2012). The term has less baggage than the word *community* and feels more socially oriented than *network*, which has more technical connotations. For Michael Warner (2002), publics form around texts, and specifically around the practices of shared interpretation. Texts play a key role in publics—as well as counterpublics, meaning groups that are in some way marginal or subversive—because they allow for the creation of shared terms, concepts, and meetings. Thinking about craigslist in terms of publics allows us to sidestep romantic connotations of community and to avoid overemphasizing the site's technical components, looking instead at ordinary practices and politics of use.

In this book, I almost always use *politics* in the lowercase sense, as opposed to the Politics of federal or international elections, laws, and agreements. Small-*p* politics are about the daily interactions that make school, work, and neighborhood life possible—decisions about including not just dead white guys in high-school English classes, employer policies on maternity and paternity leave, and judgment calls about when and how to call the police if a crime takes place in your neighborhood. Whether or not we consider these acts to be political, they have important consequences for how we think of and treat one another in everyday life, and, moreover, can accumulate into much bigger norms and paradigms of how people are valued. Put another way, small-p politics echo the 1960s slogan, "The personal is political." An overarching goal of this book is to think about the changing norms of the web by looking at policies, practices, and perceptions as political in important (but small-p) ways.

The notion of online life as political goes back long before the appearance of sites like Facebook and Twitter. In his ethnographic account of early 1990s chat rooms (called MUDs, or multiuser dungeons), Julian Dibbell (1999) described the different political philosophies that emerged as controversies arose around the disruptive behavior of bad actors. In Dibbell's account, most people agreed that some punishment was needed, but deciding the process for administering it was much less clear. Some favored an anarchist ethic of total nonintervention from programmers (dubbed "wizards" in the parlance of the time), leaving everyday users to manage themselves. Others took a more libertarian view of minimal intervention, where wizards should be involved only in extreme cases. And some favored democratic processes of decision-making and consensus, with elected representatives to step in when tensions arose. People used words like *anarchism* and *democracy* to represent their values, underscoring both how expressly political these issues were at the time, and how early on these discussions were being had in the history of the internet. The conversations and debates Dibbell described are alive and well in the present, as evidenced in everything from shifting policies on moderating content (Crawford and Gillespie 2016) to controversies like Gamergate, when women game designers and journalists were harassed and threatened across multiple platforms and over months or even years (Schulten 2014).

Platform is an umbrella term for describing the many tech enterprises that host online conversations and connections, including social media companies. The word also has nontechnological connotations, particularly in the realm of politics, where it is used to describe politicians' ideological foundations (Gillespie 2010). Interestingly, the implication in the social-media arena is the opposite—referring to a site as a platform suggests that it's just a neutral stage where people come to perform, share, and voice opinions (Gillespie 2018a). For social-media companies, the term is appealing because it allows them to portray their relationship to content as agnostic, or not ideologically invested in or responsible for the views of any individual user. Alongside the concept of Web 2.0, the term "platform" became popular in the early 2000s as part of Silicon Valley's efforts to rebrand the internet after the dot-com crash; the new vocabulary helped create some rhetorical distance from the slew of failed 1990s web companies. On the technical side, websites were becoming increasingly complex and bundled together as social-network sites, and at the same time, users were increasingly publishing and mashing up content rather than simply reading it (see Helmond 2015; Jenkins 2006; Marwick 2015). Thinking of social-network sites as platforms jived with this shift from read-only to read-and-write functionality.

A platform binds a wide set of actors together: tech companies, politicians, law enforcement, and everyday people, which includes good actors and bad, "n00bs" (newbies) and experts, dupes and cons. As an object to study, a platform can be useful because it provides a broader context for reflection, a way of scaling up and down a sociopolitical-technical chain of stakeholders. In this book, I cover a range of actors with a stake in craigslist's operations, from its founder and early employees to its everyday users and scammers, from lawyers and regulators to competitors and detractors. Beyond painting a well-rounded portrait of craigslist, my goal in raising these different perspectives is to set up a more robust discussion of the changing norms of online publics and platform politics. The various tensions and tactics that have taken shape on craigslist can point us to some key debates about the web as a whole.

In the course of everyday life online, we typically encounter many publics across many platforms, each with different political norms for how we interact and get things done. A key argument of this book is that as the web has stabilized, platforms have become more commercial and less democratic. It may be that more people have access to the internet now, but modes of surveillance have become more sophisticated and less visible. Despite powerful counterexamples like Wikipedia and Linux, it's become the norm to assume that tech initiatives must be oriented toward profit. People are encouraged to post content, but they don't retain the rights to that content once it has been shared, and platforms can sell user data to third parties, often in ways that users hadn't imagined (or understood from dense legal agreements masquerading as terms of service). As the internet has gentrified, sites like craigslist start to feel not just outdated but dangerous and sleazy. To build my critique of the gentrified internet, I'll take us on a tour of craigslist, stopping to look at the institutions it has disrupted and the legal precedents it has set, as well as its buyers and sellers, devotees and pranksters, and the competitors that tend to have more features, slicker designs, and more corporate orientations.

Studying craigslist: Notes on Methods

There are a number of ways to tell a story about a platform like craigslist. I could give a purely historical account of when and how craigslist developed over time. I could take a user-experience (UX) approach, evaluating its aesthetics or usability. A social-affordances approach would consider how the platform's policies encourage some behaviors and practices over others. I have opted for an approach that includes all three: a discussion of craigslist's historical and legal context, user accounts of everyday successes and failures, and thinking about craigslist's design and policies.

This book relies heavily on interviews. In addition to interviewing the site's founder, Craig Newmark, I have spoken with employees from craigslist's early days and key players in the Bay Area tech scene of the 1990s. These viewpoints help us understand the initial vision of craigslist, as well as the wider tech industry that shaped the company's goals and assumptions. I have also interviewed journalists, legal experts, and security specialists for perspectives on craigslist's role in shaping certain legal precedents around platform responsibility and data ownership. Craigslist runs a public-facing blog that dates to 2005, mostly penned by current CEO Jim Buckmaster, which I analyzed for information about how the company sees itself and its responsibilities.

These sources are all centered on insiders, people who have built craigslist as a platform and have a depth of knowledge about how the site works from the inside out. But in order to understand craigslist as a platform, it's also crucial to gather accounts from ordinary users. With my collaborator Jen Ayres, I interviewed people who buy and sell used goods on craigslist, as well as competing services like Free Your Stuff, eBay, and TaskRabbit. I have also conducted interviews with people who look for work on craigslist, using the platform to find jobs and gigs. A third set of interviews focused on craigslist personals and people who have gone online to find friends, hookups and long-term partners. In addition to interviews, I conducted a small ($n = 102$) online survey to gather descriptive statistics on craigslist, which helped me understand the most common uses of (and complaints about) the platform. Two other data sources of user experience are the craigslist help forum, which I analyzed for references to cons and fraud, and a data scrape of a Reddit thread devoted to craigslist. These different entry points provide a rich set of narratives about craigslist—its design and legal history, norms of use, and moments of failure. With this multilayered approach, I show the breadth of interactions that take shape on craigslist, and also how the policies and politics around those interactions reflect an earlier ethos of the internet, a set of politics that contrasts with the contemporary paradigm of the web as increasingly closed off, homogeneous, and commercialized. Additional notes on interviews, data collection, and analysis are available in the methods appendix.

Outline

This book is divided into two parts: the first provides historical lenses for understanding craigslist, and the second dives into how people use craigslist in everyday life. In other words, the first part of the book gives critical information on *what craigslist is*—technically, historically, and legally—and the second part looks at *how craigslist is used*, by good actors as well as bad.

In chapter 1, I describe craigslist's transformation from an e-mail list to a massively popular online marketplace. I start with the role of the San Francisco Bay Area in the development of craigslist's purpose and ideology. During this early phase of the tech industry, democratic values of openness and access held sway, values that have shaped craigslist's look and feel ever since. Using interviews and textual analysis of craigslist's public-facing blog, I describe the site's basic features and rules, as well as the company's values and policies. My goal is to explain how the San Francisco tech scene shaped craigslist's ideas about online publics and politics.

How do online classified ads fit into the larger history of people and media? The limited body of research within media studies on classified ads (e.g., Bader 2005; Cocks 2009) hasn't been connected to online platforms, even though the web has become far more popular than print as a way to post ads. Meanwhile, craigslist has been blamed for destabilizing newspapers' advertising models, with heavy costs for local papers (e.g., Blodget 2008a; Reinan 2014; Weiss 2013). In chapter 2, I trace a media history of craigslist by examining the development of classified and personal ads through the arrival of the digital age. Craigslist has played a key role in the struggle of legacy media like newspapers to stay afloat, disrupting what had previously been an easily overlooked but crucially reliable source of funding.

Although often overlooked as a serious tech-industry player, craigslist has helped establish some crucial legal precedents with wide-sweeping implications. In chapter 3, I describe two key strands of legal arguments that craigslist has repeatedly—and, for the most part, successfully—made: first, that websites cannot be held responsible for the behavior or activities of its users, and second, that a platform's data should be protected from third parties, particularly tech companies looking to make new products. Craigslist's legal battles present a complicated picture of its politics. On the one hand, the company has shown a commitment to freedom of expression and user agency. On the other, craigslist has quashed experimentation and creativity when it comes to other parties trying to use its data, even for projects that do not compete commercially with the platform. These legal battles show what happens when craigslist's politics run up against legal complaints, exposing the platform's view of responsibility, or what it owes to its users.

The second part of this book shifts from what craigslist is to how it is used by everyday people. Many different kinds of interactions take place on craigslist every day, from neighborhood gossip and soapbox rants to buying and selling goods to looking for jobs and employees. The chapters in this part each focus on a different set of tasks, relationships, and connections that unfold on craigslist every day. Craigslist's platform politics manifest in top-down decision-making about design and policy, but also in the norms that take shape as people bring craigslist into their everyday lives.

For most people, craigslist is mostly a marketplace. In chapter 4, I focus on craigslist's role as a secondary marketplace for used goods, meaning a market that operates outside of formal businesses and vendors. Drawing on interviews with users, I describe motivations for using craigslist to buy and sell used goods. These reasons range from community building and limiting waste to economizing and entrepreneurialism. Interviews also revealed different ideas of value that emerge in secondary markets, meaning both the monetary value that has to be decided on when there is no vendor acting as a middleman, and the social value attached to pre-owned goods. The second half of this chapter looks at what I call the "mash-up catalogs" of craigslist, meaning the digital accounts dedicated to archiving craigslist exchanges. Having gathered over one hundred accounts from Tumblr, YouTube, Twitter, and Facebook, I analyze these efforts to document craigslist as an entry point for theorizing the social lives of craigslist's things. The politics of buying and selling incorporate a range of economic, environmental, and social motivations, with negotiations of value that can alternately re-create and critique mainstream markets.

In chapter 5, I look at the hustle to find work on craigslist. Using interviews with craigslist users recruited through the site's gigs section, I put craigslist job searching in the context of shifting norms around work, like the reliance on digital tools to find employment, and moving away from long-term careers toward a string of short-term gigs. Understanding craigslist's jobs and gigs also points us to a discussion of class. Many participants saw craigslist as part of the "poor people's internet," and described a form of stigma around the jobs found on the site. While early narratives around the internet assumed that access to digital media could overcome class divides, the class bias associated with craigslist's gigs shows how these assumptions fall flat.

If talking about work and employment opens up class politics, talking about personal ads opens up questions of sexual politics and the stigma around online dating generally and craigslist specifically. Craigslist shut down its personals section in March 2018, following the passage of the Allow States and Victims to Fight Online Sex Trafficking Act (FOSTA), a bill that holds platforms responsible for crimes involving human traffickers. FOSTA is just the most recent in a long series of laws around acceptable online behavior. Human relationships have always provoked rules and norms, which are sharpened and crystallized in the design and policies of online platforms like craigslist. Drawing on interviews and an analysis of a Reddit forum dedicated to craigslist, in chapter 6 I look at what made craigslist personals distinctive from other online dating platforms, focusing on shifting norms around anonymity and a persistent social stigma.

Chapter 7 examines the problems that are created and solved as people connect with, sell to, exploit, and protect one another on craigslist. I draw on interviews with craigslist users and a scrape of craigslist's help forum to analyze the ways that people negotiate violations of platform policies. For the most part craigslist transactions go smoothly, but moments of success and failure are important to understanding the politics of everyday online life. When things go right, it's because formal and tacit policies are in place, and because a steady stream of users are working anonymously and without pay to enforce rules and norms. When things go wrong, however, we see the limits of policies around community moderation. Listening to interviews and reading through the craigslist help forum has allowed me to make sense of how users connect through and negotiate craigslist's policies around community moderation and flagging. In particular, I focus on craigslist's commitment to user anonymity, which can alternately be seen as a tool for privacy or a threatening way of being online.

Throughout *An Internet for the People*, I point out the different politics that surface in everyday online encounters. In a moment where online platforms are being questioned for their ability to support or threaten the quality of political life (Kreiss 2016; Persily 2017), it's worth taking a broad view of how democracy works online. In the concluding chapter, I describe how craigslist lives up to the democratic possibilities of the web, how it falls short, and how the site offers important lessons for holding on to an open, accessible, serendipitously messy internet.

There are two main areas of craigslist that I have left out of this book: housing and discussion forums. Beyond the fact that no research project can cover a platform completely, these sections are missing from this book for different reasons. In terms of housing, many of the people I interviewed about used goods, work, and dating had also used craigslist to find apartments and roommates. But none of these conversations about housing turned up the ideological tensions attached to buying and selling used goods, the class distinctions about work, or the character judgments about personals. Arguably, my framework of a gentrifying internet makes the omission of housing searches especially ironic. But in the interviews I conducted, housing was the least contested use of the platform, making it less relevant for my research questions on craigslist's contributions to digital culture. Discussion forums presented a different issue. In the online survey I conducted, just 2 percent of respondents reported using the forums. During interviews, very few people mentioned reading the forums and no one reported having posted to one. Another omission in this book is the lack of focus outside of the United States. Craigslist is a global website, active in seven hundred cities across the world, but 90 percent of its visitors are from the United States (Alexa, n.d.), which is a key reason for the geographic limitation of my analysis. Given that this is the first academic monograph on craigslist, I have opted to investigate the parts of the platform that are both familiar and provocative, although I certainly hope others will pursue research on the topics that I don't focus on here.

This book argues that craigslist helps us understand how the web has changed in the past quarter century, and it might seem as though I'm setting up craigslist as a white knight meant to save us from evil corporate profiteers, or that I'm nostalgic for a simpler, purer internet. But the story I tell in this book is much less straightforward than a zero-sum game of good guys and bad guys. The fact that craigslist has kept its look, feel, and core features intact for almost three decades makes it a useful object of study, but it doesn't make it perfect. For example, I disagree with how craigslist has handled requests to use its data. It's one thing to fight other companies' monetizing of user-generated content posted to craigslist, but it's another to go after people who simply want to play around with craigslist's data (Opsahl 2013). The site has struggled to overcome a reputation for fraud and crime through a somewhat naïve notion that it can doggedly work with law enforcement behind the scenes and expect users and the broader public to notice. Although I argue that there are democratic values in maintaining a simple design, I definitely do not want the entire internet to look like craigslist. What I do want is to consider what it means to have a site like craigslist endure on the web for so long, and to think about how its policies and practices can help us understand important changes in online politics.

Chances are either you or someone you know has sold something on craigslist. Maybe you sold a used car without worrying too much about the potential for fraud, or maybe you went to great lengths to protect yourself and your privacy when it came to meeting a buyer for a used phone. In researching this book, I met a number of people who never or rarely use craigslist to buy or sell anything, but nonetheless find it useful or entertaining. Some peruse craigslist posts to check the going rate for a used item; others are simply amused by looking through the "Best of craigslist" or "Missed Connections" posts. Whichever features interest them, most people use craigslist without thinking about how the site manifests a form of technological politics. And yet, politics are always present just beneath the surface—in everything from how we describe our neighborhoods when we search for a roommate to how we respond to a suspected scam. From craigslist's perspective, many of its policies also have a political bent, most clearly in decisions such as not allowing the sale of guns or military paraphernalia, but also in more subtle conflicts: in frictions between lawsuit litigants, between different kinds of sellers, between fraudsters and dupes, between craigslist and its competitors.

In my tour through the marketplaces, moderation battles, and court cases of craigslist, I tease out a number of claims about politics and online publics. Developing a multifaceted account of craigslist gives us an in-depth understanding of a site where you can get almost anything, from a free eighteen-foot sailboat (assuming you can get it out of a backyard pool in Phoenix, Arizona, without damaging the lawn) to Tom Cruise–impersonation lessons. On its own, craigslist makes for an interesting case study as the internet's longest-running garage sale, but tracing the site's history also presents a framework for considering how digital culture has changed. With its long history, stable business model, and almost unchanging aesthetic, craigslist is like an island that has stayed mostly the same while the web around it has changed. By looking at the politics and promises of craigslist, we can reflect on how the web has evolved in the past twenty-five years, how it has stayed the same, what we might want to protect, and what we should think about changing when it comes to everyday life online.

Part I

What exactly is craigslist and where did it come from? What technologies did it disrupt and what happens when its politics are challenged? The chapters in part I provide background on how craigslist came to be, its media history, and its legal battles. Chapter 1 provides background information on craigslist's transformation from an e-mail list to a massively popular online marketplace. The platform's history is technological as well as geographic—craigslist grew out of a 1990s Bay Area ethos in terms of its purpose and ideology. In this early phase of the tech industry, democratic values of openness and access held sway, values that have shaped craigslist's look and feel ever since. In addition to interviews, textual analysis of craigslist's public-facing blog helped me analyze the site's basic features and rules, as well as the company's values and goals.

Craigslist did not emerge from a vacuum. By looking at the development of classified ads, chapter 2 traces the media history of craigslist, beginning with the print newspapers the platform disrupted. There is a small body of research within media studies on classified ads (e.g., Bader 2005; Cocks 2009), but this scholarship mostly ignores what happened as classified ads came online. The popular narrative that craigslist killed print newspapers has some truth in it, and this chapter looks at classified ads as the media format craigslist replicated, and legacy media as the industry it challenged.

Although often overlooked in terms of serious tech-industry players, craigslist has helped establish some crucial legal precedents. In chapter 3, I describe two key battles that craigslist has repeatedly waged in court: The first set of cases has to do with whether or not websites can be held responsible for the behavior or activities of their users. In the second set, craigslist has fiercely protected its data from third parties, especially tech companies seeking to make new products. Both strands of legal decisions have had important ramifications for the tech industry in terms of insisting that platforms are not legally liable for bad acts of users or policing ownership over data. Looking at these cases helps us understand craigslist's definition of platform responsibility, meaning what a website owes its users, and what a fair relationship between people and platform looks like.

Before we get to how people use craigslist in everyday life, it's important to understand where craigslist came from in terms of the tech industry, its media history, and its battles in the courtroom. Across the chapters in part I, I come back to questions about craigslist's politics, which first emerged as the company launched in the tech sector heyday of the 1990s. In terms of its finances, policies, and aesthetics, craigslist has stayed remarkably stable over its history, preserving some of the early web politics that have become increasingly marginal over the past three decades.

1

Becoming Craig's List

SAN FRANCISCO ROOTS AND
WEB 1.0 ETHICS

Stop me when this sounds familiar: A couple of guys working out of a San Francisco apartment launch a web platform to create local social connections. The company takes off, building a loyal following and disrupting traditional industry, surpassing expectations to become a household name. Well before it became a cliché of start-up success, the narrative of San Francisco as tech incubator described craigslist's rise to fame. Although the story feels familiar in a landscape since flooded with start-ups, craigslist has deviated from the popular path of successful tech companies. To understand where craigslist came from, we need to think through how the different politics and norms of the tech industry have stabilized over the past quarter century. When craigslist first launched as a website in the 1990s, it reflected commonly held ideas and beliefs about what the internet is for and how it should be used. As the industry around it has grown and changed, the platform has become increasingly out of step with the contemporary web. This chapter offers a social history of craigslist, starting with a discussion of how San Francisco and California have given rise to a particular blend of technological ethics. With this background in mind, I turn to craigslist's early days, drawing on interviews with the company's founder, Craig Newmark, and early employees. From there, I lay out craigslist's core values as a platform: craigslist explicitly embraced Web 1.0 values of access, reach, and privacy, which explains the company's resistance to banner ads and monetizing user data.

San Francisco Tech, Then and Now

California looms large in mainstream narratives about digital technology, but its relationship to the industry has shifted in important ways, both ideologically and geographically. Two related concepts help describe ideological changes in the tech industry: Web 2.0 and the California Ideology. One way of framing the social and technological shifts from the 1990s to now is to periodize them, labeling the mid-1990s to around 2004 as Web. 1.0, and calling everything afterward Web 2.0. The term "Web 2.0" is typically used as a shorthand for a technical emphasis on platform interoperability, where everyday users can push content to one another rather than just having it pushed to them (O'Reilly 2005). Web 2.0 also contains an implied critique of the websites and norms that came before it. As Megan Sapnar-Ankerson (2010, 174) put it, "The very notion of 'Web 2.0' propagates an understanding of 'Web 1.0' as the outdated, buggy past, one that needs an upgrade in order to function smoothly." Web 2.0 is partly about the technical capacity to support the production and exchange of user-generated content, so key to platforms like Instagram and Snapchat. But the term "Web 2.0" is also meant to rewrite earlier narratives about the internet and tech industry. As Alice Marwick noted in her account of San Francisco's tech scene, Web 2.0 "began as a marketing ploy to differentiate a new crop of tech companies from their failed counterparts. Web 2.0 is firmly grounded in a history of labor that emphasizes creative capitalism, personal fulfillment through work and entrepreneurialism" (2015, 27). Marwick's point is that Web 2.0 brings with it a set of political and economic values, assumptions about what the web is for, and how—and by whom—it should be used.

No one paradigm encapsulates an entire corporation, let alone an entire industry. There are always devotees and detractors, with beliefs and politics unevenly distributed. Still, dominant narratives and common assumptions surface and persist. The connections between California and the tech industry have produced a quasi-economic, quasi-technological philosophy called the California Ideology. In a succinct analysis of the California Ideology, Ferrari (2019) argues that there are three key tenets. First, digital technologies are assumed to represent and support individual freedom and collective democracy (Barbrook and Cameron 1996; Mosco 2004; Streeter 2005; Turner 2010). Second, this ideology sees technology—rather than legislation or policy—as a solution to social problems (Morozov 2013; Robins 1996). Third, however disruptive tech companies might claim to be, as a whole, the industry is "fully embedded into and functional to dominant political-economic arrangements, i.e. neoliberalism" (Ferrari, 2019; see also Dean 2005; McChesney 2013; Mosco 2004). The California Ideology is ruled by a belief in meritocracy. A dominant belief in Silicon Valley is that technical know-how can overcome racism, homophobia, sexism, classism, ableism, and other forms of discrimination (Marwick 2015). The philosophy draws together a libertarian view of economics and vaguely spiritual sense of self-empowerment, a combination "only made possible through a nearly universal belief in technological determinism" (Barbrook and Cameron 1996, 50), which is based on "a profound faith in the emancipatory potential of the new information technologies" (45). The California Ideology justifies a continual nudging toward devices and products that promote interpersonal connection, continual self-disclosure, and the steady integration of online technologies into everyday life.

California wasn't always ground zero for tech culture. From the Industrial Revolution to the mid-twentieth century, technological innovation was associated with the Northeast, from Upstate New York and Cambridge, Massachusetts, to Edison, New Jersey, and Philadelphia, Pennsylvania. It's beyond the scope of this chapter to provide a detailed account of how and why the tech industry took hold in Northern California, which has been covered extensively in both the academic and general-audience press (Ankerson 2012; Isaacson 2014; Marwick 2015; Turner 2010). But to touch on some key points, Don Hoefler, writing in *Micro Electronics News*, coined the term "Silicon Valley" in 1971 to highlight the number of microelectronics companies in the South Bay (Bernard 2017). The Bay Area tech industry first took hold during the 1940s, thanks to a stream of World War II defense contracts. Local engineering expertise came from nearby universities like Stanford and the University of California at Berkeley. In contrast to these macro narratives, a much more micro-level origin story of the shift from East to West credits William Shockley, the creator of the transistor, who moved the Shockley Semiconductor Laboratory from New Jersey to Mountain View, California, to live closer to his ailing mother in Palo Alto (Isaacson 2014). From there, Shockley led an East Coast exodus to California, encouraged by the area's cultural reputation for social informality and intellectual creativity.

Companies like Intel, Hewlett-Packard, and IBM gave Silicon Valley its name, signaling the early emphasis on hardware before companies like Google, Facebook, and Yahoo! launched search engines and social-media platforms from their headquarters in Mountain View and Menlo Park. Around 2008, industry influence began to shift to San Francisco. At this time, tech innovation was becoming increasingly attached to cities, not just in the movement from the South Bay to San Francisco, but also in the development of tech centers in cities like Vancouver, New York, and Pittsburgh. The economic recession made urban real estate cheap, allowing young people to move and start businesses inside city limits. Also because of the recession, a wave of workers from the beleaguered financial industry saw new opportunities in the tech sector, bringing with them a distinctly profit-oriented (as opposed to tech-oriented) perspective. According to industry insiders like Ellen Pao, this shift had powerful consequences in terms of culture:

> In 2008, when the markets crashed, all those people who are motivated by money ended up coming out to Silicon Valley. . . . And that's when values shifted more. There was, like, an optimism early around good coming out of the internet that ended up getting completely distorted in the 2000s, when you had these people coming in with a different idea and a different set of goals. (Quoted in Kulwin 2018)

For Pao, 2008 signaled an inflection point from the tech industry, with new priorities, politics, and even geographic preferences. A core argument of this book is that using craigslist as a lens helps us think through the changes that Pao pinpointed in terms of industry culture. With its long online history and its financial and aesthetic stability, craigslist is simultaneously a success story and a holdout, a time capsule of the internet in its early days and a counterfactual to assumptions about what it takes to be valuable in a Web 2.0 world.

From List to URL: The Early Days of craigslist

When craigslist got its start, there wasn't really a coherent digital tech industry, just a bunch of people looking to build things. In August 2017 I spoke with Anthony Batt, who was an early collaborator with Newmark on craigslist, after meeting him in the WELL (Whole Earth 'Lectronic Link), a legendary message board connecting web enthusiasts in the 1990s. Batt reflected on the excitement around technology at the time: "We were building the early internet, we were figuring out what the internet would turn into." To be clear, the internet has always had corporate connections and impulses—from the first online exchange packets, corporations and investors saw massive potential in internet technologies. But in the early days of the publicly available internet, it wasn't at all clear how the web would transition from hobbyists and tinkerers to a conglomerate of major corporations.

It seems obvious today that an online platform looking to make waves would start in San Francisco. But in 1995, as Newmark was sending the first e-mails that would eventually become a website, the center of the tech industry was still fifty miles south in Silicon Valley. Batt described San Francisco as completely lacking a tech scene at the moment when he and Newmark first met:

> San Francisco didn't have a tech scene. The hardcore tech people, like people working at Apple and Intel, were south of San Francisco. San Francisco had a creative scene, artists, writers, people working for early *Wired*. There were probably a couple hundred folks that understood digital culture, but like through the lens of a CD-ROM [rather than internet]. San Francisco's tech scene at the time was computer people who had a huge bent towards creative culture. But today's San Francisco tech scene is more like Wall Street. It's all sold out. If you look to the music industry as an analogue, San Francisco is more like Taylor Swift and the Weekend rather than Soundgarden or Mudhoney or Nirvana. (Interview with author, August 3, 2017)

There's likely a degree of nostalgia in Batt's recollection of San Francisco in the 1990s, as anyone from a countercultural community tends to imprint a more authentic image onto the past. But Batt's emphasis on prioritizing profits over artistic creativity encapsulates the same shifts that Pao pointed to earlier. Because the industry is the same and the geography is close, it's easy to assume that Northern California's relationship to technology has stayed the same over the past fifty years, even as the major players have shifted from hardware manufacturers like Xerox and Hewlett-Packard to software companies like Facebook and Google. In fact, changes have been significant, from motivations for making stuff to business models and design values.

Facebook has Mark Zuckerberg; Amazon has Jeff Bezos; Microsoft has Bill Gates. For better or worse, company founders often become poster kids for tech culture, representing a corporation's values and politics. Although Newmark is fairly well known in the tech industry, many people are unaware that there is actually a Craig behind craigslist. Born in 1952 in Morristown, New Jersey, Newmark embraced the internet early. He completed both undergraduate and graduate degrees at Case Western Reserve in Cleveland, before beginning a seventeen-year career with IBM, which took him to

Boca Raton, Detroit, and Pittsburgh. He then took a job with Charles Schwab in San Francisco, which he left in 1995 for contract work with companies like Bank of America, Xircom (now Intel), and Sun Microsystems. That same year, Newmark launched the e-mail list that would grow into craigslist. Many journalists have remarked on Newmark's self-effacing, awkward personality (Blitstein 2005; Richtel 2004). He began our first interview with a kind of nerd disclaimer, apologetically explaining, "I have no social awareness of norms. I regard this as dysfunctional" (interview with author, May 16, 2017). Having spent time in the tech industry, I found Newmark to be a fairly familiar engineering archetype—smart, unassuming, wanting to connect socially without always knowing how to be sociable. As a technology, craigslist reflects many of these same characteristics of wanting to connect people without a lot of finesse or complexity.

The website started as a simple mailing list, a way to connect people in the Bay Area to one another and stay in the loop about local events, job opportunities, and technological developments. At the time, mailing lists had to be scripted by hand, and maintaining the e-mail list took a lot of work. On a technical level, the email list was scripted in CC and Pine, but the code could only handle around 250 email addresses, at which point Newmark switched to Majordomo—"People would email stuff, and I'd read it using Pine. Then I would pipe it to Perl scripts, which would convert it to HTML. This was at the end of '96. Through 1998, into '99, my database program was Pine, and my system involved deleting older emails, which would open up space" (interview with author, May 16, 2017). The e-mail list required significant work to maintain and provided no monetary compensation, but it reflected an early web excitement about connecting electronically. As Batt described: "Craig was really studious in maintaining these threaded conversations . . . where we could communicate among like-minded people" (interview with author, August 3, 2017).

Once online as a website, craigslist kept its local roots, at first operating exclusively in San Francisco. Offline, craigslist also hosted parties and events to promote networking and charitable giving in the tech scene. Christina Murphy was involved with craigslist from its early days, and she recalled local enthusiasm for tech events: "We started planning parties, because this was pre social [media], and people really wanted to meet. . . . It felt like a small community in San Francisco, it felt like a club—people were excited about using craigslist, they wanted to meet people and put a face to the name" (interview with author, August 17, 2017). Tech parties in the 1990s were not like the parties that would follow thirty years later. Rather than the extravagant holiday parties of Amazon (with a twenty-thousand-plus guest list), Twitter (featuring robot bartenders), or Google (which lined up Cirque de Soleil as entertainment [Stone 2014]), craigslist's parties mostly featured a lot of pizza and a cash bar. As one tech reporter described a craigslist party in 2000, "Small, sedate groups gathered around tables and munched pizza. . . . The booze wasn't free, so nobody had gotten hopelessly soused yet. Craig was standing in the front of the room, talking quietly into a microphone about how craigslist is now expanding into other cities" (Newitz 2000).

As craigslist shifted from an e-mail list to a website, the internet was still very much in the process of developing into an industry, and people were still trying to make sense of it as a technology. Batt explained:

> There was no tech scene, but that's why craigslist mattered. Since the scene was not a scene, Craig was trying to connect people. We were getting questions about the internet, from like the *San Francisco Chronicle*. [At one point] we had a meeting with them, and in the middle they said, "so, you guys are the internet." That's how uniformed they were, they thought the internet was a person. (Interview with author, August 3, 2017)

Although many were still unclear about the internet on a technical level, there was a lot of enthusiasm and cash for investment. As Murphy described the industry climate of the mid-1990s, "People had a lot of money and wanted to get involved, but didn't always know what they were doing. People were getting a lot of funding, for ideas that weren't solidified. There was such an influx of money, it was nutty" (interview with author, August 17, 2017). General understanding of online technologies lagged far behind industry enthusiasm. Before search engines, it was hard even to know how to navigate the web when looking for jobs or local events. Simply by having a lot of content that was logically ordered, craigslist quickly developed a following.

Migrating from an e-mail list to a URL required a name, and according to Newmark, settling on the name "craigslist" was almost accidental: "I had inadvertently created a brand, and decided to call it 'craigslist' to signal that quirkiness" (interview with author, May 16, 2017). Batt provided some additional context on giving the new website a name:

> We were sharing a card table and a loft in South of Market, we weren't thinking of it as a business, it was just a way to connect, like, 20 people. . . . As I recall, we were working in the office and we were trying to come up with names. I said, just call it craigslist. I think we started just using

it as a variable. But we did some mock-ups, which stuck, and the name stuck. (Interview with author, August 3, 2017)

Over time, the question of whether and how to think of craigslist as a business would produce a number of disputes and arguments, reflecting the status of an industry still coming to terms with the politics of putting design values into practice.

After a brief experiment with running the site on a volunteer basis in 1998, craigslist was converted into a for-profit company in 1999. Craigslist stayed rooted in San Francisco until June 2000, when it added its second city, Boston, and then expanded to other major metropolitan cities in August 2000 (Crunchbase, n.d.). For a brief period Nancy Melone acted as CEO, but in September 2000 a legal dispute erupted between Melone and craigslist. According to a tech blogger at the time, "Melone, who worked two years on the site during its infancy, said she was ousted in the spring of 2000 and got $32,000 and the List Foundation URL (listfoundation.org) as part of her severance pay" (Johnsville News 2005). Listfoundation.org had for some time been an alternate address for craigslist.org, with both directing users to the same craigslist home page. When Melone launched a job site called MetroVox.com, it not only looked similar to craigslist but also rerouted the listfoundation.org URL to MetroVox, meaning that people who had grown accustomed to reaching craigslist via listfoundation.org now found themselves on a competing site. Craigslist sued Melone over the issue of the URL redirect, and the case was settled in arbitration.

With Melone gone, Newmark took over as CEO, but that didn't last long. According to Newmark, "In 2000, people helped me understand that I wasn't the best manager, and that's when I turned things over to Jim. I then went over to Customer Service and began to help out there" (interview with author, May 16, 2017). Mostly this consists of responding to website users who suspect fraud or have complaints about the site. The idea of a tech-company founder spending his time doing customer service is almost unthinkable at any other company and can be explained only by Newmark's compulsive need to respond to complaints, suggestions, and requests. In an article from 2004, a journalist noted that Newmark "has a kind of condition: obsessive customer-service disorder. He is not totally at peace if there are e-mail messages in his in-box complaining that someone is falsely advertising, defacing or hacking into the site or blanketing various forums or channels with sales spam" (Richtel 2004). As of 2019, Newmark continues to do customer-service work, although on a reduced scale. Newmark is a self-described "techno-optimist," and during our conversations he seemed determined to avoid negative or pessimistic topics, preferring to focus on what is fixable—he continually pointed to himself as an engineer who wants to solve problems as literally as possible. At present, he devotes most of his time to various philanthropic causes—in particular, supporting families of veterans, voting rights, freedom of the press, and bird sanctuaries (Bereznak 2017; Elizabeth 2017; Newmark 2017; Streitfeld 2018).

Before he became CEO, Buckmaster had previously found apartments and furniture on craigslist, and then eventually uploaded his résumé to the jobs section, looking for work as a software engineer. Craigslist scooped him up and eventually, according to Newmark, Buckmaster "made himself obvious" as the best candidate for CEO. Buckmaster declined to be interviewed for this book, but it's clear from conversations with Newmark, press coverage, and trial proceedings that the two are in sync when it comes to what the company is and how it should be run. At one time they shared an office, where they worked on separate projects in amiable silence (Richtel 2004). Although their values are similar, Buckmaster's promotion to CEO came with a slew of changes, and in many ways he was largely responsible for turning the website into a company. As Buckmaster noted in a 2004 interview:

> In 1999, craigslist was running on a PC. I took it to a multi-server environment. I took it to a number of other cities. When I came in, there were about a dozen classified categories. There was no search engine and no discussion boards. Every posting was reviewed and posted manually. I moved the site to a self-service model. I added the flag system, where users are able to flag a potential problem. (Quoted in Hempel 2004)

Since Buckmaster took over, the company has been incredibly stable, both because Buckmaster has been at the helm for so long and because he's committed to holding on to craigslist's features, appearance, and politics.

Clues to craigslist's corporate culture can be gleaned from its hiring page. Like a lot of tech companies, craigslist offers perks like a "wellness stipend" and weekly in-office yoga, but there are also key differences from the kind of hypercompetitive tech culture that has been satirized in pop culture. Craigslist describes itself as a "tech nirvana, no VCs, MBAs, sales, marketing, biz dev, or pivoting," with "an unusually philanthropic company mission and philosophy" (craigslist n.d.[a]). Craigslist employees have to accept that the company may never go public, meaning that they can't anticipate cashing in on a future public offering of shares. But the trade-off is a tech-industry job that focuses on coding and developing software rather than courting media hype and constantly shifting programming timetables.

In December 2017, I met with Newmark in the company's headquarters, which is on the top floor of a fairly normal-looking office building in the Nob Hill neighborhood of downtown San Francisco. (In 2010, the company moved from its original headquarters in an old Victorian house in the Sunset District [Temple 2010].) Like a lot of modern workplaces, the layout is open, with a couple dozen desks clustered in the middle of the room and a ring of glassy offices around the edge—Buckmaster claimed a corner office, where he worked at a standing desk. The office boasted hallmarks of hipster office aesthetics: wall-mounted bike racks in the entrance, strands of Edison bulbs, and one of the open-layout desks has been swapped out for a drum kit and upright piano. Newmark currently splits his time between San Francisco and New York City, but although he's only in the office periodically, his presence provoked no visible reaction among craigslist employees, let alone the fanfare that follows an office appearance by corporate leaders like Mark Zuckerberg or Satya Nadella.

For a while, craigslist seemed like a darling of the internet, an example of a tech company that held on to its local roots and community commitment even as it grew and expanded. In 2006, the Electronic Frontier Foundation (EFF) honored craigslist in its fifteenth annual Pioneer Awards, explaining that "craigslist is the world's most-used classified forum in any medium, serving as a non-commercial community service. craigslist focuses on helping people with their basic needs—starting with housing and jobs—with a pervasive culture of trust" (EFF 2006). The idea of celebrating craigslist's "pervasive culture of trust" would unravel over the next decade, but for the first ten years of its life online, the platform stood out as an example of a digital community that spanned online and offline contexts. In the mid-2000s, Newmark received a number of awards, being named Webby Person of the Year in 2005, one of the world's hundred most influential people by *Time* magazine in 2005, one of the fifty most important people on the web by *PC World* in 2007, and one of the twenty-five most influential people on the web by Bloomberg in 2008 (Bloomberg n.d.). Beyond craigslist's emphasis on interpersonal connection and everyday entrepreneurialism, the website reflected a broader excitement about all of the ordinary transactions that stood to change because of the web.

A precise date is difficult to pinpoint, but craigslist arguably peaked in popularity between 2007 and 2010, when social-media sites like Facebook and Twitter were coming into full force, and an increasing number of people were integrating the web into everyday life. More and more people online meant that bad actors had a growing number of targets, and alarm over web-based crime, from sexual predation to financial fraud, grew louder (Marwick 2008). Throughout 2008 and 2009, state attorneys general across the country made a concerted effort to clamp down on sex workers and human trafficking facilitated by craigslist personals (Associated Press 2010). Reports of prostitution, coupled with the platform's role in some sensational acts of violence—cases detailed in chapter 3—caused craigslist's reputation to nose-dive between 2009 and 2010. While millions of people continued to use the site to search for used goods, jobs, and hookups, a dark narrative of violence and scams had taken hold that would never entirely be shaken.

Craigslist's Platform Politics

Craigslist might have predicted a shift in tech culture from the South Bay to San Francisco, but as it gained more industry neighbors, a gap emerged between the platform's politics and those of the mainstream tech sector. The decision not to update its appearance and its caution in rolling out new features began to seem out of step for users who had come to expect continual upgrades. While selling user data to third parties and paid advertising became the financial lifeline of Web 2.0 platforms, craigslist continued its straightforward approach of charging users small fees to post certain kinds of ads. And while most start-ups dreamed of taking their companies public and cashing in on company stock, craigslist has stubbornly resisted outside investment. In short, craigslist's critique of the mainstream internet isn't in the form of a manifesto or a political campaign, but in its design values, monetization strategies, and industry relationships.

Design Values: Keep It Simple, Stupid

Craigslist's refusal to update its appearance has become one of its distinguishing features. One user I interviewed, Rob, described the platform as "bare bones," noting that craigslist's design "is a very light web experience. Just background, no images, text, not a lot of, there's no banners, right? There's no graphic ads." It's almost hard to describe craigslist's design aesthetic as deliberate, given that the site still looks much as it did in the late 1990s, when programmers were very limited in terms of visual design. Although the technical ability to design more sophisticated features and aesthetics has long since been available, craigslist has stayed the same, aside from minor tweaks in functionality. According to Murphy, the plan was always to keep the platform's interface simple and usable:

> Craig was really big on craigslist not looking commercial, on it not looking slick. [He'd say,] "I just want it to be a list"—maybe that's the tech guy in him. . . . He wanted it to be easy to use, he wanted it to be something that everyone could use. He wanted it to show that a community member built it. I think it still resonates with people that it feels home grown. It's a community place rather than a company that's trying to make money, I think it still feels that way. (Interview with author, August 17, 2017)

While platforms like Facebook and Snapchat race to add features and update aesthetics, craigslist has retained its text-based home page in Times New Roman font. This is a bit like a car company deciding not to integrate features like Bluetooth navigation and impact sensors because it simply prefers to keep marketing an older, less sophisticated, but very reliable model.

The commitment to old-school design has both advocates and detractors. Craigslist's design values make perfect sense from an engineering perspective. As Newmark told me in an interview, "You could say there are two approaches to site design: fast, efficient, and simple, or heavy, slow, and complicated" (interview with author, May 16, 2017). Buckmaster expressed a similar view on the craigslist blog, where a number of posts reference the site's speed, such as this entry from March 2008:

> Serving 10 billion page views on a few hundred servers, craigslist leads the internet industry by orders of magnitude when it comes to efficient use of electricity. The last time I checked we were clocking something like 175,000 page views per kilowatt-hour. Compare this to single digit thousands of pages-per-kwhr for most large sites, which typically run tens to hundreds of thousands of servers. Have said it before, and will say it again: pound-for-pound our tech team is the best in the business. (Buckmaster 2008a).

According to craigslist's leadership, being the best in the business isn't about sexy design or new features, it's about efficient, lightweight programming. From a purely functional viewpoint, the resilience of craigslist's appearance demonstrates its efficiency—for old-school software engineers form follows function, and too much emphasis on aesthetics is a waste of time.

As the tech industry continued to develop, craigslist began to seem more and more like a relic. In 2006, a South by Southwest (SXSW) panel presented six design visions for remaking craigslist, focusing on using less memory and a cleaner layout (Douglas 2006). Three years later, *Wired* magazine ran a series of articles about craigslist, which included an invitation for esteemed designers to give the site a makeover (Wired staff 2009). Respondents described craigslist as "cluttered," "claustrophobic," and "confusing," complaining that the site had too much text and too many links and lacked a clear organizing principle. Their proposed revisions mostly focused on making craigslist prettier and easier to use on a mobile phone. But there is value in holding on to web aesthetics from the past. In my earlier work on countercultural communities and digital technologies (Lingel 2017a) I argued that there can be disadvantages in trying to adapt the look and feel of alternative platforms to keep pace with mainstream technologies. Major design overhauls can lead to what I've called "mainstream creep," or the idea that a platform loses some of its countercultural "street cred." Part of my original interest in craigslist was to think of it as a platform that resists continual redesign and feature rollouts.

While stability is part of craigslist's reputation, the site has in fact changed over time. Categories have come and gone, and new features have been added, like the ability to include images in ads and map-based searching. In 2012, the platform made a number of design improvements, including pushing out versions of its website optimized for mobile and tablet browsers, increasing the number of images allowed in a listing from four to eight, and rolling out a Hover Zoom–like feature that allows users to preview images from a post before clicking on an individual listing (Dave 2012). But these changes are minor in contrast to platforms and devices that continually roll out new features. In my interviews with craigslist users, many saw the site's throwback vibe as a positive thing. For example, Yma saw the site's minimalism as enjoyable in its simplicity: "I think it's kind of fun because it's more stark. It's just the listings and you click." For longtime internet users, craigslist's stability harkens back to an earlier aesthetic of the web. As Nathaniel explained, "You know, it seems somewhat old-fashioned to me now because it's very straight-forward, which I like. It's a simple interface, it's easy to use. I don't know, I guess just that it feels like the old internet a little bit."

There's a nostalgic dimension to Nathaniel's claim that craigslist "feels like the old internet." It isn't just that craigslist has been online for over twenty years, it's that the site looks the same as it did twenty years ago. Justin

Peters is a tech journalist who has written articles about craigslist in *Wired* and *Slate*, and I interviewed him on January 15, 2018. According to Peters:

> For people who remember Web 1.0, the nostalgia factor is definitely meaningful. . . . I have to imagine if craigslist remains viable and presumably profitable that it's not just [meant] for me, who's been online for 25 years, but there must be some younger people around who are using it not out of any nostalgia for something they remember, but who are using it because it works. And then also perhaps secondarily because it reminds them of some sort of past that they know existed but never actually got to experience themselves. Like children of the eighties going to 1950s themed diners.

In my interviews with craigslist users, I did meet a number of young people in their twenties who use craigslist alongside Web 2.0 platforms like Instagram and Indeed. Like the people I interviewed generally, younger participants saw both the value and the drawbacks of craigslist's design, appreciating the lack of frills while also wanting more features. Participants also associated the site's aesthetic simplicity with a respect for user privacy, which brings us to the next feature of craigslist's platform politics: monetization.

Minimal-Profit Politics

Many craigslist users never pay for an ad, and because of its .org URL, people often assume that the company is nonprofit—a misperception, although the company does have a charity associated with it, Craig Newmark Philanthropies. So how does craigslist make money? Over time, the company has developed different strategies for keeping the site mostly free, generating profits from nominal fees for posting certain ads. The first major test came in 2001, when the dot-com bubble burst. A suddenly wobbly tech sector destabilized job listings as the platform's sole source of revenue, and craigslist made an appeal to users for suggestions on how to keep the site alive. Running banner ads was off the table, but users came up with a number of alternate revenue sources: increasing fees for posting employment listings; seeking voluntary support (a "virtual tip jar") from users; and charging fees for services (like household help and moving), personals, or for items for sale, perhaps on a sliding scale based on the value of the item. Finally, users suggested fees for posting, but not viewing or responding to, housing ads, the logic being that realtors and landlords, who could presumably afford the modest cost of $10, would be the ones posting ads (D. Robinson et al. 2006).

Craigslist implemented this last suggestion in a small number of cities, which has gradually increased. Costs vary by location, loosely corresponding to the size and wealth of the city.

At the time of writing, most ads are still free to post, but there are some exceptions. In addition to fees for real-estate ads in certain cities, it's $7 to post a gig, regardless of the city a user posts from. Users also pay to post ads in the employment-wanted section. Although posting items for sale as an owner is free, posting as a dealer costs between $3 and $5. These charges are craigslist's entire revenue stream. While craigslist is a for-profit company that demands content- and community-moderation work from users, it has so far resisted the lure of banner ads and monetizing user behavior. Peters argued that refusing to advertise or sell user data has become an important draw for craigslist in comparison to competing sites:

> I think partially that [not going after users' data] is why people consciously or subconsciously don't take to other sites as much. Because if there's not a lot of venture capital like behind you, and you've got these ambitions of becoming a unicorn company, you're not going to get there by just selling used furniture. There's got to be something else to monetize, and it's going to be the user. (Interview with author, January 15, 2018)

Craigslist isn't entirely free to use, but its model is straightforward and transparent: a small number of ads cost a set amount of money to post. This contrasts sharply with monetization strategies that operate behind the scenes, are invisible to users, and can change without explanation.

Craigslist's Financial Structure and the Eight-Year Battle with eBay

Craigslist's financial structure is much less transparent than its monetization strategy. Largely because the company is privately held, there is very little official data on craigslist's finances. A company goes public by selling a portion of the business in an initial public offering, whereas a private company can still sell shares to individuals and corporations, just not offer those shares up for sale publicly. In 2008, *Business Insider* estimated craigslist's annual revenue at $80 million and its value at $5 billion (Blodget 2008b). In my interviews with Newmark, he declined to give information about the company's monetary value (or his, for that matter) but he said that most of the estimates he'd seen of craigslist's revenues and his own net worth were far too high. Although the exact numbers are a mystery, it's clear that craigslist is determined to remain privately held. From reviewing court cases, it seems that the company has never had more than three shareholders, with the largest number of shares owned by Newmark and Buckmaster. While craigslist will never see the huge stock-option payoffs of successful start-ups, its financial independence also means that the company stays free from shareholder interference in decisions about design or services offerings. Craigslist has resisted outside investment, with one key exception: eBay.

In 2004, eBay purchased nearly one-third of craigslist's shares. Eight years later, the two companies severed their business ties, having spent most of the intervening time locked in a fraught legal battle. What happened? Why did these two companies spend so much on suits and countersuits, and how did eBay come to own part of craigslist in the first place? It's helpful to think about the relationship between eBay and craigslist because they compete for users who want to buy and sell used goods online, and because contrasting the two sets up important comparisons in terms of their corporate philosophies.

The story starts in 2002 with a breakdown in priorities among the three key craigslist shareholders: Newmark, Buckmaster, and Phillip Knowlton, who according to Newmark obtained shares during the company's early days, without really expecting the shares to accumulate financial value. As Newmark described in a 2004 blog post, "With the idea of establishing checks and balances, mostly on myself, I entrusted some equity in craigslist to a guy who was working with me at the time. . . . I figured it didn't matter, since everyone agreed that the equity had only symbolic value, not dollar value." Years later, craigslist was turning a profit, and while Newmark and Buckmaster were content to have most people use the site for free, Knowlton saw the potential for monetization. By 2003, Knowlton was shopping his shares around for potential buyers.

At the time, eBay was looking to enter the online-classifieds market, and craigslist looked like an ideal entry point. Early in 2004, eBay approached Knowlton about buying his shares. In order to get approval from Newmark and Buckmaster, eBay founder Pierre Omidyar and CEO Meg Whitman made repeated assurances that they embraced craigslist's "public-service" ethic, and had no interest in a takeover. By August, Knowlton had settled for $16 million from eBay, which paid an additional $8 million each to Newmark and Buckmaster (West 2010).[1] The new ownership structure left Newmark with 42.6 percent of shares, Buckmaster with 39 percent, and eBay with 28.4 percent. At the time, Buckmaster explained the appeal of eBay in terms of antiscamming know-how and helping to expand outside the United States:

> With eBay, we hope to be able to do a better job at consumer protection. eBay has the resources to put people behind bars. . . . Also, we would like to bring craigslist's services wherever people are requesting them. We get a lot of requests from people internationally—eBay is relatively sophisticated in that regard. (Quoted in Hempel 2004)

No one at craigslist was aware that eBay was already working on launching its own online classifieds operation, Kijiji, nicknamed the "craigslist Killer" in private memos between eBay executives (Ames 2015).

Over the next four years, it grew increasingly obvious that eBay wanted to acquire full ownership of craigslist. At one point, Price told Buckmaster that eBay's takeover was "inevitable" and that Buckmaster and Newmark "were mortal, but eBay was not, and eBay would acquire 100 percent of craigslist whether it took decades and, if necessary, over Newmark's and Buckmaster's dead bodies" (quoted in Ames 2014). A key breaking point came in June 2007, when eBay launched Kijiji in the United States—the site had already launched in countries where craigslist didn't have a web presence. Craigslist immediately responded with a notice of competitive activity. In addition, craigslist pursued a series of structural changes to regain control, with the effect of squeezing eBay members off its board and diluting eBay's shares from 28.4 to just under 25 percent. Those actions sparked a pair of lawsuits in 2008: eBay filed a corporate-governance lawsuit in Delaware against craigslist, seeking to restore its board seat and its watered-down shares, and craigslist filed a civil-fraud lawsuit against eBay in San Francisco.

The trial proceedings provide some of the only available details into craigslist's financial workings, such as the breakdown of shares between Buckmaster and Newmark. They also set up a stark contrast in platform politics between craigslist and eBay. For example, in his ninety-one-page decision, Delaware chancellor William Chandler III noted the "curious" circumstances of two companies that were so ideologically different being linked through share acquisition.[2] Chandler also described craigslist and eBay as having a David and Goliath dynamic:

> For most of its history, craigslist has not focused on "monetizing" its site. The relatively small amount of monetization craigslist has pursued . . . does not approach what many craigslist competitors would consider an optimal or even minimally acceptable level. Nevertheless, craigslist's

unique business strategy continues to be successful, even if it does run counter to the strategies used by the titans of online commerce. . . . It might be said that "eBay" is a moniker for monetization, and that "craigslist" is anything but.[3]

Chandler ultimately issued a split ruling, reinstating eBay's share of craigslist stock, but not restoring eBay's seat on craigslist's board. The second lawsuit, in California, was eventually settled in arbitration, and in 2015 eBay sold back its 28.4 percent stake in craigslist for an undisclosed amount (Bensinger 2015).

What do the lawsuits between craigslist and eBay show us about the former's platform politics? First, we see craigslist's refusal to adopt mainstream monetization strategies. Of course, craigslist is far from an anarchist rejection of industry—after all, these two very profitable companies hashed out their problems in courtrooms. But the fraught relationship between craigslist and eBay presents a clear contrast of corporate priorities and platform politics. The lawsuits also expose a degree of naïveté from Buckmaster and Newmark. With the advantage of hindsight, the idea that eBay would be content with a 30 percent stake in craigslist without any ulterior motives seems ludicrous. Then again, eBay's interest in craigslist also seems flawed—eBay kept seeking internal data to identify craigslist's "secret sauce"—but for many users a key part of craigslist's appeal is the very things that make it different from eBay.

Conclusions

As a company that has always been headquartered in San Francisco, craigslist has been witness to the city's changing and increasingly fraught relationship to the tech industry. Like San Francisco, the internet has gentrified over the past twenty-five years, attempting to smooth over frictions and fractures, and develop new norms of aesthetics and use. Craigslist is one of many companies that burst into public view during the excitement and uncertainty of the 1990s. Decades later, the site looks and feels the same, while the rest of the web has largely moved on. Craigslist reflects a certain set of assumptions about the online publics and politics, assumptions that were prevalent in the mid-1990s but have since become less common and more outdated. In other words, when craigslist first went online, the goal wasn't to oppose mainstream values of the internet, because there wasn't yet a clear sense of what the internet would turn into. Craigslist was always quirky, but this quality only became a form of criticism as the mainstream web evolved, largely leaving craigslist's early web values behind.

How does craigslist speak back to the mainstream web? As *Wired* observed in 2009, "craigslist is one of the strangest monopolies in history, where customers are locked in by fees set at zero and where the ambiance of neglect is not a way to extract more profit but the expression of a world-view" (Wired staff 2009). That world view believes in user autonomy, update minimalism, and transparent monetization. If a company can be profitable without embracing mainstream platform politics wholesale, the fact that it exists at all, let alone remains popular, becomes its own form of protest. Craigslist's platform politics can't necessarily be deployed universally across the internet. But the fact that they can be stable and successful matters in an industry dominated by views like "privacy is dead" and "move fast and break things."

While I see craigslist as an exemplar of Web 1.0 ethics in a Web 2.0 indus-try, this view risks romanticizing the 1990s web and simplifying differences among companies that got their start early on. After all, craigslist and eBay launched within a year of each other and as the lawsuits between the two companies made clear, they have very different politics. The important thing about craigslist, however, is that it didn't just get its start in a Web 1.0 moment, it has refused to let go of Web 1.0 values, in its design, business model, or industry relationships. Like Sapnar-Ankerson (2010), I see draw-ing distinctions between Web 1.0 and 2.0 as not "an exercise in nostalgia but a way to illuminate a discursive web connecting aesthetics, ideologies, economies, and industries" (190). This chapter has looked at craigslist as a connective thread between important shifts—technical, economic, social, and geographic—of the internet over the past twenty-five years.

When I asked Newmark about whether and how the California tech industry had changed over time, he was circumspect and cautious: "The ratio of people thinking only to make money versus people with mixed ideology has shifted [toward the former]" (interview with author, May 16, 2017). By "mixed ideology," Newmark was referring to the company's profit-minimalism approach and to its rejection of Silicon Valley business models. Craigslist reflects some parts of the California Ideology and rejects others. Collective democracy is a key tenet of craigslist, but it operates at the level of accomplishing daily tasks and building neighborhood connections rather than the level of state or national politics. While craigslist might see itself as helping to solve local problems, this takes place in terms of finding jobs and activity partners, rather than larger social ills like racism or providing better education. Craigslist is something like an oasis in the midst of a constantly shifting digital desert, where stability and simplicity are features rather than bugs of platform politics.

While this chapter has described craigslist's origins and its relation to a broader tech industry, the next two chapters provide a media history and legal discussion of craigslist's development since 1995. Together, these chapters present a multifaceted account of where craigslist came from, the industry it has disrupted, and the legal battles the company has waged. The platform politics I've described in this chapter take on new complexities when we turn to craigslist's vexed relationship with newspapers and its problems in the courtroom.

2

The Death and Life of Classified Ads

A MEDIA HISTORY OF CRAIGSLIST

Although it has been compared with a number of things and places over the years—job fair, flea market, local pub—craigslist has always thought of itself as a website for getting classified ads online. But what are classified ads? Why do they matter in the context of newspapers, reading publics, and craigslist? Easily overlooked compared with their sexier marketing-ad counterparts, classifieds are actually crucial to the economics of local newspapers, and they also have an important history in allowing regular people to reach a wide audience while retaining their anonymity. Like craigslist, classified ads are simultaneously a tool for local businesses and important links for marginalized communities. In this chapter, my goal is to place craigslist within a broader context of advertising and interpersonal connection, and to recognize what it reproduced and what it disrupted as it grew into the most popular platform—at any time, in any medium—for writing and reading classified ads.

The Classified Ad as a Media Form

What is the role of online classified ads in the larger history of reading publics and technology? How can our understanding of craigslist be historicized by looking at changing tools and practices of classified ads as they transitioned from print to online media? Although there is a small body of research on classified ads (e.g., Bader 2005; Cocks 2009), this scholarship has largely ignored the transition to online platforms. While peer-to-peer exchange (see chapter 4), the gig economy (see chapter 5), and online dating (chapter 6) can feel like inventions of digital technologies, they all have precursors in print media. For over two centuries, the classified ad has been a crucial link connecting buyers and sellers, employers with workers, and single people looking for romance and friendship.

Classified advertising has been a nearly ubiquitous feature of the modern American newspaper since at least the mid-nineteenth century (Lorimor 1977), or even earlier if we take a loose definition of the format (see Cocks 2004). Despite—or perhaps because of—their ubiquity, classifieds have largely escaped serious scholarly attention, either in terms of media history or their social meaning (Lorimor 1977). What academics have written about classifieds in the United States tends to focus on their linguistic features (Bruthiaux 1996) or the legal uncertainty surrounding their use (Stevens 1990), or else uses them as a convenient data source to explore gender dynamics (Deaux and Hanna 1984; Nair 1992), queer romantic expectations (Laner 1978; Lumby 1978), or marketing principles (Hirschman 1987), especially in the case of personal ads. In the limited scholarship on craigslist, similarly limited categories emerge, particularly around personal ads as a vehicle for investigating queer dating life (e.g., Grov et al. 2013; Reynolds 2017; Robinson and Vidal-Ortiz 2013).

As a form, the classified ad evolved in a different direction from the marketing ads used by companies to sell products, with four important distinctions. First, the classified is marked by a person-to-person rather than company-to-person relationship (Lorimor 1977). Foreshadowing social-media platforms to come, the classified ad was largely meant to be a casual rather than professional exchange. Second, unlike display ads, classifieds require sustained attention and local knowledge to be read and understood. Cocks (2004) noted that in Victorian Britain, manuals were published to teach people how to respond to classifieds. Similarly, how-to books about entrepreneurialism and craigslist include detailed descriptions of how to post and respond to online ads (e.g., Buelow 2013; Landahl 2006). Third, for some readers, classifieds are mainly a source of amusement or entertainment, even (or especially) when earnest ad writers had no intention of being funny. Not unlike the mildly macabre practice of perusing obituaries (M. Johnson 2007), looking through classified ads can easily take on a voyeuristic character (Merskin 1995). Finally, the space constraints of classified ads have produced unique linguistic characteristics (Bruthiaux 1996). Because newspapers traditionally charged customers per character, classified ads were historically an exercise in extreme brevity. While many of these constraints fell away with the emergence of craigslist—which didn't charge the writer at all for most ads, let alone per character—some conventions of abbreviation and coding persisted online, particularly in personal ads (for a comprehensive list of abbreviations used in craigslist personal ads, see Lloyd [2009, 227–30]).

Although the sparse scholarship on classifieds doesn't tell us much about their historical importance in everyday life, we can still identify their economic relevance to the financial stability of newspapers (Merskin 1995). Text-only marketing had been present in British newspapers since the 1600s, and Czech newspapers have carried classifieds since the 1700s (Gammelgaard 2010). Classifieds took off in the mid-1800s (Cocks 2004), but this involved overcoming a degree of suspicion from newspaper and magazine editors. Lorimor (1977) argued that ever since colonial times, consumer demand has been the driving force behind classified ads. Initially, publishers were reluctant to incorporate the idiosyncratic messiness of classifieds into the neat pages of a newspaper. Things began to change at the beginning of the twentieth century, when the classifieds became part of the revenue-generating strategies of newspapers.

Classified Ads and Counterpublics

Of the many kinds of classifieds, personal ads have historically been the most controversial. Seeking employment or looking for a used car can fit in to narratives of industriousness and thrift, but searching for romance or even just companionship through a newspaper has long provoked suspicion and stigma—a topic I'll come back to in chapter 6. From a media-studies perspective, personal ads contain more than individual messages of interests and desires—they also reflect norms of dating, sexuality, and gender identity. In his study of personal ads in Britain, Cocks (2004) showed how moral anxieties came to shape how lawmakers, activist groups, and the press interpreted classifieds. Both the ubiquity and anonymity of personal ads seemed to highlight a decline in moral standards that was deemed particularly threatening to women. While studies of the content of personals have focused on how such ads reproduce mainstream stereotypes about gender and sexuality (Deaux and Hanna 1984), it's important to think about how classifieds and personals carved out small pockets of subversive resistance at the margins of mainstream newspapers.

Because Victorian culture treated women as standard-bearers of morality and because of long-standing (and enduring) fears of women's physical and moral vulnerability in the public sphere, early classified ads were commonly seen as particularly dangerous for women, with the potential to lure them into inappropriate social connections. Cocks pointed out the capacity for classified ads to enable anonymous connection that could dodge the close surveillance of women's romantic communication:

> We can see that the classifieds were not only an area of danger, but also the location for meetings of diverse subcultures, partly because they represented a small space in which policing was problematic, and because they circumvented the moral surveillance which after 1914 was increasingly directed against freedoms which seemed to contain dangers of racial and sexual degeneration. (2004, 3–4)

With fewer editorial constraints, personal ads offered discursive spaces of potential experimentation, play, and community building, in which the voices of marginalized readers—even within the constraints of the form and of newspapers' interventions—could be expressed and directly addressed to other readers.

Personal ads can be used to defy sexual norms. Cocks (2004) pointed out that personals in early twentieth-century Britain were often used for selling pornography covertly. But personal ads can also be used for political subversion in the midst of oppression. For example, Führer's (2012) analysis of matrimonial ads by German Jews in Nazi Germany, which were published in the only daily newspaper not wholly controlled by the regime, shows how the personal columns defied and questioned anti-Semitic propaganda. German Jews used the classifieds to display their professional and personal qualifications, painting a radically different picture from the one imposed by Nazis. As Führer contends: "a few of them read almost like a public statement, meant as a protest of principle against the very idea that the question of 'race' should be taken into consideration in business matters" (2012, 69). German Jews under Nazism used the classifieds of the *Frankfurter Zeitung* to challenge—covertly but publicly—the regime's propaganda and violence. These acts of textual subversion remind us that readers have always had a degree of agency in shaping the content of the newspaper through classifieds ads, which can be considered "a social network avant la lettre since they offer an opportunity for individuals to address an anonymous mass in private matters" (74).

In the twentieth century, mainstream disdain for classified personal ads gave them a subversive cachet among countercultural and marginalized groups. Personal ads became a fixture in underground and alternative publications that emerged beginning in the 1960s. Some of the highest-circulating alternative publications—for example, the *Village Voice* and underground newspapers of the 1960s and 1970s like the *Berkeley Barb* and the *Los Angeles Free Press*—carried a large number of personal ads, including sexually explicit ones (McMillian 2011). As Cocks noted, "The ambiguity of the small ad . . . allowed people to experiment with new freedoms" (2009, 189). For Cocks, personal ads retained a countercultural investment in experimenting with new identities and desires, while running less of a risk of direct intervention from the authorities:

> One of the successes of the [1960s] counterculture, one that was to catch on as a medium for love, sex and adventure with increasing force over the following twenty years, remained relatively unnoticed: the small ad. Ads were crucial to the self-identity of the counterculture, and as a result they carried on the long tradition of personal advertising as a subversive medium. This sense of continued defiance among the classifieds was reinforced by the attacks of the police and courts on their wilder outposts. (172)

The alternative weeklies that blossomed all over the United States in the 1980s continued to offer "thick classifieds section[s]" (McMillian 2011, 181), which were both a form of self-expression for individuals and an important source of revenue for countercultural publications.

The personal ad's popularity in countercultural and alternative publications helps explain some of the institutional resistance documented by Merskin (1995) in her survey of classifieds editors. While the majority of editors carried personal ads, some felt that such ads compromised the image of their papers. Those who did carry personals often placed restrictions on the content of ads, particularly for ads that referenced lifestyles alternative to heterosexual monogamy. As a whole, mainstream newspapers' policies had a significant impact on the kind of ads that could be placed (for legal implications, see Stevens [1990]). Meanwhile, personal ads by individuals seeking same-sex partners flourished in LGBT publications such as the *Advocate* (Lumby 1978) and the *Wishing Well* (Laner 1978). According to Merskin (1995), mainstream daily newspapers in the United States only began to carry personals in the late 1980s and early 1990s. The moral judgments surrounding personal ads in newspapers have a parallel with the mainstream social resistance to online dating, where romantic encounters that start through mediated dating sites, regardless of whether that site is a newspaper ad or a website like OkCupid, are stigmatized as antisocial or perverse (Cali, Coleman, and Campbell 2013).

Without overstating the freedom and subversiveness of the classifieds, it's clear that the cultural and political questions they raised are still relevant today in the context of digital media. Internet-studies researchers have pointed out the advantages of online publics for folks on the margins. Queer youth have found support and solidarity through the web (Gray 2009; Kitzie 2018), while Black Twitter provides an important venue for people of color to express shared cultural norms and political beliefs (Brock 2012; Jackson 2016). Michael Warner (2002) used the terms publics and counterpublics to talk about forms of social connection that are tied to media objects like newspapers and novels. For people on the margins, classified ads were an important tool for finding one another, acting as a beacon of mutual recognition.

Another connection between print classified ads and online communication has to do with fears around anonymity and authenticity. The moral objections described by Cocks (2004) revolved around whether classified ads—and their authors—could be trusted. Were ad authors who they claimed to be, and were their intentions legitimate? These concerns—about trust, authenticity, and anonymity—have important connections to rules and norms of online publics and will resurface in the next chapter as part of craigslist's politics around platform responsibility. As Lorimor (1977) pointed out, classifieds in general—and personals in particular—raise issues of trust between readers and publications, issues that endure in more contemporary panics surrounding fraud, hacking, and the circulation of fake information online.

Every technology brings with it a set of suspicions around proper versus improper use (Marvin 1988), and part of figuring out the social role of a new media form, whether it's a classified ad or an online message board, involves thinking about the capacity for bad actors. Some of the fears about traditional classified ads were little more than an excuse for classism, sexism, and homophobia. Yet it is also important to acknowledge that fears around the classified ad have roots in real acts of crime and violence. There is a somewhat grisly history of violent crimes plotted with the help of classified ads dating back at least as far as Belle Sorenson Gunness, who lured men to her Indiana farm using the "matrimonial columns" of local Chicago newspapers and is estimated to have killed between twenty-five and forty people between 1884 and 1908 (Cyriax 2009). Newspaper classified ads are still a source for potential scams—scammers have used everything from personals to ads for puppies as cover for criminal intent. Even newspaper staff members have taken advantage of the classified ad's potential for fraud: in 2017, the Bureau of Alcohol, Tobacco, Firearms and Explosives busted a newspaper editor for using classified ads to traffic guns (K. Christensen 2017).

Legally, uncertainty about whether publishers can or should be held responsible for the fraudulent or criminal content of classifieds placed in their papers (Stevens 1990) has parallels with debates on the liability of online intermediaries, to be discussed in more depth in the next chapter. I'll come back to themes of trust, anonymity, and safety in chapter 7 as part of a discussion of craigslist's approach to problems of scams and deceptions. For now, I want to wrap up this examination of craigslist's classified-ad roots by discussing how the website's arrival presented problems for newspapers who had come to rely on classified ads as a source of revenue.

Unwelcome Disruptions: Craigslist, Classifieds, and the Newspaper Industry's Bottom Line

In the battle between print and online media, a common narrative pits amateur bloggers and independent journalists against professional news writers with expertise and training (e.g., Benilde 2010; Walker 2005). As getting content online became easier, traditional media outlets felt threatened by bloggers and DIY journalists. Craigslist presented a different threat to the newspaper industry: the bottom line of advertising income. Craigslist offered a free alternative to print classified ads, which had become a consistent, low-overhead means of supporting newspapers. Journalists making sense of craigslist in its early days drew direct comparisons to classified ads, while emphasizing new affordances that came with the web. For example, as craigslist launched in Boulder, Colorado, a local journalist described the site's resonances with its print predecessor:

> For 22-year-old Jessica Matzuk, her move to Boulder this fall was made easier with craigslist.org. While she still lived thousands of miles away in Virginia, Matzuk said she could easily contact people in Boulder with apartments through craigslist.org. "It's better than the newspaper (classifieds), because it's free and people can include a lot more detail on

craigslist, and it's easier to search," Matzuk said. "For anything that's happening, the Internet is now the first source that I check." That growing sentiment, particularly among the younger generations, has many print publications scrambling to see how they can increase their role in the Internet world of people communication. (Clucas 2004)

While newspapers struggled to figure out whether and how much to charge for reading their content online, another battle was brewing over how to keep control of classified ads. To compete in the new marketplace, some local newspapers experimented with bringing their classified sections online. In November 2003, two major newspaper publishers, Knight Ridder and the Washington Post Company, invested $6.3 million in the online people-networking website Tribe.net, with hopes of boosting their online classifieds business (Clucas 2004).

The stakes for the newspaper industry were high. In the pre-web era, classifieds accounted for 25 percent of all newspaper revenue (Lorimor 1977). Classified-ad income was more predictable and came with fewer overheads than market-based advertising, a win-win revenue source from the perspective of local newspapers. The popularity of classified ads grew substantially in the United States between the 1980s and the 2000s, but by 2004 a combination of the digital-media boom and a sluggish economy had led to a 20 percent drop in print revenue from classified ads and a 40 percent drop in job ads (Clucas 2004). Media theorist R. G. Picard has argued that since the mid-2000s classified advertising in newspapers has been declining for the simple reason that ads are "more effective on the Internet than in print" (2008, 705). By 2009, the traditional financial model for newspapers had been destabilized to the point that a Pew Research report stated that online ads had "devastated a key revenue source for traditional newspapers" (Jones 2009, 4). In terms of the specific contribution that craigslist made to this decline, Seamans and Zhu (2014) used a natural experiment to estimate the impact of craigslist's introduction in 308 local-newspaper markets in the United States. The authors found that when craigslist launched in a new city, local newspapers saw their classified-ad rates drop by about 20 percent. Expanding into a new geographic area meant a minimal cost for craigslist, but presented a real loss for local newspapers.

Disruption is often held up as an ethos of the tech industry (Christensen, Raynor, and McDonald 2015) and craigslist was one of many websites—along with Autotrader and Backpage—to disrupt print media's revenue streams. While entrepreneurs in Silicon Valley embrace an "innovate first, ask questions later" approach to building new technologies, disruption comes with the cost of upsetting existing industries. Part of the growing animosity toward craigslist as a "newspaper killer" was wrapped up in a larger narrative of digital technologies transforming information and media systems. As Weiss (2013) succinctly put it:

> Craigslist is (a) where young urban people conduct much of the traffic of their lives, including renting apartments, finding lost pets, and getting laid in the middle of the day, and is (b) thereby destroying classified revenues for big-city newspapers, which are already in crisis, and so it has become (c) the symbol of the transformation of the information industry.

More than competing for advertising, craigslist symbolized an upheaval in how people read the news, got information, and connected to their neighborhoods.

It's clear that craigslist affects local newspapers by eating away at their revenue from classified ads, and even those with an immense fondness for craigslist could wonder about the social benefits of the site (and its roughly forty employees) weighed against the value of thousands of local newspapers. Significant blame in the decline of local newspapers has been attached to the internet generally and craigslist specifically, but this argument ignores some of the larger issues that have plagued newspapers for nearly a century. As media analyst Thomas Baekdal explained in a Twitter post, "blaming craigslist [for the decline in newspaper revenue] . . . is disingenuous. They listened to the market, and created something people wanted. The US newspapers can only blame itself [*sic*] for completely missing what was very plainly happening all around them."[1] Like Baekdal, Pickard has argued that blaming online classifieds for destabilizing print newspapers ignores the fact that papers relied on a vulnerable business model: "Since the late 19th century, journalism has been primarily supported by advertising revenues. But this model is increasingly unsustainable as audiences and advertisers migrate to the Internet, where ads sell for a mere fraction of their paper-based counterparts" (2014, 154). Although journalism is arguably a public service, the dominant funding structure in the United States has been based on commercial advertising—in Pickard's view, a flawed business model.

The blame game of who killed traditional newspapers is based on having clear-cut heroes (local newspapers) and villains (craigslist). But socio-technical shifts in power and influence rarely unfold in straightforward, linear paths. For example, Autotrader is a website that allows people to post ads for buying and selling used cars and has eaten into the classified revenue of print newspapers. But Autotrader is owned by Cox Enterprises, a privately held media conglomerate that owns a number of newspapers, in addition to radio and broadcast-television stations. So even though Autotrader eats into classified revenues of newspapers, the website's profits ultimately support a media company that owns print newspapers. Any argument that blames online classifieds sites for diminishing newspaper profits must take into account the complex economies of media industries.[2]

Tensions around craigslist's role in the decline of print media resurfaced in 2018, when Craig Newmark Philanthropies made a $20 million donation to the City University of New York's School of Journalism. For years, Craig Newmark Philanthropies has donated to nonprofits that support a free press (Peiser 2018), but many of CUNY's alumni questioned the move, "calling out the irony in naming a journalism school after the man who founded a company that went on to cost newspapers $50 million in missed revenue in 2004 because of the so-called craigslist effect" (L. Johnson 2018). It's outside the scope of this book to dig into all of the complexities of print media and journalism in the wake of digital media (see McChesney and Pickard [2011] for an important account of the journalism industry), but I do want to consider how craigslist's disruption of print classified ads has shaped the relationship between the site and the media.

In interviews, Newmark has suggested that competition over the classifieds market has led to a sense of resentment from print-media journalists, leading to skewed perceptions of craigslist in the press. About 15 percent of Jim Buckmaster's two-hundred-plus blog posts reference the media, typically taking a tone of frustration with perceived inaccuracies in reporting. For example, in a 2010 post, Buckmaster lashed out at a CNN journalist for "ambushing" Newmark during a charity event meant to highlight craigslist's charitable donations, and instead asking questions about fraud on the site:

> There is a class of "journalists" known for gratuitously trashing respected organizations and individuals, ignoring readily available facts in favor of rank sensationalism and self-promotion. They work for tabloid media. Your stunt has veteran news pros we know recoiling in journalistic horror, some of them chalking it up to a decline in CNN's standards, which is unfortunate.

In questioning the integrity and ethics of journalists, Buckmaster voiced a sense of frustration and victimhood, suggesting that journalists prefer sensational headlines over a more complicated story. By leading with rare but dramatic cases of violence, journalists, Buckmaster insisted, ignore both the statistical unlikelihood of fraud on craigslist and the efforts the site has made to work against misuse. Buckmaster's blog posts frequently attempt to correct the record, at least from a pro-craigslist perspective, whether by calling out journalists for perceived bias or by demanding apologies from policy makers.

As I noted in the previous chapter, one of several moral panics about the web surfaced around 2009, stoking fears of sexual depravity and financial fraud. While the company was struggling to rebrand itself as a community resource, higher-ups at craigslist saw the site as undermined by a popular press eager to dig in to stories of sex and violence. The reality is that the press had focused on craigslist's facilitation of hookups and kinky interests well before high-profile cases of sexual violence (e.g., Loustalot 2003; Sohn 2003). But when stories about sex shifted from quirky to horrific, Newmark and Buckmaster began to see their platform as misunderstood at best and, at worst, maligned in a moral panic. It's impossible to know if press coverage of sexual violence on craigslist was rooted in an industry-wide resentment of the platform or a general tendency to sensationalize. But the relationship between craigslist and newspapers is complex, encompassing cultural traditions of anonymous connection and producing a reliable source of income.

Conclusions

The transition of classified ads from the printed page to the web wasn't exactly smooth, reflecting a broader set of disruptions around digital technology and print media. There are some important takeaways from the history of classified ads. First, while craigslist is often described as a free-for-all of idiosyncrasies, quirkiness, risk, and desire, these characteristics have a legacy in the print classified ad, which underscores the tendency of media technologies to reproduce rather than replace their predecessors. Classified ads have always been contested texts when it comes to authenticity and appropriate behavior. Second, classified ads have consistently drawn together a wide range of readers, what Warner (2002) would call publics and counterpublics. For Warner, texts can play a crucial role in anchoring a community, particularly for people who are in some way marginalized. Classified ads give people a way to reach a mass audience, to seek out and communicate with people who share an interest, a desire, or an experience of otherness. While anonymity can be useful for people looking to use classified ads to communicate during conditions surveillance or stigma, the same feature means that classifieds can be used for deceptive and sometimes violent ends, which feeds into panics about safety and anonymity. Finally, the aesthetic simplicity of classified ads belies their financial importance. Classified ads had long been overlooked as an important or interesting part of newspaper work, despite their profitability. The importance of print classified ads only became obvious when their existence was threatened by a less expensive, less edited, and more easily accessible online alternative.

For a seemingly straightforward media object, classified ads support a complex array of social relations, from the pragmatic to the subversive, the mundane to the violent. With the web, the reach of ads expanded and rules around content became looser. On the one hand, this meant that more people than ever could produce, read, and be entertained by classified ads, without the geographic or editorial constraints of print newspapers. On the other hand, the massive reach of online platforms made it easier than ever to swindle, scam, and lie. Working through the history of classified ads helps us see what craigslist inherited and what it introduced as it brought personal, employment, and for-sale ads online.

Looking at the history of classified ads has given us a clearer sense of what came before craigslist, and which industries were disrupted as the site expanded into multiple cities and became increasingly popular. In the next chapter, I'll examine some of the battles over appropriate versus inappropriate uses of craigslist by reviewing the company's key court cases. The courtroom offers another vantage point for thinking about how craigslist fits into a wider digital culture and industry. As both a plaintiff and a defendant, craigslist has outlined its expectations of how the site should be used, producing at times conflicting political visions of free expression and legitimate use.

3

From Sex Workers to Data Hacks
CRAIGSLIST'S COURTROOM BATTLES

Craig Newmark does not particularly like talking about the occasionally bad behavior of craigslist users. When I approached the subject with him in an interview, he explained that "the Internet can allow people of bad faith to get together, but it also does a lot of good, connecting good people and fostering understanding" (interview with author, May 16, 2017). Although Newmark recognizes that the internet can be used for deception and violence, he prefers a more optimistic vision that emphasizes self-determination, free expression, and community building. All these aspects are part of the internet's power, but so is the capacity for fraud, scams, and violence. Sometimes bad behavior on craigslist is blatantly obvious and horrifically violent, like the rare cases of assault and murder. Other times, bad behavior is much less sensational but still clashes with craigslist's politics, such as taking the platform's data and using it to build new tools and products. Both kinds of problems test the company's politics, and by looking at craigslist's legal battles we get a clearer picture of the platform's sense of its responsibilities to users.

Craigslist works as intended most of the time for most people. But on rare occasions, exchanges can go very, very wrong. A look at craigslist's legal history sheds light on the dangerous and potentially violent capacities of the web in general and craigslist in particular. Picking apart legal controversies also shows us what happens when craigslist's view of platform responsibility is tested in court. By platform responsibility, I mean the obligations that platforms have to people who are affected by their policies and practices.

As online platforms have grown more complex and integrated into everyday life, their responsibilities have become harder to pin down (see Gillespie 2018a). Court cases and legal decisions help sharpen the fuzziness of platform responsibilities, giving shape to the specific rules that apply to people, companies, and data online.

Of the many lawsuits that have involved craigslist, I focus on the two problems mentioned above: determining platform responsibility for user behavior, and dealing with unauthorized uses of data. These issues emerged as the most salient legal matters after analyzing Jim Buckmaster's public-facing blog, press releases from the EFF, and LexisNexis search results for the terms *craigslist* and *lawsuit*. I also draw on legal journalists' coverage of these cases and interviews I conducted with experts in the arena of platform responsibility and copyright law. Legal professionals look at case law to help make specific legal claims and to understand prior precedents as decided by the courts. For me, craigslist's lawsuits are interesting and important because of what they can tell us about evolving debates over technology and culture. Although craigslist is just one node in a dense network of industry players, at key moments it has had a significant impact on discussions about whether platforms are responsible for the behavior of users, and what rights tech companies have over their data. When users post problematic content or engage in violent behavior, what responsibility do platforms have to keep people safe? Who has the right to decide what kinds of data use are fair and what kinds are a problem?

Platforms Don't Hurt People, People Hurt People: Regulating Online Behavior

To understand craigslist's vision of platform responsibility, we need to look at the Communications Decency Act (CDA), and specifically section 230, commonly called CDA 230. Of major legislation covering the internet, CDA 230 is probably the most famous, simultaneously a touchstone for free-speech advocates, tech entrepreneurs, and provocative troublemakers. Passed in 1996, the CDA as a whole was meant to clarify the ways that people could legally use the web, whether for academic, entrepreneurial, or entertainment purposes (Mendels 1996). Section 230 is usually held up as a beacon of internet freedom, outlining legal protections for internet service providers and platforms, with the goal of encouraging free speech, technological innovation, and user control over information. Under CDA 230, platforms cannot be held liable for the actions of users. The law means that

Facebook isn't legally responsible for users who harass or threaten someone online and that YouTube can't be sued for hosting videos about terrorism. Platforms like Facebook, Twitter, and YouTube would likely never have gotten off the ground if companies could be held liable for content that was false, obscene, subversive, or extreme. The law reflects a long-standing tenet of the early web, that online content should be open, accessible, and diverse.

In 2017, the US Congress passed the Allow States and Victims to Fight Online Sex Trafficking Act (FOSTA), which is arguably the first major limitation to the freedoms gained by platforms with CDA 230. Support for FOSTA was overwhelming, with the only nay votes in the Senate coming from long-standing privacy advocates Rand Paul and Ron Wyden. FOSTA is "aimed at curbing online sex trafficking by holding online platforms legally liable for any content found to 'knowingly assist, facilitate, or support sex trafficking'" (Chávez 2018). The bill allows people to take legal action against a platform if its users violate federal sex-trafficking laws. In other words, platforms are not liable for the bad behavior of users, unless users are involved in human trafficking. Within days of FOSTA's passage, a number of companies changed their policies, including Reddit, which had threads dedicated to sex work, and online dating sites like Tinder (I will come back to FOSTA and craigslist personals in chapter 6). But craigslist had a particular relationship to the new law, having argued for decades that platforms couldn't be held responsible for the acts of users, specifically when it comes to sex work. In fact, when considering internet law in the United States, craigslist is probably the best platform for thinking through the shift from CDA 230 to FOSTA, and how legal battles around sex, sex work, and violence have shaped ideas about platform responsibility.

For craigslist, questions about liability have most frequently been attached to sex work, sexual violence, and human trafficking. Like their predecessors on the printed page, craigslist personal ads had always attracted attention (e.g., Loustalot 2003; Sohn 2003), which became a frenzy when cases of sexual violence surfaced. As more and more people got online to do more and more everyday things, craigslist became one of the first websites to undergo a public as well as a legal trial about what it owed its users. I concentrate on two key controversies in craigslist's battles around sex work: the confrontation between craigslist and a Chicago sheriff, and the first high-profile murder that involved craigslist ads. Both of these events transpired in 2009, which turned out to be a pivotal year for testing craigslist's politics and its ideas of platform responsibility.

Thomas Dart has served as the sheriff of Cook County, Illinois, since 2007, making him the chief executive of the second-largest law enforcement department in the United States (after Los Angeles). In 2009, Dart filed a lawsuit against craigslist, demanding a shutdown of what was then called the "Erotic Services" section. The suit had two counts: an accusation that craigslist constituted a public nuisance by facilitating prostitution, and an injunction requiring craigslist to cease all conduct related to illegal sex work. Craigslist anchored its defense in CDA 230, arguing that it could not be held liable for the content of ads posted by users. As in previous cases where craigslist had been sued for the content of its ads (e.g., *Chicago Lawyers' Committee For Civil Rights Under Law v. craigslist*),[1] the court ruled that craigslist was ultimately not responsible for the content posted to its platform.

In the text of the Dart decision, we see a court grappling with the consequences of the increasing integration of the web into every part of social life, including sex and sex work. The decision relies on the idea of platform neutrality, positioning craigslist as a neutral entity that merely publishes user behavior, rather than shaping it:

> Nothing in the service craigslist offers induces anyone to post any particular listing or express a preference for discrimination; for example, craigslist does not offer a lower price to people who include discriminatory statements in their postings. If craigslist "causes" the discriminatory notices, then so do phone companies and courier services (and, for that matter, the firms that make the computers and software that owners use to post their notices online), yet no one could think that Microsoft and Dell are liable for "causing" discriminatory advertisements.[2]

In his work on user moderation on Facebook and YouTube, Gillespie (2018a, b, c) has argued that platforms have a vested interest in presenting themselves as ideologically agnostic, a standpoint that allows them to sidestep questions about their role in mitigating online harassment or crime (see also Gillespie 2010). Decisions like *Dart v. craigslist* provide a legal rationale bolstering this perspective, suggesting that online platforms are simply the empty vessels into which users pour their thoughts, ideas, and data.

In some ways, Dart's lawsuit seemed more like a publicity stunt than a serious attempt to hold platforms accountable. Craigslist had already instituted changes intended to make personal ads safer. The company started charging fees for adult-services ads in 2008 as part of a settlement with forty state attorneys general, with the immediate effect of a massive drop in ads (Buckmaster 2008b). A blog post from Buckmaster on March 9, 2009, claimed that ads had dropped between 90 and 95 percent in major urban areas. In addition, the company had put new moderation rules in place, and Buckmaster argued that "the ads that remain on the site are much improved in their compliance with our Terms of Use and local laws, in part due to screening measures developed in collaboration with the Attorneys General and law enforcement" (Buckmaster 2009). Some felt that Dart's attack on craigslist was hypocritical, given that craigslist's cooperation with law enforcement enabled his and other sheriffs' offices around the country to prosecute illegal sex work and human traffickers. As one blogger noted at the time:

> It's telling that Dart is making a big, public stink about prostitution on craigslist. If his goal were stopping prostitution, he'd want to keep craigslist open, providing his department with a steady source of leads. It's easier than staking out street corners. No, Dart needs to be seen as stopping prostitution. And that requires calling out craigslist. (Thomas 2009)

In 2008, craigslist argued that it was being scapegoated while lawmakers looked to score political points in fighting the scourge of a sex trade that had moved online (see Hazen 2010; Masnick 2009). Dart's suit seemed like an uptick in what craigslist viewed as misinformed antagonism.

Just one month after Dart filed suit, his complaints took on a new urgency following a series of crimes involving victims found through craigslist's Erotic Services section. Over the course of a week in April, three violent attacks took place in Boston and surrounding cities, allegedly committed by Philip Markoff, a twenty-three-year-old medical student at Boston University.[3] Trisha Leffler, a sex worker, had flown in from Las Vegas to Boston and posted an ad on craigslist. She later identified Markoff as the man who answered the ad, came to her room at the Westin Copley Place in downtown Boston, threatened her with a gun, restrained her with rope, and stole her cash—in addition to two pairs of her panties. Five days later, on April 14, Julissa Brisman, a twenty-five-year-old from New York City, was attacked and murdered at the Marriott Copley, also in downtown Boston. She had posted an ad for erotic massage to Boston's Erotic Services section, to which Markoff allegedly responded. On April 16, Corinne Stout, another sex worker from Las Vegas, placed an ad on craigslist, offering lap dances out of her hotel room near a casino close to Boston. Like Leffler, she identified Markoff as the man who responded to her ad, came to her room, and attempted to rob her. Markoff was arrested by the police on April 20. Evidence against him was significant—Leffler and Stout identified him as the attacker, he left fingerprints at the crime scenes, his home IP address was matched to messages sent to the victims, and possessions of the attacked women were found in Markoff's apartment. Some journalists, after turning up information on Markoff's activity on fetish websites, suggested sexual deviance as a motivation. Others pointed to his gambling habits and personal debt as motivations for his alleged crimes (LaRosa and Cramer 2009).

As horrific and senseless as the attacks attributed to Markoff were, the fears stoked by this crime spree were boosted by broader anxieties about socio-technical change. The quick succession of crimes and Markoff's background as a young, white medical student with an apparently oblivious fiancée fed into the media frenzy, but so did the use of craigslist to locate victims. As LaRosa and Cramer noted in their account of the crimes, "So many people use craigslist and feel so comfortable with it that it was upsetting to hear that a killer was using it to pick out victims like the rest of us might pick out a used kitchen table" (2009, 64).

By 2009, the tech industry had recovered from its late 1990s crash and social-media platforms like Facebook, Myspace, and Twitter had taken hold in everyday life. Yet the popularity of these platforms didn't necessarily translate into a sense of comfort—for many, it was clear that web-based technologies were here to stay, but it was much less clear who should be using them and how. As with technological innovations that came before, social uncertainty around the web often crystallized around young people and sexual activity (Marwick 2008; see also Marvin 1988; Malin 2014). As journalists, educators, parents, and regular internet users looked to make sense of technologies that weren't so much new as newly popular, edge cases of deviant and criminal behavior became particularly fixating. While violence against women, and particularly sex workers, is sadly nothing new, when combined with Markoff's clean-cut image and use of new technology, we get an ideal recipe for media panic and public outrage.

In the aftermath of the crimes against Leffler, Brisman, and Stout, a significant amount of blame landed on craigslist. Although the platform had cooperated with police and had in fact provided a crucial means for apprehending Markoff, a number of journalists and policy makers called for substantive changes to online personal ads (e.g., Corbin 2009; Moore 2009). Craigslist responded by renaming "Erotic Services" as "Adult Services," and the posting fee for ads in the category was increased from $5 to $10—charging more was meant to decrease the number of ads. These efforts weren't enough to stem public complaints, which ranged from moral disapproval of casual sex to concerns about human trafficking and forced prostitution.

Violence against women, human trafficking, and coercive sex are unacceptable acts that need to be met with a strong legal response. But in thinking about the different stakeholders involved, deciding who should be held responsible becomes difficult. Dart offered a vision of platform responsibility where sites like craigslist were on the hook for facilitating illegal behavior. Craigslist preferred to consider itself as a protector of free speech and liberal sexual politics, and, like many in Silicon Valley, saw complaints about adult services as a conservative attack on the web's democratic values of self-expression and tolerance. Dropping out of the narrative was what kind of responsibility sex workers expected from platforms and law enforcement.

While craigslist was negotiating its adult-services policies in 2009, journalist and former sex worker Melissa Gira Grant defended the platform as a better alternative to its less responsible peers. Gira Grant (2009) argued that it was:

> wrong to reduce the now-shuttered erotic-services section to an "online red-light district." . . . Far from unregulated public sex, each interaction had to begin with a few emails and, often, a light background check. These transactions might not always have gone as advertised, but they were rarely harmful or resulted in headlines.

Rather than a free-for-all, Gira Grant described craigslist as a middleman that allowed sex workers to screen potential clients. In support of Gira Grant's claims, sociologists and economists who have studied sex workers' relationship to the internet have found that online platforms actually make sex work safer (Cunningham and Kendall, 2010). When platforms like craigslist and Backpage shut down, sex workers have fewer tools to screen customers and are forced to rely on pimps.

However sex workers themselves saw platform responsibility, the law ultimately sided with law enforcement. FOSTA represents a victory for people like Dart and a rebuke of platforms like craigslist. The high-profile crimes in 2009 were part of a substantive shift in craigslist's reputation from a scrappy upstart for community building into a refuge for scams and violence.[4] Reflecting on this reputational shift ten years later, platform responsibility emerges along a number of fronts. Craigslist wanted to support free speech and sexual freedom and saw itself as responsible for promoting these values through its platform policies. CDA 230 was crucial in maintaining this vision of platform responsibility—as became clear with the passage of FOSTA, craigslist could only stand by its free-expression defense when it wasn't legally liable for the behavior of its users. Craigslist also offered a narrative of responsibility in pointing to its active cooperation with law enforcement, contrasting its policies with those of less responsible peers— a narrative that was ultimately inadequate in the face of growing pressure from antitrafficking activists and lawmakers.

You Can Access, Just Don't Use: Politics of Platform Data Control

In chapter 1, we saw that common complaints about craigslist emphasized its minimal design and slow pace of updating features. Not content with just pointing out design flaws, users and companies have occasionally taken these complaints to the next level by making new tools and apps based on craigslist data. For example, users have written software to automate running searches and posting ads, rather than doing so manually, one search or post at a time. A quick search of the coding library GitHub shows that for anyone with basic coding skills, tools for tweaking craigslist are easily available. Yet scraping data is in violation of craigslist's terms of use, and the company has repeatedly fought for control over its data when outside actors have attempted to leverage that data to build tools and apps. More than just tech-industry infighting, these lawsuits matter when it comes to characterizing—and monetizing—user-generated content (UGC). A 2013 lawsuit with a company called 3taps demonstrates how craigslist's view of data use runs up against Web 1.0 values that privilege not just access to but reworking and circulation of information.[5]

The entire business model of 3taps involves walking a fine line between using and misusing data. 3taps is "an exchange platform dedicated to keeping public facts publicly accessible. [They] collect, organize, and distribute exchange-related data for developer use" (3taps, n.d.). Think of 3taps as a middleman that specializes in data scraping, building tools to gather data from platforms like eBay and craigslist, and packaging them for other companies. The company's self-description emphasizes that it gathers "facts" that are public, issues at the core of its lawsuit with craigslist. Tensions between craigslist and 3taps began in 2011, when 3taps and a second company, PadMapper, partnered up to create a map-based platform for browsing craigslist's housing ads. At the time, craigslist's real-estate listings didn't display as a map, meaning that users had to create their own maps of apartment listings, for example on Google Maps or on paper. PadMapper wanted to cut out the cartographic middleman and used 3taps to create a more sophisticated, map-based interface for searching apartment listings (see figure 3.1). Craigslist sent each company a cease-and-desist letter and blocked their IP addresses in 2012. When 3taps continued scraping data by rerouting requests through other IP addresses, craigslist sued, and the case went to court in 2013.

Craigslist's main advantage over its many competitors is market share—it launched at a moment when there were few (or really no) competitors. Although 3taps and PadMapper relied on craigslist data, their platforms represented a crucial shift. Rather than being directly involved, craigslist ads were now indirect, with PadMapper rather than craigslist as the main platform. For craigslist, the problem wasn't just that 3taps was *accessing* data but that it was *using* data in a new way, to support a competing platform.

Fundamentally, *craigslist v. 3taps* addresses the limits of the mantra "information wants to be free," a dominant narrative of early tech culture (see Wagner 2003). Underlying alternative copyright movements, whistle-blowers, white-hat hackers (meaning hackers who cooperate with or support law enforcement), and the free and open-source software community, this ethos demands open access to and use of information across the web, irrespective of whether those data come from a public library or a privately owned company. Participatory culture (Jenkins 2006), remixes (Sinnreich 2010), and memes (Shifman 2014) are all massively popular cultural forms attached to an information-wants-to-be-free ethic. But for companies looking to monetize UGC, user information can't be free, at least not all the time or for everyone. How much authority do platforms have over the ways people use their data? Are some uses of platform data more legitimate than others? How much weight do documents like terms of service (TOS) and terms of use (TOU) carry in the eyes of the law? These questions point us to the politics and logics shaping how tech companies envision their responsibilities to users when it comes to data.

It's unclear when the first TOU went online, but one of the earliest controversies between platforms and users goes back to 1994, when AOL sold users' detailed personal information to direct marketers without notifying customers (Nollinger 1995). Over the next three years, AOL crafted an agreement of service for its users, advising them that (among other things) it sold their information to third parties. TOU—written largely by lawyers and at a grad-student reading level (Steinmetz 2015)—would become a default feature of online platforms. I've argued elsewhere that TOU could be a powerful tool of connecting with users and reflecting their (rather than platforms')

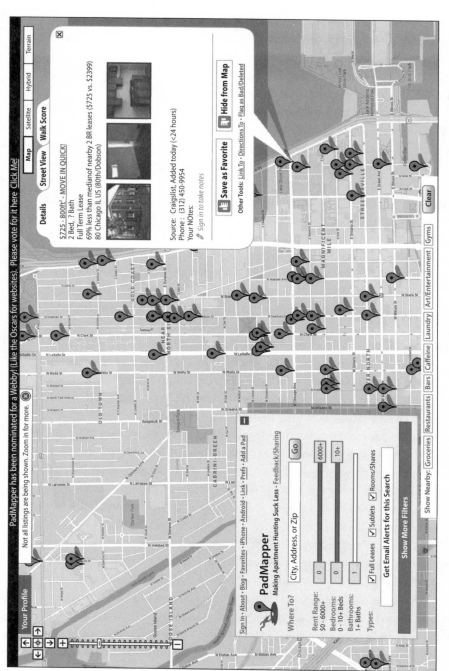

FIGURE 3.1. During its short lifespan of 2011 to 2013, PadMapper promised to "automatically generate a beautiful craigslist ad with high-res pictures and location maps" (quoted in Zekas 2012). At the time, craigslist displayed ads as a list ranked by date of posting, with no functionality for sorting by location or even linking to a map.

interests and values (Lingel 2017a). But for the most part, platforms have opted to treat these documents as preemptive litigation frameworks rather than as potential points of dialogue between everyday users and platform administrators.

The first available URL for craigslist on the Wayback Machine is from 1998, when the site already had a "Policies" link, a document of under three hundred words that focused mostly on condemning spam, written at an eleventh-grade reading level. By 2011, when 3taps was scraping data, the TOS had been formalized into a much longer (4,633 words) and more complex (an undergraduate reading level) document, in keeping with practices across the web more broadly. By this point, TOS were part of a landscape of "clickwrap" agreements that most users rarely read. Whether or not the individual developers who wrote the 3taps script for scraping craigslist data had read the site's TOS, they almost certainly knew that, strictly speaking, their scrape was against the rules—but they probably assumed that the rules, like TOU everywhere, didn't matter. For the court, craigslist essentially deauthorized 3taps from accessing data via its cease-and-desist letters, so when 3taps subsequently used different IP addresses to access the site, the company demonstrated an awareness that it lacked the authority to scrape content. From 3taps' perspective, the key issue in the suit was copyright. 3taps argued that craigslist posts were facts rather than copyrightable content, and thus part of public domain. In the court's decision, copyright proved to be less important than the difference between access and use.

As a first step, the court clarified that authorization is ultimately at the discretion of the platform, with a take-it-or-leave-it option for users. 3taps (along with advocates like the EFF) maintained that online information wasn't meant to be just accessed and read but *used*. District-court judge Charles R. Breyer was unconvinced by 3taps' arguments that craigslist's actions represented a model of web access that would render creative web work—from hacks to mash-ups—as illegal use:

> Nor does prohibiting people from accessing websites they have been banned from threaten to criminalize large swaths of ordinary behavior. It is uncommon to navigate contemporary life without purportedly agreeing to some cryptic private use policy governing an employer's computers or governing access to a computer connected to the internet. In contrast, the average person does not use "anonymous proxies" to bypass an IP block set up to enforce a banning communicated via

personally-addressed cease-and-desist letter. . . . Thus, a meaningful distinction exists between restricting uses of a website for a certain purpose and selectively restricting access to a website altogether.[6]

The court sets up a contrast here between users who simply access the site and more elaborate tactics developed after a user has already been blocked. Breyer compares platforms to store owners who "open their doors to the public, but occasionally find it necessary to ban disruptive individuals from the premises."[7] Just as store owners have the right to refuse service, platforms have the right to deauthorize problematic users. Limited agency is assigned to users who access platforms, regardless of whether they've read or agreed with the TOU, while platforms retain control over the site, the code, and the content.

Before I get to the consequences of this lawsuit for craigslist and for platform responsibility in general, I want to point out a couple of issues that the case did not resolve. The court agreed that craigslist had the right to protect its data from being reused by 3taps. But it's unclear if or how much it mattered that the defendant was a corporation rather than a person. What happens when it's activists, journalists, and researchers who use social-media data? Another unresolved question concerns craigslist's reliance on cease-and-desist letters to "deauthorize" use. One of the EFF's key complaints was that craigslist's use of cease-and-desist letters amounted to bullying small-time players, but the court stayed silent on the ethics of such letters as a corporate tactic. Finally, given that the court essentially dismissed TOU as "cryptic," what other measures exist for platforms to lay out their responsibilities to users? And do these measures ever allow users to speak back to platforms?

In the settlement, 3taps gave $1 million to craigslist on condition that it be donated to the EFF. Immediately following the lawsuit, press coverage suggested that 3taps would shut down (Farivar 2015), but the site has continued to offer data-scraping services to developers, pulling from platforms like eBay, Backpage, and Letgo. Another key outcome of the case was the reputational hit that craigslist suffered in squaring off against data scraping, which becomes clear if we consider the EFF's changing views on craigslist as a platform. Over the years, the EFF has oscillated between celebrating craigslist as a tool for community building and decrying their attacks on open use of data. In 2006, the EFF gave Craig Newmark its annual Pioneer Award, praising the site's focus "on helping people with their basic needs—starting with housing and jobs—with a pervasive culture of trust" (EFF

2006). EFF also supported craigslist when it came to mounting a CDA 230 defense in cases during 2007 and 2009.

3taps provoked a harsh pivot in the nonprofit's treatment of craigslist. In their amicus brief to the United States District Court for the Northern District of California regarding the case, lawyers from the EFF argued that:

> website owners should necessarily expect to tolerate some loss of autonomy that the owner of a password protected computer system retains. . . . craigslist's enormous success is a result of its openness: anyone anywhere can access any of its websites and obtain information about apartments for rent, new jobs or cars for sale. Its openness means that craigslist is the go to place on the web for classified ads; it [sic] users post on craigslist because they know their ads will reach the largest audience.[8]

EFF took issue with both craigslist's claim of total ownership over its data and the way the platform responded to perceived threats, arguing that a cease-and-desist letter "cannot be the basis of . . . liability because it permits private entities to dictate what is and is not a crime based on their own business interests" (Opsahl 2013, 5). Craigslist's zealous protection of its data contradicts a paradigm of online openness, and the company's use of cease-and-desist letters enforces its values outside the purview of the courtroom. If *Dart v. craigslist* came from an increasingly common fear that craigslist was dangerous and lewd, the 3taps suit prompted a different loss of reputation and status among internet freedom advocates like EFF.

Conclusions

Much of the contemporary dialogue about platform responsibility is about Politics rather than politics, about influencing elections rather than rules for individual behaviors. But both kinds of politics are at stake when it comes to platform responsibility. For craigslist, responsibility means safeguarding the freedom to post and also protecting data from other platforms. I have argued that craigslist has embraced a Web 1.0 paradigm of platform politics, emphasizing anticensorship and giving users the ability to say whatever they want, a right bolstered by CDA 230—and limited (in part) by FOSTA. The leeway that craigslist emphasizes as free expression only extends so far, however. For craigslist, users can post kinky personal ads, but they can't make tools to scrape or tweak craigslist data without facing the threat of a potential lawsuit. Craigslist has been fiercely protective of its data, seeing any tweaks or hacks as a threat to its market share. This proprietary stance suggests a very different kind of responsibility, where users are held responsible for violating craigslist's TOU. With 3taps we see the hard stop of craigslist's beliefs about openness: building tools and apps with craigslist data.

The norms we have for thinking about platform responsibility were not inevitable—they are the result of tensions, accidents, missteps, and, on occasion, lawsuits. At different moments, lawsuits have forced craigslist to articulate its relationships to law enforcement, sex workers, start-ups, and hackers. The rulings that came from these cases have had an important impact in terms of craigslist's user policies and its reputation within the tech community. Both FOSTA and the 3taps suits assign control to platforms, holding them accountable for bad actors (at least in the case of sex trafficking) and giving them the right to sue users for (mis)using data. In a context where the government is unlikely to develop guidelines and individual users have little power, it is the platforms that will dictate what access, authority, and agency look like. Before we can decide what we need to ask of platforms like craigslist (or Facebook or Google), we need to understand how we got to the frameworks that are currently in place. Looking at two key legal battles throughout craigslist's long life online, we can see some of the formative moments in understanding what responsibility means, with implications that are legal as well as social and technological.

Part II

Every day, hundreds of thousands of people go on craigslist. The platform has more daily visits than the websites of PayPal, ESPN, or the *New York Times*. People come to craigslist for different reasons. Many have used goods to buy or sell, others are looking for work, while some people show up to lurk on the discussion forums, to daydream about a new car or apartment, or because they get a kick out of "Missed Connections." Every facet of craigslist's platform opens up a set of norms and responsibilities, the stuff of small-*p* politics. Chapters 4, 5, and 6 each investigate a category of craigslist functions: marketplace, job hub, and dating site. More than just identifying how people use the platform to do different things, I'm interested in the underlying norms and values that are supported and discouraged by craigslist's policies and politics. For example, buying and selling on craigslist (the focus of chapter 4) isn't about just matching supply and demand, it's about developing logics of value without the middleman of a bricks-and-mortar store. Finding a job on craigslist (chapter 5) means negotiating expectations of employers and employees, but also of a wider online public that often dismisses craigslist as part of the "poor people's internet." Despite a general thaw in the public's view toward online dating, craigslist personals provoked intense suspicion and stigma (chapter 6), right up to the moment the section was shut down in response to US federal legislation about sex trafficking. Each section of craigslist has rules and policies, and in chapter 7 I look at moments of failure and violation. The winners and losers on craigslist are shaped by the platform's efforts to protect users through flagging and anonymity, design and policy decisions that demonstrate a particular vision of responsibility. The concluding chapter of this book steps back to reflect on the interviews and account of craigslist's history and use to ask: What can craigslist's politics, successes, and failures tell us about contemporary digital culture? I'll argue that even as craigslist falls short of its ideals, it nonetheless offers important lessons for holding on to an open, accessible, serendipitously messy internet.

4

Craigslist, the Secondary Market, and Politics of Value

The first time my mom took me to a thrift store, I was immediately overcome with a wave of embarrassment. As one of four children, I was used to hand-me-downs, but Goodwill felt totally different—the mishmash of clothing and unfamiliar smells left me feeling that this was *not* how clothes should be purchased. Looking back now after having long embraced a love of thrifting, I'm struck by how immediate my response was, how quickly I felt, even if I couldn't explain, a capitalist critique of used goods. By the age of seven, before I had any money, I had already internalized a narrative that put new things above used, the sanitized over the secondhand.

Powerful assumptions about consumption and exchange were baked into my childhood suspicions of thrifting. Historically, people have always found ways to repurpose, barter, and gift previously owned goods (Dalton 1982), and the idea that goods should be bought brand new (rather than secondhand) and then thrown away (rather than reused) is a fairly recent development in human society. Secondhand clothing stores present a challenge to mainstream capitalism, although this threat is more ideological than financial. People who study secondhand stores have pointed out the ways thrift stores and vintage shops are deeply invested in capitalist goals of profit and exchange (Gregson and Crewe 2003). But on an ideological level, buying secondhand rejects throw-away-and-replace culture, in favor of reusing, upcycling, and buying used.

When it comes to buying and selling goods online, we might think of platforms like Amazon and PayPal or traditional brick-and-mortar stores with a strong online presence in the marketplace. But online technologies also play an important role in the secondary market, or the interpersonal exchange of goods and services without formal vendors. And the secondary market plays a huge role on craigslist, acting as a major draw for the platform. People buy and sell used goods for many reasons, some more in keeping with the primary market than others. The secondary marketplace both resists and reproduces the primary market, and by looking at buying and selling on craigslist, we can see the politics that come out of ordinary decisions like setting prices, writing ads, and finding sellers. Shopping in the secondary market doesn't require brand new rules or customs, but it does open up spaces of renegotiating expectations, norms, and values. Without formal price guides or a paid salesforce, how do people in secondary markets set prices and arrange sales? How do online platforms for buying and selling reshape relationships between people and objects?

To get a sense of how the secondary market works on craigslist, I first walk through the process of posting "For Sale" ads on craigslist. Then I zoom out to consider the secondary economy, and the different motivations for peer-to-peer exchange, drawing on interviews with people who spend significant amounts of time buying, selling, and donating used goods on craigslist, as well as other sites like Facebook Marketplace, OfferUp, and Buy Nothing. Interviews were conducted during the summer of 2017 in collaboration with Jen Ayres, an American-studies scholar who researches thrifting. By drawing on interviews with die-hard enthusiasts as well as fierce critics of craigslist, my goal is to articulate how the secondary market fits into digital culture, and how craigslist fits into the landscape of peer-to-peer exchange sites and apps. (More details on interviews and analysis are available in the methods appendix.)

Interviews revealed tensions around the social lives of objects, ethics of selling versus donating previously owned goods, and strategies for determining price and value. I then shift from interviews to what I call craigslist's "mash-up catalogs." By mash-up catalogs, I mean the hundreds of blogs, photo collections, and video channels based on collecting craigslist ads. Instead of physically circulating used goods, digital representations of craigslist objects circulate online, with different kinds of consumers and norms of value. While interviews help us think through the physical circulation of goods, mash-up catalogs offer a nonmaterial form of value based on shared enthusiasm for anime, video games, or poetry. By thinking about the circulation of physical goods as well as digital objects, we get a more robust understanding of the politics around use and reuse in online platforms.

The Basics: Buying and Selling on craigslist

To post an ad on craigslist, a user starts by clicking a "Post to classifieds" link on the site's home page. From there, a user opts between jobs, housing, for sale, services, community, and events. An important division in buying and selling has to do with owners versus dealers, meaning people selling items that they own personally versus people who buy and sell items in bulk or as part of a business. Posting items as an owner is free, while there's a small cost (between $5 and $7 per post) for dealers. Searching for items on craigslist is always free, regardless of whether the item is from a dealer or the owner. After identifying as a dealer or owner, the next step is choosing a category. The "For Sale" section contains dozens of subcategories, from motorcycle parts to books to video games, and categories are the same across the different cities in which craigslist is available. Then a seller moves on to writing the ad, which involves filling out a series of text boxes. Some text boxes are the same across categories, like posting title, price, and location, while others are specific to a category—for example, furniture ads ask for a manufacturer and model, plus the item's dimensions.

Users are required to provide an e-mail address, which they can decide to make visible or have craigslist cloak it in their ad. Users can also opt to be contacted by phone calls or text and to provide a contact name. In addition to making decisions about contact information, users can decide how much information to provide about the pickup location, giving a ZIP code or a street address, with the option to include the location on a map. On the next page, users can choose to include photos, and then confirm the text of their ad. Users receive an e-mail that asks them to accept the platform's TOU, and (if the ad requires a fee) a payment page. Users can create an account for managing multiple posts, or they can just use an e-mail address to access a management page for revising, deleting, or reposting a single ad. Ads are listed chronologically, with the newest ads at the top. Interested buyers can search within categories, or do a general search across all categories. Buyers contact sellers by e-mail or phone, arrange a pickup date, and confirm a price. As with other features on the platform, craigslist's involvement with the logistics of buying and selling is minimal—it provides a point of connection for buyers and sellers to find each other, but leaves it up to users to negotiate the details.

Sharing Economies and Peer-to-Peer Exchange

As a technology, the internet has always involved sharing, linking people and ideas as much as terminals and code. In his account of different forms of socio-technical sharing, Nicholas John (2017) noted that early computing required intense allocation of resources, known as time sharing (see also McCarthy 1983). Sharing has less technical and more psychosocial connotations on social-media sites, which encourage users to share content—partly so that platforms can, in turn, share advertising. While commodification has become an important way of generating profits for online platforms, the internet also supports much more literal exchanges in the marketplace. Two of the most common terms for this type of web-based commercial activity are peer-to-peer exchange and the sharing economy.

While the two terms are sometimes used interchangeably, peer-to-peer exchange originally referred to content sharing on user-run servers. Early examples from the 1990s include Napster and mp3.com, followed by bittorrent sites in the 2000s (Catalano 2018; Lamont 2013). A looser understanding of the term "peer to peer" de-emphasizes servers specifically to include any resource-sharing or exchange platform that is digitally mediated (see Lund 2017). If peer-to-peer exchange is an activity, the sharing economy is the broader set of norms and practices in which peer-to-peer exchange operates. Along these lines, Sundararajan defined the sharing economy as having five key characteristics: it is (1) market based, with (2) the goal of generating high-impact capital; it (3) relies on "crowd-based 'networks' rather than centralized institutions or 'hierarchies,'" and (4) participation tends to blur the boundaries between personal and professional connection, with an emphasis on personal service and interpersonal relationships. Finally, a sharing economy (5) blurs the lines between full employment and casual labor (2016, 27).

Early internet-studies scholars saw democratic potential in connecting users across geographic distance (e.g., Castells 1997), while scholars like Sundararajan (2016) see the marketplace as a key site for democratic access. Both see technology as a tool for democratic access, with a key distinction that what's being accessed is capital rather than information. Sundararajan cites examples of scrappy entrepreneurs and inventive lifehackers, contrasting sharply with researchers who see the sharing economy as exploitative, and reproducing rather than challenging economic inequality (e.g., Duffy 2015; Gray et al. 2016; Irani 2015; Shapiro 2017). In my interviews with people who used craigslist and other peer-to-peer sites, some saw secondary markets as an entrepreneurial paradise for finding deals and making money, while others wanted to use online platforms as a way of resisting the capitalist norms of the primary market.

Secondary Markets and the Web: Motivations and Social Norms

People opt in to secondary marketplaces for a range of reasons, sometimes echoing an early-web emphasis on community building and resource sharing, and at other times emphasizing economizing and entrepreneurialism. Among peer-to-peer folks I interviewed, motivations for circulating used goods fell into three broad categories: environmental responsibility, building local community, and saving or making money (see table 4.1). The lines between these categories were porous. For example, many participants emphasized environmental politics but also mentioned cost cutting, and others noted that a shared commitment to reducing waste could be a source of community building. I also saw a range in how much time and energy people invest in the secondary market. While some people described themselves as occasionally motivated by saving money on cheaper goods or making money with one-off selling gigs, others were building a reliable income through buying and reselling used goods.

For some participants, sites like craigslist were part of a commitment to environmental politics of reducing waste. Mimi was the most extreme in her commitment to using peer-to-peer exchange as a tool for avoiding consumption. She described herself as a dedicated "street picker," explaining, "we live in a sea of discarded and reclaimed objects that are constantly in motion, and . . . you can actively try not to participate, but for me, it's a sport all day, every day." Craigslist's "Free" section, where people post ads for items that can be picked up at no cost, was a regular treasure chest for participants like Mimi. During the course of our interview, she described finding everything from clothing and underwear to furniture, food, and cleaning supplies on the street, and, more than saving money, her goal was to keep items out of trash bins and landfills.

For Molly, secondary markets helped build local social ties, where circulating used goods was intended to forge or strengthen ties to the neighborhood. Similarly, Lou explained that the main appeal of the secondary marketplace was "being involved in your community and recycling goods within your community." Jax also described a preference for keeping things local, with selling online as a combination of practicality and creating the

TABLE 4.1. Motivations for Buying and Selling in Secondary Markets

Motivation	Illustrative Quote
Environmental	"I like that mentality of reducing, that ecological part of reusing and recycling objects. Just doing more [to make a difference]. Unfortunately, I don't believe it's impacting manufacturing, but ideally, I hope it would. There's so much that doesn't need to be manufactured that is and just sits in [someone's house]." (Flo)
Local community	"We want [used] things to go hand to hand, because you meet your neighbors. You form friendships and bonds with people you might not have met otherwise." (Molly)
Entrepreneurial	"I realized that I could go to thrift stores and junk shops and find random things that people would pay my rent for buying, because it was valuable and sitting there gathering dust. If we have to live in a capitalist society, we might as well turn garbage into rent." (Jax)

potential for community ties: "Local's always better for so many different reasons. Practical, meaning you don't have to ship it. You don't have to deal with it getting lost. You get your money right away. . . . [Selling local is] also more fun. There's a certain fun element to somebody showing up at your door. 'Hey, here's those fabric cubes you wanted. Have fun!'" Participants like Molly, Lou, and Jax saw the secondary market as a way of knitting neighbors together, where distributing used goods locally is a sign of a caring neighborhood community.

Other participants cared mostly about saving or making money. For example, Deena talked about a fierce reluctance to buy new, which she saw as a waste of money: "If I'm buying it [new], I'm angry about it. Because if this [pointing at a piece of furniture in her house], is at a yard sale, and someone doesn't want it, or they're moving—people move all the time—and they're like, 'I need it gone. Please take it.' So I feel like a chump when I buy something." A more entrepreneurial logic emerged for Micah, for whom sites like craigslist were largely tools that helped pay the bills. In contrast to Mimi, who saw city streets as a playground for finding and repurposing discarded goods, to Micah and participants like him, salvaging was phase one of a reselling—rather than reusing—process.

The online secondary market contains many platforms, and no one I interviewed was so devoted to a single platform that they used it to the exclusion of all others. Instead, people saw platforms as having strengths and weaknesses that guided what kinds of items to buy and sell there. In terms of how craigslist fit into the landscape of peer-to-peer exchange platforms, participants tended to emphasize pragmatism and locality. For example, Jax explained, "craigslist is only good for local, very practical stuff. You wouldn't put an antiquity on there, but you would put an old iPhone, or a table." Micah agreed, focusing on a reluctance to ship heavy objects: "Bigger stuff that you might not want to ship is good for craigslist. Things around the house are good for craigslist, large items, furniture, chairs, and stuff like that. . . . For the most part, most of the things that I sell on craigslist are larger items that I can't ship." Without a specific area of focus (like AptDeco, which focuses solely on furniture) and with its local emphasis (unlike eBay, which assumes people will ship items to each other), craigslist's strength is connecting people in a city for a wide range of used goods. Like all platforms that operate in the secondary market, craigslist supports a less formal set of exchanges than the primary market. How do strangers who may have different motivations for peer-to-peer exchange approach the buying and selling process? What logics and processes emerge, and what do these practices tell us about the primary market?

Things Are for Use

The first law of library science, according to famed librarian S. R. Ranganathan, is that books are for use (1931). Rather than stocking shelves with books meant to sit untouched and unread, Ranganathan saw the circulation of books as the key measure of a library's value. Secondary marketplaces are governed by a similar principle, and many of the people I interviewed emphasized circulation and distribution as a key reason for using craigslist. For example, Renee saw the secondary market as a way of avoiding mainstream capitalism, or, as she put it, "Amazon capitalism," which emphasizes continually replacing electronics and objects rather than reusing them: "Having these things switch hands and be—something that may have been useful to one person and no longer is—taking on a new life, almost, being useful to somebody else, and reducing the need to participate in, like, Amazon capitalism or things like that." In these accounts, peer-to-peer exchange makes sense in terms of both reducing waste and circulating goods to where they could be *used* rather than just *owned*.

Of all the participants I spoke with, Molly was the most adamant that peer-to-peer exchange should get things to a home where they could be

used. From an environmental stance, exchanging goods was always preferable to buying new, but in addition, Molly strongly preferred giving things
away to reselling them:

> I do know some people who just compulsively take stuff off of the free
> sites. They're not reselling it, they're not really using it, they just want to
> have it, and it's just accumulating in their houses. It's just crazy amounts
> of stuff. Maybe it makes them happy, but if somebody else could have it,
> and use it, I wish that they would just let them.

Molly disliked the idea of commercializing peer-to-peer exchange or turning
it into a smaller version of the primary market, and she was very critical of
folks who collected or hoarded used goods rather than using them.

A tension that surfaced repeatedly in interviews had to do with selling
versus giving away used goods, which tended to pit community-building
folks against those looking to make money. Sundararajan noted that as peer-
to-peer exchange platforms become increasingly commercialized, tensions
between community and profits tend to emerge: "The infusion of venture
capital and the emergence of platforms with large corporate investors lead
many to believe that any ideals associated with a . . . sharing economy
cannot be sustained" because of contradictions between building "community" among users and making profits for shareholders (2016, 26). As
someone who emphasized the community-building role of the secondary
market, Molly found the reselling of free or underpriced goods particularly
problematic:

> Some of these people that sweep through [free bins and thrift stores] like
> locusts, they probably have great houses and a lot of really nice stuff that
> they would never sell, but they're only too happy to try to profit from
> this other stuff. I don't like those people very much. If I found one thing,
> and then decided to resell it, it was really great, that's one thing. I'm not
> going to go and snatch everything out from under everybody every day.
> I'm not going to go and undermine somebody else getting something
> great just so I could hoard things.

Themes of keeping things circulating and in use are central to Molly's perspective on used goods, as opposed to "locusts" motivated primarily by
profit, with little or no concern for either the items themselves or local community members who might need them.

Focusing on consumption and community over resale value contrasts
sharply with more entrepreneurial logics of peer-to-peer exchange. Jax was

largely interested in using craigslist as a way to supplement his income, but he was definitely aware of the "no-reselling" ethic. In the process of describing how he came to appreciate scavenging and salvaging, he pointed to the complexities of selling versus giving away used goods:

> The point is, that's when it really dawned on me, people don't care [about the economic value of things they throw out]. They just don't care, and it's so easy to either grab a thing, keep it, or grab a thing and sell it, which a lot of people don't approve of, but sorry, I don't care. . . . Honestly, I think that there's a certain amount of envy behind getting angry at someone for reselling something that was given to them. It belongs to me now. I'm going to do with it as I choose, and I don't particularly care how someone feels about that. . . . I'm sometimes more reluctant to take it if it's [from] a free box, but I'm not going to lie. If I see something and I'm like, "That's clearly worth $100," I'm going to take it and sell it. If it's like a purse that I could maybe get 5 or 10 bucks for, I'm going to leave it there for somebody who actually wants a purse.

Jax offers a nuanced rubric for deciding how to treat used goods, based on value and opportunity. While Molly privileged use over reselling or hoarding, for Jax a certain level of potential profit dictated his treatment of salvaged objects. What emerges here is a spectrum of secondary-market politics: for some people things are always for use, while, for others, things are always for sale, and for many there's an in-between negotiation based on pragmatism, ideology, and opportunism.

Provenance and the Social Lives of Used Goods

People have different motivations for participating in the secondary market, and to an extent my interviews showed that relationships to objects mapped loosely onto people's categories of motivation. For those concerned with environmental damage and limiting waste, objects were meant to be salvaged and reused, preventing the purchase of new goods. For people concerned primarily with building community, a common theme emerged around viewing used goods as having a social history, a cumulative ledger of ownership that produced a particular social value. For people motivated by profit, used goods were thought of in utilitarian terms: objects are meant to be identified, evaluated, and shipped off for as much profit as possible. In this section, I focus on the value that people assigned to used goods based on the biography value as well as previous ownership. Borrowing the term "provenance" from library science, I want to dig into the meaning assigned to previous ownership within peer-to-peer exchange.

In library and archive terminology, "provenance" refers to an artifact's history of ownership (Millar 2002). Provenance is crucial for determining value, as well as whether or not an artifact's acquisition is ethical, because gaps in ownership can trigger concerns around how an artifact was obtained or transferred (Spencer and Sesser 2013). The secondary market doesn't usually require an archival process of documenting changes in ownership, but, as a concept provenance helps describe relationships between people and used objects. On craigslist, unlike eBay or Amazon, in-person exchanges mean that buyers and sellers can see glimpses of each other's lives, with momentary insight into a used item's origin and ownership.

I opened this chapter with a description of my initial suspicions of thrift-store clothes as too uncertain in their origins, but many of the people I spoke to about peer-to-peer exchange saw this uncertainty as preferable to the sterility of new goods. This was particularly true for clothing and household goods, where "much of the value is located in the imagined histories and biographies of consumption" (Gregson and Crew 2003, 5). Smish described an instance of feeling connected to a person selling her a table on craigslist:

> Me and my boyfriend went to pick up this beautiful small kitchen table. . . . It was this lady and she said, "I must have been about your age when I got this table, happy I'm handing it off to you guys." She told us that's when her and her husband got this table when they were a little bit out of college, and it was their first kitchenette table. I was like, "I'm so happy I have it now. That's really sweet."

Whether buying or selling, participants frequently described forming a sense of attachment to previous and future owners based on a sense of connection or affinity, giving used objects meaning through a ledger of ownership.

In their study of thrift and vintage stores in the United Kingdom, Gregson and Crewe (2003) found it was mostly men who described imagined histories of secondhand goods. But in my interviews, I found that references to provenance came mainly from women. Often, these participants emphasized that buying used goods on sites like craigslist felt more ethical than buying items that were new:

> I'm scared of the new stuff. I'm like, "Where did this come from? Why? Who made it? Were they getting paid enough?" I get nervous to buy new

because I feel like there's something scary behind it. Whereas buying old, it's like, "This is some junk nobody wants, and it has a funky look and story behind it." That's way more comfortable for me.

Deena here flips mainstream narratives of consumption, where used goods are viewed as dangerously unsterile and new goods are morally unblemished. Instead, used goods have a more interesting social history and a higher likelihood of ethical production.

Participants also described being reluctant to hand off or sell their used goods to people who, in their judgment, wouldn't contribute to a colorful provenance of a given item. Smish described a sense of regret in selling objects to people who lacked the style or expertise to appreciate a beloved object:

I recently sold a pair of leather clogs I had to a kind of lame girl . . . and I was kind of bummed because those were really cool shoes that should have gone to someone with personality but I just really needed money at that point, so it just went to a pretty boring person.

Smish had never worn the leather clogs in question, but nonetheless felt that she'd essentially failed the shoes by not finding a more fitting home (meaning a more interesting buyer) for them. Yma expressed similar concerns with vetting people before agreeing to sell or give away items: "I have things for similar reasons that I can't part with because it feels like a disservice to the person [who owned it before] and the garment itself to be done with it." In these accounts, used goods become meaningful through use, acquiring a kind of cultural patina that distinguishes them from items that have never been owned or used, and thus have no stories to tell. A nonmonetary form of value emerges here, where participants treated provenance as having meaning and weight. Other saw value in much more conventional and economic terms, as I describe next.

Negotiations of Value

What is a used item worth? Without the middleman of a retailer, how do people figure out prices in secondary markets? As Gregson and Crewe pointed out, "the relationship between rubbish and value is unclear, complex, convoluted; transfers and shifts occur between and across these cultural categories which are themselves fuzzy and striated" (2003, 115).

Provenance describes a process of assigning emotional value to used objects by drawing on biographies of previous ownership. But people involved in peer-to-peer exchange also determine financial value, drawing on a range of tools and practices.

People with a more entrepreneurial interest in peer-to-peer exchange tended to be the most systematic in setting prices. For example, Micah described the range of apps and automated software that he used in order to determine the value of used goods, particularly books:

> There are repricers out there that run on actions. It will always be looking to see if it needs to take an action, or be a reaction from an action. Let's say someone lowers their price by a penny, it will constantly look at that and react to it. Whereas the software I'm using is a little bit cheaper but still gets the job done. It'll only reprice and look at what needs to reprice at specific times. This repricer allows me to have it reprice 20 times a day.

Micah's process for pricing doesn't make room for emotional or psychological value and focuses solely on retail value. With his entrepreneurial politics, Micah is essentially replicating approaches and tools of major retailers on a smaller scale.

Most people I interviewed didn't use Micah's sophisticated pricing tools, relying instead on personal expertise. For example, Deena described her frustration with craigslist ads that had typos or lacked information: "Sometimes people spell things wrong, or something. [*Laughs.*] That's always a mystery to me, when someone doesn't describe things well on craigslist. I'm just bummed out for them. I'm like, 'You're not going to sell this if you don't write what it really is.'" Jax was so committed to his understanding of value that he described occasions when he would reach out to people on craigslist or Internet Yardsale to suggest a higher or lower price:

> They're asking for $150 more than that laptop is worth, and I want them to sell their laptop. I genuinely want them to make some money, but I know they're not going to if they don't bring the price down. . . . In this one case, I linked to a recently sold one on eBay. I was like, "Dude, this sells for like 100 or 120 bucks." They thanked me, but they continue to leave it at the same price. I feel bad because they're not going to win this. They're not going to sell it for the price that they want.

Seeing himself as an expert in secondary-market pricing, Jax wanted to correct what he saw as market miscalculations. Deena experienced similar encounters with objects that were mispriced, and described wanting to understand variance in pricing used goods:

> I'll try to figure out why [an ad isn't well written]. I'll be like, "Is this a designer or something I don't know about?" Or I'll look it up. Some people do just post [overpriced] things online, because people just don't understand that even though you bought this gown for $2,000, no one wants a used gown you wore, and it's not a designer and it's not that nice looking, and it fit just you and you're looking for [a lot of money].

Pricing became a way of identifying rookie sellers, who could alternately be taken advantage of or protected by those with more experience in the secondary market.

In addition to individual expertise, a number of participants described using sites like craigslist and eBay as crowdsourced pricing guides for the secondary market. As Zara described, the going rate on eBay dictates whether a price point is too high or low:

> It's total bullshit when people are just like, "This is the new value of it, so I'm selling it to you for this price," when you could go on eBay and look up how much people have paid for it for the past year. . . . eBay, right now, is like the blue book for finding the realistic [price of used goods].

Participants also described using craigslist as an informal pricing guide, with the caveat that craigslist was often the end of the line for used goods, meaning that sellers were often highly motivated and prices could be negotiated. As Opal explained, "craigslist is the only place I'll totally lowball people, because I think that people are more motivated to get rid of their stuff. I set my prices on craigslist similarly. I'm willing to take a lowball offer if I post things on craigslist." Although haggling was commonly seen as highly irritating, people often saw craigslist as a platform where selling something quickly was more important than selling something for the best price.

As much as pricing could be rational or analytical, participants also talked about moments when emotional attachment outranked monetary value. When asked how she decided if something was a good deal on craigslist, Smish responded, "How much I want it. That's literally it. I don't care if it's damaged or if it's a little bit overpriced or whatever. But then it's always nice to have someone selling something that they don't know how much it's worth." On the one hand, Smish argued that value was based solely on personal desire for a given item. On the other, she couldn't help being aware of price, and searching the secondary market meant always holding out hope for underpriced goods. Jax shared similar thoughts on the way that emotional attachment could overcome economic sensibilities:

> If I'm buying something for myself, it's all about how much I'm willing to pay to have it, which is usually not much, unless it's . . . like a laptop that I want to last for seven years. Or [if] it's like, "Oh, there is that flexible figurine from a video game from my youth that I'm never going to find anywhere else, and it's $40, which is outrageous, but I want it," which is a rare occasion.

Emotional or highly personalized relationships to price are far removed from the pricing tools that Micah uses to keep ahead of competitors. The different modes of value that surfaced in interviews about peer-to-peer exchange speak to the flexibility of the secondary market to accommodate different relationships between people and things.

Replication or Resisting: Secondary Markets and Capitalism

Secondary markets both reproduce and resist capitalist norms of buying and selling. The degree to which any given peer-to-peer exchange falls more on the replication or the resistance side of the spectrum depends largely on someone's primary motivation for using secondary markets. People like Micah and Jax largely saw platforms like craigslist as offering loopholes and work-arounds for profit making. With some work and some savvy, secondary markets provided a way to salvage used goods and remarket them on craigslist, eBay, and other online sites for peer-to-peer exchange. The secondary market may operate on the margins for these buyers and sellers, but it often retains key components of the primary market. Participants like Micah and Jax saw themselves as maneuvering within and taking advantage of micro-gaps in a capitalist system. In a way, their entrepreneurial efforts sought to correct momentary lapses in the market—bringing discarded goods back into exchange and assigning prices that reflect conventional definitions of value. In this view, secondary markets are a way of working within the existing market, of identifying ways to save or make money, and don't really critique the underlying system of the marketplace.

People who see the secondary market as a means of ethical consumption or community building offer more of a critique of the primary market. As an example, Renee saw the secondary market as an alternative set of relationships to capitalism:

In its own way, even if people who exchange goods and services this way aren't doing it for this reason, I think it's a pretty radical project in resisting capitalism. Especially because with things like disposability culture and planned obsolescence of technology, and other objects—like, something breaks: throw it out get new shit. Or there is a thing you don't use—it's easy to just throw it out, leave it on the side of the road kind of thing.

Concerns about consumption, waste, and ethical production led some people to avoid the primary market as much as possible. A defiant critique of capitalist markets emerges from this perspective, which sees the mainstream market as valuing profits over people or the planet, and mainstream consumers as ignorant of the environmental and societal harms of their buying habits. Yet even for people who saw peer-to-peer sites as tools for resisting capitalism, value played a role, although in nonmonetary ways. Used goods could become valuable through provenance, where emotional or social value accrued through previous ownership, or simply because of a highly personal interest in an artifact. Both logics of used goods defy rational norms of the primary market.

The internet has been held accountable for fostering a "buy-it-now" mentality of continuous, instant consumption (Alt 2018; Thoumrungroje 2014), and it's also been blamed for reducing intimacy (Hu et al. 2004). Different motivations for using online secondary markets mean that platforms like craigslist can simultaneously reproduce and undermine mainstream consumption cycles, while also acting as a tool of community building. For environmentalists and community builders, we see a mode of leveraging online technologies to reject or augment mainstream markets, and to value an object's social history over its capacity for profit.

Mash-up Catalogs of craigslist

So far, all of the exchanges I've described involve a shift between online and real life—people either find items on the street, in their homes, or in a thrift store and decide to post them online, or they find items on sites like craigslist that they want to bring into their houses. But craigslist is also connected to a very different kind of circulation, where craigslist ads become artifacts that are remade and exchanged, taking on value for their sense of quirkiness, silliness, and serendipity. For a more robust account of the relationships between people, objects, and value on craigslist, I want to take us on a tour of the mash-up catalogs of craigslist.

People create mash-ups by weaving together a collection of media clips into a single artifact. Also called remixing (Lessig 2008), convergence culture (Jenkins 2006), and configurable media (Sinnreich 2010), mash-ups are "premised on the notion of *recognizability* and *critique of pop culture*" (Sinnreich, 2010, 143; italics in original). Mash-ups bring together different pop-culture elements from music, film, or art, and part of the enjoyment is in creating an artifact that is simultaneously familiar and brand new. Mash-ups can be album length, like *The Grey Album*, released in 2004 by Danger Mouse as a remix of an a cappella version of rapper Jay-Z's *The Black Album* with samples from The Beatles' LP *The Beatles*, commonly known as "The White Album." Or they can be one-off singles—for example, the mash-up of Avicii's 2013 hit "Wake Me Up" and Rick Astley's 1987 single "Never Gonna Give You Up," with an added hook from a third song, the 1990s party anthem "Tubthumping" by Chumbawamba. For good pop-culture measure, the video includes well-timed clips of famous dance sequences, pulled from popular TV shows like *The Fresh Prince of Bel-air* and *Scrubs*. Mash-ups draw from an internet culture that prizes cross-pollination and play, where outcomes are measured in views, comments, and further remixes rather than monetary gain per se.

On Facebook, Twitter, Tumblr, YouTube, and Instagram, there are dozens and dozens of accounts dedicated to craigslist. Perhaps the most famous is "craigslist Mirrors," a project created by Eric Oglander in 2013 (see figure 4.1). A Brooklyn-based artist, Oglander was a longtime craigslist user who at first noticed and then became somewhat obsessed by images from craigslist ads for mirrors. Speaking to a journalist in 2016, Oglander explained the allure of mirror photos as a balance between the casual nature of a craigslist ad and the haunting capacity of mirrors: "I'm interested in the lack of attention in the photographs. These people as far as I'm aware have absolutely zero interest in creating a beautiful image and unbeknownst to them, these photos are so striking" (quoted in Garrett 2016). In 2015, Oglander published a book version of his blog, with seventy full-color images from his catalog of mirror ads posted to craigslist.

I interviewed Oglander on May 18, 2018, to ask about "craigslist Mirrors," and specifically about the value he saw in the project: "For me, and maybe for the other people as well, it's the inadvertent nature of the photographs. . . . I think it's just the simple fact that the original posters weren't attempting to make anything profound." Oglander also emphasized the cross-platform nature of the project as part of its power: "The thing that I liked about the craigslist mirrors project is that the simple act of dragging a photo from

FIGURE 4.1. A screengrab from Oglander's Tumblr page, featuring his collection of ads posted to craigslist selling mirrors.

one website onto another rendered it as art. Recontextualization in art is all over the damn place . . . taking things out of context makes them more potent." To Oglander, "craigslist Mirrors" gains artistic value from two key components—the unassuming nature of the ad imagery and the movement of content between platforms. These ingredients—mundane content and cross-platform flow—are key in thinking about the value of craigslist mash-up catalogs.

To find craigslist mash-up catalogs, I searched mainstream social-media platforms using "craigslist" as a keyword. In total, I found over two hundred blogs, Facebook groups, Tumblr accounts, and YouTube channels. Looking across these catalogs, underlying goals range from calling out bad behavior (like identifying unethical treatment of animals) to amplifying the quirkiness of craigslist ads. A major division shapes up between mash-ups and collections that are culled or curated, but not actually mash-ups. In the second case, users create an edited assortment of craigslist ads, usually organized by geography or for collectors. For example, "SF Rooms" on Tumblr gathers "the newest available rooms in San Francisco all in one place; only neighborhoods you'd actually want to live in for under $1000 a month" ("SF Rooms," n.d.). On YouTube, "craigslist Game Finds" posts videos to help viewers find rare and valuable video games being sold on craigslist.

In contrast, mash-up collections are meant to entertain rather than to sell. Mash-up catalogs use craigslist ads to produce a new creative form. For example, Tumblr's "Haiku Hotel" posts poems taken from, directed to, or inspired by craigslist ads. ("Haiku Hotel" is the name of a long-standing craigslist forum dedicated to haiku.) Similarly, "Real Missed Connections" on Tumblr lists poems created from the text of "Missed Connections" ads, which are posts that allow strangers to reach out to one another after a missed opportunity to talk, flirt, or exchange personal contact information (for more on "Missed Connections" and craigslist personals, see chapter 6). Some craigslist mash-up catalogs combine craigslist content with popular-culture memes, creating contrasts between the original craigslist content and a new presentation as a blog. "Westeros Personals" (also on Tumblr; see figure 4.2) is a good example of this category, mashing up craigslist personal ads with still images from the massively popular book and TV series *Game of Thrones*. Curated catalogs reflect an effort to cull ads in keeping with personal tastes or interests, but the initial intention of the poster—buying or selling used goods—remains. With mash-ups, people put a twist on the original ads: rather than buying or selling, the objective is to produce a new narrative or a new affect. Put another way, the value of curated catalogs is still monetary, while the value of mash-up catalogs takes shape in more cultural or countercultural terms.

What are people doing when they create catalogs of craigslist ads? Once the idea of buying and selling drops out of the picture, what value do craigslist ads have? I'm interested in mash-up catalogs because they provide a more complicated account of value and socio-technical connection, and because they reflect a remix-culture emphasis on cross-platform links and countercultural audiences. In terms of talking about craigslist's role in a wider online context, mash-up catalogs provide direct connections between craigslist and other social-media platforms like Instagram, Tumblr, and YouTube, and they can provide an anchoring point for subcultural and countercultural publics. Similar to early descriptions of digital libraries as cabinets of curiosity (Dalbello 2004), mash-up catalogs present a collection of craigslist

A SONG OF CRAIGSLIST PERSONALS   INDEX   MESSAGE   ARCHIVE   SUBMIT

MOD 1

Craigslist Personals @craigslistlove · 1h
anybody else still trying to Save the World?

POSTED ON **MAY 25TH** WITH **33 NOTES**
TAGS: JON SNOW GAME OF THRONES A SONG OF ICE AND FIRE WESTEROSPERSONAL
S

FIGURE 4.2. The Tumblr account "Westeros Personals" pairs text from craigslist personals ads with stills from the HBO TV series *Game of Thrones*. Although the blog was fairly successful in terms of likes and reblogs, the project was fairly short-lived, with posts only between January and June 2015.

curios. The YouTube channels, Tumblr logs, and Twitter feeds dedicated to craigslist ads produce a digital afterlife that extends beyond craigslist itself, with nonmonetary logics of use and value.

Earlier I used "interesting" to describe craigslist mash-up catalogs, which picks up on Sianne Ngai's (2015) work on aesthetic categories of popular culture. Ngai's theories of cultural aesthetics are meant to unpack the significance of undervalued cultural judgments—the cute, the zany, and the interesting. All three of Ngai's categories speak to some part of craigslist generally, and mash-up catalogs specifically. But while cuteness and zaniness surface throughout the platform, it's the judgment of being interesting that most neatly maps onto the digital catalogs of craigslist ads.

For Ngai, things become interesting through external reference points, and not as an innate quality of interesting objects themselves. Sometimes, she argues, we call something interesting as a placeholder until another descriptor emerges. Other times, we describe things as interesting when we identify a difference between the expectation and the reality, even if the gap between the two is difficult to name: "what is striking is the consistency of the judgment's function: that of ascribing value to that which seems to differ, in a yet-to-be-conceptualized way, from a general expectation or norm whose exact concept may itself be missing at the moment of judgment" (2015, 112). Without knowing the source of the poached content from "Real Missed Connections," the poems may be fun or weird, but with context they become interesting. In general, mash-ups require familiarity with remixed content to appreciate them fully. You can enjoy Danger Mouse's *Grey Album* without knowing its origin story, but context makes the album interesting.

Another feature of craigslist mash-ups is the role of repetition and continuity. One "Westeros Personals" ad is funny, but the long sequence of ads parallels the exhausting repetition of craigslist itself, with its daily barrage of ads, inquiries, jokes, and scams. Repetition, too, has a connection to Ngai's idea of what makes something interesting: "what is unique about the judgment 'interesting' is that it inevitably diverts attention away from itself so as to throw the spotlight entirely on the question of its own legitimation. It is a judgment that . . . hurries past the first moment in its eagerness to arrive at the next" (2015, 169). Craigslist ads are meant to be ephemeral, but in mash-ups we see a desire to curate and preserve, to produce new publics through the creation and circulation of media content.

By publics, I mean the different subcultural or countercultural groups that can come together around a text (or set of texts) as a focal point.[1] In his influential paper on publics and counterpublics, Warner saw texts as having the ability to bind people together in social and political relations: "Attention is the principal sorting category by which members and nonmembers are discriminated. . . . The existence of a public is contingent on its members' activity, however notional or compromised" (2002, 61). In chapter 2, I argued that personal ads have an important history of connecting people on the margins. In conditions of surveillance or inequality, countercultural media can be a powerful binding agent. Mash-up catalogs can also act as a shared text connecting people who share an experience of marginalization or a niche interest. Returning again to Ngai (2015), mash-up catalogs are binding agents of interest, because " 'interesting' is both what makes 'serious' subcultural groups cohere in the first place and what makes it possible for people to belong to many of them, creating the webs of filiation that [make] these interest groups overlap" (172). As a group, craigslist mash-up catalogs have a mixed record of sustaining attention. While "craigslist Mirrors" and "Westeros Personals" get hundreds or sometimes thousands of likes and reblogs per post, "Haiku Hotel" poems have almost none, which is the case for most of the blogs, channels, and Twitter feeds I identified. Given the frequently short life-spans of the catalogs I analyzed, publics may fail to materialize or persist. But the photos and videos themselves survive as long as the platform does, meaning that there's also an enduring possibility of future viewers, followers, clicks, and retweets. Even the least popular mash-up catalog could simply be waiting for the right counterpublic to assemble.

Mash-up catalogs help us think through different registers for value and use. Originally, Craig Newmark set out to connect people in a local area, and craigslist was guided by practical goals of publicizing events and matching job seekers with potential employees. But the internet rarely limits itself to one intention, and while many people still have decidedly pragmatic goals for craigslist, Ngai (2015) and Warner (2002) give us the frameworks for thinking about very different uses for craigslist ads. Amid the pragmatism of buying and selling used goods, mash-up catalogs return us to the random messiness of digital culture, to a form of value that takes shape in remixing content and pulling together fans, whether they share a love of Persian rugs (https://craigslistpersianrugs.tumblr.com/) or manga porn (https://fateseriespersonals.tumblr.com/). Circulating physical goods in the secondary marketplace plays a huge role in craigslist's popularity. Mash-up catalogs have a different kind of value, rooting publics to texts.

Conclusions

Whether based in the physical trade-offs of goods or in the online circulation of texts and likes, craigslist's ads call for a public. Sometimes this public is straightforward: a call to pick up a coffee table from the curb or a call to buy a slightly used laptop. Sometimes the publics that craigslist summons are less direct and more obscure, mashing up craigslist personals and pop culture references, or crafting poetry from "Missed Connections" ads. The first category reflects craigslist's long-standing investment in the local. As Newmark explained to me in an interview, his original motive with craigslist was "helping people do everyday tasks in their lives, like putting food on the table, or getting a table to put that food on, or getting a roof under which to put that table" (interview with author, May 16, 2017). The publics created in craigslist's "For Sale" ads are fleeting and pragmatic, but nonetheless have specific norms and practices of exchange and value. Publics that take shape through mash-up catalogs are more persistent, but still ephemeral, in that the publics assembled by "Hotel Haiku" and "Westeros Personals" are groups constituted by reading, commenting, and circulating, but rarely (if ever) meeting or even talking directly to one another.

For Warner (2002), the circulation of texts is a crucial means of bringing publics together. Some of the most obvious counterpublics that craigslist has supported over its history are queer men and women, who may feel excluded from mainstream online dating sites, or groups that use discussion forums to talk about polyamory, eating vegan, or frugal living. But there are also political dimensions to publics in the secondary marketplace, to resisting or replicating the mainstream economy, or in circulating pop-culture texts and insisting on their value. By connecting buyers and sellers, craigslist supports different political ideologies about consumption and marketplaces. Craigslist also provides the building blocks for mash-ups, drawing together different fan groups and subcultures.

Do things have politics? Some of the most basic forms of everyday politics come through in the ordinariness of craigslist ads, in the contingent judgments of price and value, in the ideological registers of environmental protection, community care, or entrepreneurial innovation. Small-p politics are about personal commitments to causes like protecting the environment by reducing consumption, or the social investment in neighborhoods and neighbors, or about finding ways to be an entrepreneur in the midst of a capitalist marketplace. When it comes to mash-ups, politics take on a more cultural form. As Sinnreich noted in his work on mash-ups, people who engage in remixing may not necessarily see themselves as "being engaged in any process larger than their own immediate needs and ambitions," yet the work of mash-ups "engenders resistance to . . . regulation at every intersection of institutional site (legal, ideological, commercial) and community site (aesthetics, praxis, technology)" (2010, 182). Political resistance doesn't necessarily require a fully articulated platform or direct action in the streets. Subtler and more ordinary forms of political life take place every day as we buy, sell, and share goods, and as we find and circulate media content.

Buying and selling used goods are the most common reasons people use craigslist. This chapter has unpacked the ordinary work of buying and selling on craigslist, as well as the online lives of ads, which can get remixed and reworked into poetry, porn, and memes. Like other platforms connected to the informal economy, craigslist ads reflect the different politics that accumulate in things, whether physical or digital, with monetary or cultural value. The secondary market opens a window into the everyday lives of objects and the people who own them, and it also exposes the gaps and critiques of the primary market. Buying and selling used goods gives rise to informal rules and processes that surface when strangers meet up to exchange those goods, circulations of consumption that take shape outside of formal vendors or brick-and-mortar shops. For used goods, craigslist is just one stop along a path of peer-to-peer exchange, an entry in their provenance as they move from person to person and home to home. And long after an object has been exchanged in person for the last time, the ads that facilitated its sale can continue circulating online as part of an online public, taking on new forms of value and exchange.

5

Craigslist Gigs, Class Politics, and a Gentrifying Internet

From the beginning, craigslist has seen itself as a platform for finding jobs. In the early days, this meant tech jobs in San Francisco, but as the site grew geographically, it diversified the kinds of jobs being advertised, and before long everything from short-order cooks to nannies to video-game designers were being recruited on craigslist. Craigslist divvies up its employment section into two categories: "Jobs" and "Gigs." Perusing the Jobs ads on Philadelphia's craigslist site, project engineers are wanted for a fabrication shop, a research associate in biochemical assays is being sought by a pharmaceutical company, and a county library is looking for a bookmobile librarian. Like many other ads, the jobs I've described are all full-time and advertise benefits. While the Gigs section is smaller in terms of subsections (thirty-one to eight), common perceptions of craigslist's employment opportunities skew toward short-term, one-off jobs. In talking to people about jobs and craigslist, a recurring assumption is that the site only offers "low-caliber" employment (to quote one participant) meaning a job rather than a profession, a gig rather than a career.

In this chapter, I look at gig work on craigslist as a starting point for thinking through how workplace norms have changed alongside shifts in technology. Assumptions about craigslist and employment also point to craigslist's persistent reputation problem, meaning common judgments about the kinds of people who post and respond to craigslist ads. Drawing on participants' accounts of employment opportunities on craigslist, I build an argument about online publics and class politics through a lens of gentrification. I'll argue that craigslist's changing reputation about employment foreshadowed many of the power struggles around the gig economy, none of which can be analyzed without talking about class.

Changing perceptions about craigslist's job listings are in line with a broader economic shift away from long-term, stable employment toward short-term freelancing and gigs. Sometimes called the "gig economy," this type of work is tied to online platforms that allow people to find contract positions or one-off projects, usually without opportunities for advancement or benefits. The gig economy increasingly relies on platforms to connect workers and employers and has drawn on Silicon Valley tech culture to promote a set of beliefs about employment and risk. Many people continue to find traditional work arrangements on craigslist, but in interviews, participants described the platform's reputation as geared toward blue-collar or low-paying jobs rather than high-status employment opportunities.

What does work look like on craigslist? To start, I'll describe the kinds of work that people find on craigslist and the benefits people see in looking for short-term or one-off jobs. Second, I'll turn to the labor that goes into using sites like craigslist and the expertise required to find work in the gig economy. Class politics are a key focus of this chapter. In interviews, many participants described craigslist as part of the "poor-people's internet" or "for blue-collar people." Although craigslist got its start among the tech industry's creative class, over time it has increasingly picked up a set of class markers associated with a less elite, more diverse population. In the United States, it's common to link a sense of personal self-worth or fulfillment to employability. The willingness to take certain kinds of jobs is a personal decision, but norms around employment have much broader social and economic implications. How can craigslist's working-class associations help us to think through class politics of the web? What are the consequences when a platform is labeled as belonging to or intended for the lower class?

In this chapter, I rely primarily on interviews with craigslist users recruited through the site's Gigs section. In the spring of 2018, I posted ads to the Gigs section in Philadelphia, looking to interview people who had found work using craigslist. This recruitment choice skews my analysis toward gigs rather than full-time jobs, although the two categories aren't mutually exclusive—most people who searched in the Gigs section also regularly looked for work in the Jobs category. Partly the decision to recruit through the Gigs section was a pragmatic one, in that it made more sense to classify a single qualitative interview as a gig rather than a job. Additionally, focusing on gigs helps me think about craigslist as part of the gig economy, increasingly a dominant mode of understanding relationships between technology and work. Alongside interviews with craigslist gig workers, this chapter draws on interviews with people involved in the secondary market, discussed in chapter 4, who shared experiences about the work required for buying and selling, which many of them referred to as a side gig. I also include interviews with some of craigslist's early employees to get a sense of the company's connection to employment and recruiting in the tech industry. (For additional information about interviews, see the methods appendix.) From the beginning, craigslist has wanted to be a resource for finding jobs, but the kinds of work on offer have changed somewhat since the 1990s. Over time, jobs on craigslist have lost their association with elite tech work and gained a reputation as blue-collar jobs and gigs of last resort.

Craigslist and the Gig Economy

While popular narratives of craigslist often emphasize quirky personal ads and the pragmatic exchange of used goods, when the company got its start the focus was publicizing local events and job seeking in the tech sector. Christina Murphy, then a headhunter who specialized in the San Francisco tech scene, was involved with craigslist during its launch as a website. Murphy was one of the four people (along with Nancy Melone, Louise "Weezy" Muth, and Craig Newmark) loosely gathered under craigslist's original management team (Glave 1999), and Murphy's background as a headhunter reflected craigslist's initial view that searching for jobs should be one of the site's key functions. As Murphy described it, part of craigslist's initial appeal was its affordability and its tech-savvy user base:

> There was a fair amount of buzz [when craigslist launched], because it was so affordable—$25 to put your job up. There weren't a lot of places at that time where you could post jobs. I think people got that it was a good deal. People who were using it were people who had their finger on the pulse [of the local tech industry]. (Interview with author, August 17, 2017)

The sense of exclusivity that Murphy describes is a key casualty in craigslist's transformation from serving the tech elite in San Francisco to serving a much wider array of jobseekers.

As an e-mail list, craigslist initially relied heavily on word-of-mouth advertising. As Murphy recalled, "Everything was from word of mouth—all of the candidates were people who knew somebody who knew somebody.

I think recruiters were eager to tap into that sense of exclusivity." In the early days, craigslist worked to build a following among recruiters in San Francisco's tech industry. Newmark had hazy memories of reaching out to human-resources (HR) trade magazines before eventually settling on a word-of-mouth approach. Murphy recalled the company's early advertising efforts in more detail:

> We created one mailer—I only really remember one, and I just remember it because it was kind of a funny one, it was something like, "taking the temperature of the job market?" It had a little strip inside of it where you could put it on your forehead and take your temperature. I don't remember ever buying advertising in a magazine or anything like that. They looked like a gift card, they were green, I think we just sent them to HR managers. [Job ads were] the only money we were making. (Interview with author, August 17, 2017)

As a website, craigslist has always hosted more than employment opportunities, but since the job ads actually produced revenue, it makes sense that craigslist initially concentrated its advertising on services to HR people and headhunters. Over time, craigslist started charging small fees for various kinds of ads, but job ads have always required a fee, with the logic that anyone who could afford an employee could afford a small fee for an ad. As Murphy recalled, "Craig was really adamant that job posting were for either saving money or making money [compared with other recruiting tools]. He never wanted any other part of craigslist to charge money. Since companies [were already paying elsewhere for] posting jobs, Craig was fine charging them."

Craigslist's web-based approach to job hunting came at a moment when the tech industry had become the emblem of the "new economy," or a shift in how ordinary people imagined work and the economy. In her study of New York City's tech scene in the 1990s, Gina Neff (2012) argued that the dot-com era both reflected and encouraged shifts in employment norms. In particular, the tech industry normalized contract work over long-term employment and an internalization of risk among workers. According to Gary Hall's work on the gig economy, Western society is increasingly one in which "we are encouraged to become . . . micro-entrepreneurs of the self, acting as if we are our own, precarious, freelance microenterprises in a context in which we are being steadily deprived of employment rights, public services, and welfare support" (2016, xi). Starting in the 1990s, positive and even romantic associations with risk sprung up around the booming tech industry. As Neff argued, "while taking risks at work is not new, it became newly important and found expression in the ways in which people worked in the Internet industry" (2012, 67). Initially, people saw craigslist as having the inside scoop on tech jobs. Over time, craigslist jobs were less about working in the tech sector and more about the kind of working arrangement associated with disruptive innovation. On craigslist, as elsewhere, many workers began embracing an ethic of "no risk, no reward" when it came to decisions about where and how to work.

Gig economy, platform economy, 1099 economy, on-demand economy, microwork, crowdwork—a number of terms describe the interconnections between digital technologies and changing labor norms. While microwork usually refers to short tasks with low pay, managed through platforms like Amazon Mechanical Turk (see Irani 2015; Irani and Silberman 2013; Zyskowski et al. 2015), crowdwork describes tasks that are similarly brief but typically unpaid, such as editing Wikipedia (Ford 2015; Lund 2017) or citizen science efforts (Franzoni and Sauermann 2014). The on-demand economy typically involves in-person work that's managed by smartphone apps like Uber (Rosenblat and Stark 2016) or Postmates (Shapiro 2017). Gig, platform, and 1099 work are more general terms in that they are not tied to a particular kind of work or platform, although the latter suggests work that's formal enough to file taxes (which is not the case for many of the people I spoke to about craigslist).[1] While others (e.g., Graham, Hjorth, and Lehdonvirta 2017) prefer "digital labor platforms" to describe online work, I use the term "gig economy." Partly this is because craigslist uses the word "Gigs" as a category of its job listings. And unlike Mechanical Turk, Uber, or Thumbtack, craigslist doesn't manage online gigs or communication between employers and employees. It simply allows employers to post openings and job seekers to post résumés. Craigslist predates microwork, but its Gigs section reflects a set of assumptions that took hold in the 1990s and has become increasingly normalized—that online platforms are the best tools for connecting workers and bosses, and that gigs can be an end point rather than a temporary fix for employment.

The gig economy is characterized by trade-offs—gaining flexibility but losing security, feeling a sense of independence but giving up workplace benefits. Spanning different industries and working arrangements, people I interviewed often saw gigs as opportunities to learn or hone new skills while having a lot of independence over their schedules. They typically narrated the tumult of continually finding new gigs as an acceptable trade-off for flexibility, and they tended to see themselves individually—rather than the economy generally—as responsible for their ability to find work and make a living. As a set of tools, online platforms play a key role in facilitating the search for gig work, and as an industry, the tech sector has helped to sell a relationship to work based on risk and individualism.

The Basics: Finding a Job on craigslist

To find a job on craigslist, you start by looking through the job ads in a given city. At the time of our interview, Shelly had lined up a number of jobs on craigslist: driving for Lyft, passing out flyers for a local retailer, and repeat jobs checking people in at a nearby county fair. As someone who used craigslist on a daily basis to find work, she offered a descriptive and practical account of the job-search process:

> So you see something you're interested in or something you think you're qualified for. You click up on the top corner, either email or sometimes there's a phone number. I don't like to call people, I don't like to be on the phone, I'd rather text you or email you. So if there's a phone number . . . I'll text. Or if it's something more like this [interview] I'll email. So I email them and I'll introduce myself. If it calls for a resume I'll send my resume . . . and then you just wait for a response. You know what I'm saying, they'll email you back. A lot of the times you won't get emails back, which is cool but the ones that do email you back, that's the ones that are worth it because that's the ones that make you money.

Having used craigslist for many years and in multiple cities, Shelly had a lot of confidence in her ability to parse good opportunities from bad, and saw craigslist as a useful tool in her arsenal of gig-work resources.

More than anyone else I interviewed, Shelly identified as a craigslist enthusiast, checking it at least once a day. She often structured her entire day around the site, mostly to find jobs, but also for buying and selling used goods and finding apartments. For example, on the day I interviewed her, Shelly planned on working for a number of hours as a Lyft driver and had also set up an appointment for her boyfriend at a hair-braiding studio—which she found on craigslist. She was open to a number of jobs, from retail and driving to passing out flyers. Other people I interviewed were narrower in the kinds of jobs they sought. For example, Rob stuck entirely to finding music gigs, while Shayla preferred "Warehouse jobs. Maybe stocking jobs. They got all types of jobs. Driving jobs. [Craigslist has] sales associate jobs at different stores and stuff. They've got a lot of different stuff. I only applied to warehouse jobs from craigslist, though. It's just what I like to do."

While participants like Shelly and Shayla relied on gig work for their entire income, other participants used craigslist primarily to find one-off gigs to supplement their income. For Nathaniel, looking for gigs on craigslist:

> has been ongoing as more of an occasional or one off thing. A few years ago, my wife and I had a baby, and I found myself wanting to make extra money. There was this window of time where I kind of jumped in and was trying to do everything I could.

For Jax, gig work was similarly meant to supplement to his income, although in the past it had comprised more of his time and earnings:

> I think that, right now . . . I'm intentionally doing it because that money is earmarked for things, whereas in the past, it was money that I brought in to make ends meet, to keep things more tight. I want to take my friend, Pebbles, to the beach in September. I want it to be a nice trip instead of one of those fly by night, $50 each day trips.

For Nathaniel and Jax, craigslist gigs were ways of responding to temporary fluctuations in their finances, fitting craigslist into the margins of their regular employment.

It takes work to find work. Even for people who wanted just occasional side jobs, sorting through job ads required time and expertise. Compounding the problem, most of the gig workers I talked to used multiple platforms to search for work, including Indeed, TaskRabbit, Thumbtack, and Fiverr. Many participants described frustration and fatigue as part of the search process. Arkansas noted that sometimes finding out about deals or potential jobs on platforms like craigslist was more of a burden than an opportunity: "Sometimes, I feel good that I don't know about something. If somebody is like, 'Oh, I just put all this stuff out outside my house. It's located at xyz.' I'm like [*sighs*]—Now, I got to go. I feel so tired." For Arkansas, the work of finding used goods could be exhausting, to the point that missing out on available items sometimes came as a relief. Participants valued the flexibility of online job searching and gig work, but they also found that the labor required to stay employed was substantial and ongoing, bleeding into other activities (see Ticona 2015). A trade-off in flexibility, then, is the expanding workday, which includes the job search as well as the job.

Lows and Highs in the Gig Economy:
Uncertainty, Expertise, and Independence

Uncertainty is a feature rather than a bug of the gig economy. As Van Doorn and Velthuis observed from their study of online sex work, "rather than inhibiting economic activity, . . . manufactured uncertainty is generative in the sense that it opens opportunities for entrepreneurial action, stimulating market innovation and value creation" (2018, 13). In response to uncertainty about employer expectations, job availability, and competition for jobs, participants described a trial-and-error approach to honing the application process. On craigslist, a trial-and-error approach often started with lowering expectations about the kinds of jobs that were worth applying for. As Agnes explained, "I guess your brain gets more used to reading the style of [craigslist ads] as you look through. I guess when you kinda feel like you've seen what's out there . . . and you're like, 'oh well maybe I need to adjust my expectations a little lower.'" Over time, participants learned to adjust expectations for what kinds of work were available in the gig economy. Having to settle for jobs that pay less or are personally unfulfilling points to a key gap between what gig-work hype promises (freedom and personal growth) versus what it often delivers (low pay and monotony).

As they looked for jobs, users developed a sense of expertise in evaluating and responding to ads for work, with parallels to buying and selling on craigslist. For example, participants developed a sense of whether certain cities were more likely to have jobs relevant to their interests. Denny was primarily interested in tech-related gigs that he could do remotely, like beta testing software. He searched for gigs across multiple cities, noting that some cities were better for finding work than others: "So the biggest cities I've noticed that'll have gigs for that, there's L.A., there's San Francisco, which has more of the software kind of stuff, New York, and Philadelphia." Cathy also noted specific differences in the kinds of jobs available in different cities, and felt that tech jobs on the coasts were more demanding and required more experience than jobs in the South or the Midwest. While Denny and Cathy searched out relevant jobs across the country that they could work remotely, most people I spoke with confined their searches to the local area in which they lived.

Part of the expertise required to navigate craigslist involves avoiding scams and spam, along with the process of flagging suspicious ads. I'll come back to this topic more fully in chapter 7, but, for now, it would be difficult to overstate the exasperation of participants around spam and scams. Denny saw scams as a problem across different cities, but felt it was particularly bad in New York City, estimating that "70% of New York's craigslist" was "scammy." Agnes described the process of having to filter out scams for legitimate ads in the job section:

> With jobs, there's definitely a lot of ones that you're like, what *is* this? This is definitely a multi-level marketing scheme, which is a scam. But those ones, you gotta know the words that they always use in those multi-level marketing things, they always will say "Oh, investment opportunity" and "Oh, you can build up your portfolio" and build up your whatever. You can just tell when you're reading them that this is a scam. . . . Any ad with like "job, job, job!" but it doesn't say anything about what you're gonna do with the job or the name of the job, well that's either some multi-level marketing or . . . a scam of some kind.

Over the course of days or weeks, participants built up literacy in job ads, learning to separate legitimate ads from phishing scams and pyramid schemes.

In addition to gaining expertise through trial-and-error responses to ads, some participants also took advantage of online blogs and video tutorials for the gig economy. Cathy first started looking for short-term jobs on craigslist after reading about it on a blog that she followed about gig work. She saw blogs and tutorials about the gig economy as a good investment in her time and energy, giving her ideas for self-promotion and finding new platforms to search for jobs. More cautiously, Micah described YouTube videos about "online arbitrage" as useful in learning new tips and tricks, but he felt that they came with the potential for taking advantage of newcomers:

> [YouTube videos are] good to learn. Unfortunately, with that there's another market . . . that's involved where there's "gurus" or the people who are making six, seven figures. Now they're . . . selling courses on how to be successful. You've got your newbies who aren't entrepreneurs . . . or maybe they're just starting to get into it, and they don't know what to do, or how to do it. They look up to these "gurus" and they'd pay for these mentoring classes, or pay to be in a special private group where there's better information available.

Rather than paying a fee to a "guru," Micah preferred setting up private (but free) Facebook groups with a small number of people who shared his interests in reselling. On the whole, Micah and Cathy were exceptions, in that most participants reported developing a sense of expertise pretty much on their own, relying on trial and error to develop the best strategies for finding the right gig(s).

The gig economy often demands that workers develop new skills and embrace self-promotion, labor that goes largely uncompensated, at least directly (Gregg 2013). Gig work requires a lot of hustle, which Van Doorn and Velthuis defined as "a committed and honest yet cunning form of entrepreneurship that demands certain investments, most notably time" (2018, 9). Beyond the hours that gig workers spend finding jobs and honing employable skills, participants described the continual pressure of high expectations for productivity coupled with a mismatch of minimal pay. Cathy shared an experience of struggling to meet the demands of a job that exploited a gig-worker mentality of perpetual hustle: "I've worked something off craigslist one time that I put in 80 hours and got $60 for it for one week, and [the employer was] kind of thinking this is normal to prove that you're motivated, and I just couldn't do it." One of the most exploitative features of the gig economy is the internalization of a hustle mentality; rather than faulting the job for its demanding expectations, Cathy's phrase "I just couldn't do it" shows how workers assign themselves blame for an exploitative work arrangement—Cathy assumed that it was her fault for not keeping up with an employer's expectation of continual hustle.

Gig work is precarious, with minimal paths for advancement or financial security. Why spend so much time and energy finding short-term work over the security of longer-term employment? Individual reasons vary, but many of the gig workers I spoke with emphasized a sense of personal freedom and a dislike of monotonous desk jobs, echoing earlier research on the gig economy (see Gregg 2013; Neff 2012; Shapiro 2017). Beaver preferred gig work to regular part-time jobs because it was easier to fit into his schedule:

> It's something you could do when you're not busy, and when you have like a full schedule. . . . So I can kind of do it and increment it into my schedule way better than I would say like a part-time job or something that would need more requirement of hours, or just commitment.

Although it's difficult to generalize, gigs on craigslist tend to be very fluid and autonomous, key components of their appeal. As Shelly explained:

> I hate people. Well, I hate bosses. I love people but I can't be told what to do, I wanna own my own business eventually. . . . It's plausible, it's just

very hard to do, so I do all these other things to chase my dreams. . . . I'm bipolar, like I can't sit behind a desk all day and do things that are like, trivial. I can't. I'd rather be out and managing my own life and my own time.

For many people, the work of handing out flyers, checking people into a county fair, or driving Lyft might feel monotonous or trivial, precisely the kind of work Shelly wants to avoid. Yet to her, gig work feels flexible and self-directed, and the predictability of a nine-to-five job felt stifling rather than stable. Being bipolar, Shelly also preferred constant fluctuation of jobs and work locations, which appealed to her need for stimulation.

While Shelly described gig work almost as a lifestyle, others, like Cathy, saw one-off craigslist jobs as a temporary but personally beneficial measure in between career shifts. In fact, Cathy saw craigslist as crucial in giving her an entry point to a new career that required tech skills:

> I decided to do my own contracting business and got a business name and an [employer identification number], and that's where I started getting experience in the social media and graphic design and blogging. I would just pick up projects off of craigslist and then internships and I moved on from there, that I pick up [most of my clients] almost exclusively from craigslist.

Cathy saw craigslist gigs as part of a cycle, a way to gain new skills like graphic design. Instead of getting training at a company as part of her formal employment, Cathy took it upon herself to develop skills that she could then market to other craigslist employers. In keeping with new economy narratives (see Neff 2012), Cathy viewed her DIY training as exciting and entrepreneurial rather than a burden.

Whether participants used craigslist every day or once a month, they all viewed gig work as having rewards that outweighed the risks. As Neff argued about the New York City tech sector, part of the logic of gig work involves seeing yourself as in charge of finding employment: "the lure of risk becomes a powerful mechanism pushing people to think of themselves—not their companies, not their industries, and not their economies—as solely responsible for their employment and economic well-being" (2012, 37–38). While Neff's tech workers were often chasing big payouts in the form of stock options, craigslist gig workers usually had more mundane goals of plugging financial gaps or avoiding desk jobs. Macro- and micro-level factors shape people's relationships to gig work. In the United States, a national drop in real wages over the past three decades, combined with decreasing social welfare and government support, has led employed people to seek additional work, while those outside the official labor market have sought casual work (Breslow 2013; Ivanova 2018). On an individual level, hyped narratives of entrepreneurialism encourage people to take risks and embrace fluid, uncertain work arrangements.

Beyond enjoying the flexibility of gig work, people often described the process of finding different jobs as enjoyable. After listening to Micah's in-depth account of online arbitrage, I asked if he enjoyed the work as much as it sounded. He replied:

> I do, I love it. I love business, and I love being free to find creative ways to make money, and doing it kind of outside of the box. It's my own terms. It's my own way of doing something. I'm not going to some retail job, or some desk job, or whatever, and doing tasks or specific work for a company to make money. It's almost problem solving in a way. How can I make money? [By] thinking outside the box.

Interestingly, Micah *did* have a desk job as a software developer, which is where most of his income stemmed from. Yet Micah saw his more lucrative day job as "in the box" while online arbitrage was creative problem solving. Searching for jobs on craigslist can feel tedious and anxiety ridden, but it can also feel exciting and inventive.

There are many intertwined logics behind gig work, from making money to demonstrating expertise to feeling a sense of agency. Jax described some of these interwoven motivations with a sense of pride (although not fulfillment) in finding ways to make money from his work buying and selling used goods:

> I would not describe it as creative fulfillment. There's just a thrill in— There's a certain schadenfreude to it . . . when you find something that someone has put in the garbage to send to a landfill that you know full well is worth a significant amount of money, and it will cost you nothing to profit from it, it's thrilling for multiple reasons. First of all, you've stopped something from rotting in a landfill. You've made some money. You get a little tingle from it.

As was the case for Micah, Jax found a sense of satisfaction in monetizing forgotten, thrown-out, or underpriced objects, leveraging his expertise to turn trash into profits. Craigslist has a reputation as a tool of last resort, but it can also be part of a tactical toolkit for everyday opportunism.

As participant accounts make clear, gig work is a complicated landscape of ambition, frustration, and opportunity. Is gig work exploitative? Like many researchers who study gig workers, I bring a critical lens to employment that doesn't provide security to workers. From a labor-activism standpoint, gig work reflects growing income inequality and the further erosion of workers' rights. Although digital labor platforms may manipulate their workers (Shapiro 2017) and push back fiercely on attempts at unionization (Bensinger 2017) or legislation that would offer more protection for workers (Bellafante 2018; Kerr 2017), many people nonetheless genuinely like gig work. If the goal for academics is not only to reflect on socio-technical change but to agitate for change, we have to start by recognizing the genuine appeal of the gig economy to significant parts of the labor pool.

Perceptions of work are shaped by individual personality and interests, but broader issues like class also play a significant role. Gig work offers minimal security and almost no chance of upward mobility. There is no path for rising through the ranks of Uber or Mechanical Turk, and most craigslist gigs simply lead to searching for other craigslist gigs. Yet seeing craigslist jobs as opportunities versus dead ends leans heavily on one's class background and economic circumstances. How does class shape perceptions of gig work? And what are the class politics of craigslist?

Craigslist and the Politics of Class

Early narratives about the internet emphasized egalitarianism through access, where anyone could learn new things and create new content. But promises of egalitarianism and empowerment have fallen flat, amid reports of online discrimination around gender (Rybas and Gajjala 2007), nationality (Burrell 2012), race (Nakamura 1995), sexuality (Gray 2009), and class. Surprisingly little has been written about class discrimination online or the ways that class shapes perceptions of the web. To be clear, a lot has been written about the digital divide, meaning the social, cultural, and economic implications of having versus not having access to the internet (e.g., Cullen 2001; Norris 2001; Van Dijk and Hacker 2003). Digital-divide research has helped shape important policies on tech infrastructure and education, but this scholarship has generally produced narratives that tend to emphasize *access to* rather than *perceptions of* digital technology.[2] Put another way, studies on the digital divide tend to assume that once everyone has access to technology, differences in their backgrounds will drop out. But differences in class and background matter when it comes to not just *whether* people use technology but *how*. Beyond studying socioeconomic and class implications of access to technology, what are the implications of associating certain platforms with a lower socioeconomic status? For example, what do people mean when they call craigslist the poor-people's internet?

Across interviews, I heard links between craigslist and the working class.[3] Thinking about class politics sheds light on many features and functions of craigslist, but emerges most saliently around work. As Savage and his coauthors (2013) argued, class labels are about more than income. The kind of job someone has can matter more than salary: an electrician can make more than an office manager but still be perceived as working class (and low status) rather than white collar (and high status). Status is about more than one's job, and can change as a person moves from one setting to another. For example, the same person could work as a janitor, and thus have little status at work, but could also serve as a deacon at church, giving him high status. In the United States, assumptions about class pull from many factors, including education, speech, dress, and social connections. But within the combination of factors tied to class, employment is often key.

Thousands of full-time, highly skilled, and professional jobs with benefits are advertised on craigslist every day. Yet like many people I spoke with, Agnes saw craigslist as a good place to find a gig but not a career:

> Maybe with looking for jobs, [craigslist] definitely makes it more . . . casual, and less intense. Like they don't really care who you really are. It's more likely to be more lame jobs, or, like, easy, no-experience-required-type jobs. Which is fine if that's what you're looking for, but if you're trying to find a real job, [craigslist] is not really the best place necessarily for that.

When Agnes characterizes craigslist jobs as "easy, no-experience-required-type jobs," she highlights a perception of craigslist as too inclusive and unfiltered in its listings. As I noted earlier, in craigslist's early days, the site had a reputation for publicizing precisely the kind of "real jobs" that Agnes sees as no longer available. As craigslist expanded beyond San Francisco and the internet became available to more and more people, the exclusivity that had defined craigslist in its early days eroded. Gig work, with its diverse labor pool, low wages, and operational interchangeability, represents the inverse of where craigslist started in the world of online HR.

If we wanted to divide job-search platforms by status, we might put craigslist on one side and platforms like LinkedIn or Glassdoor on the other. This division hinges precisely on what counts as a good job with a livable wage.

For someone like Gillian, a middle-class woman in her late thirties, jobs on craigslist represented minimal benefits and no room for advancement: "I feel like craigslist has never had a good reputation. It's always . . . just been a little bit shady. Even the jobs are shady, right? It's like, 20 dollars an hour." Gillian's skepticism about whether craigslist gigs can reliably provide a good quality of life is reasonable, but for some of the people who making a living on craigslist, jobs that paid $20 per hour were seen as the upper echelon of available employment opportunities. Throughout my interview with Shelly, for example, she referenced $20 an hour as the high-water mark of her gigs:

> I get paid $20 an hour through Lyft. No matter how you slice it, whatever time of the day I work, if I work five hours straight I'll make $100. That's lit, that's paying my bills. That paid my gas bill on Monday. You know what I'm saying, it pays my half of the rent.

A working mom who lived with her boyfriend, Shelly was responsible for a significant portion of the bills, and was able to make ends meet solely through gig work. For Shelly, being able to pay bills is the definition of a good job; rather than Agnes's earlier division of "real jobs" and "lame jobs," we might instead think of jobs that are rewarding beyond making ends meet and jobs that just make ends meet.

Even when people cobbled together a livable wage on craigslist, they still had to contend with its reputation as a platform for the working class. For example, Cathy shared her experiences with the stigma around using craigslist to find work:

> Yeah, I don't think anybody would discuss it that's white collar, is a good way to put it. . . . I don't think anybody white collar would talk about [using craigslist]. Blue collar [people] might brag, . . . it depends on the person. Yeah, it is about craigslist in particular. I do get a sneer out of a lot of the wealthy ones. I had to keep it private, and actually I have brought this up [as a way to find] employment, that gets a sneer out of most of the wealthier ones, but middle to poor class actually look at this as an opportunity on the job ads and the sale stuff.

For Cathy, craigslist represents a way for working-class people to find jobs, but she felt that wealthy folks saw the platform very differently, as a last resort rather than an opportunity. Cathy also implied that craigslist is used by wealthy people who are reluctant to admit using the platform, just as she has learned to keep her use of the site private to avoid skepticism and "sneers."

Almost everyone I spoke with thought of craigslist as having a reputation problem. Seb described craigslist as "the poor people's internet," explaining that the "internet now is colonized. That's just the primary agenda." Seb saw craigslist as a holdout of an earlier internet, a sort of ghetto that was increasingly used only by working-class people. Yet it was hard to pin down exact roots and causes for the platform's class connotations. Rob offered a range of explanations for craigslist's problematic reputation:

> I do think that there's something about the class of craigslist. Even though craigslist is used by, I presume, whole classes of people, I think that there's an undercurrent of classism with craigslist like, "oh, you got that on craigslist" or "oh, you're never going to find a good job on craigslist." craigslist is associated with lower caliber interactions . . . maybe because it's cheap, it's free relatively? Maybe because it's plied with bots, maybe because it's ugly, basic? I don't know. Maybe because it's so available, maybe it's like an exclusivity thing.

Rob's explanations for craigslist's "low-caliber" connotations focused less on the actual content of ads and more on the site's aesthetics and interface. On the one hand, craigslist is valued for its accessibility and simplicity. On the other, the site can feel cluttered with spam and bots, a by-product of low barriers to entry.

Craigslist's working-class reputation points us to shifting norms and priorities between Web 1.0 and 2.0 politics. Craigslist's platform politics emphasize access, dating back to an earlier vision of the internet, where access was supposed to ensure that anyone with an internet connection could learn something new or find new opportunities. But in Rob's brainstorming of what might be driving craigslist's lower-class stigma, he suggested that instead of a positive form of *inclusion*, accessibility has a negative connotation as a *lack of exclusivity*. This is a problem in a web dominated by self-promotion and status (Lampel and Bhalla 2007; Marwick 2015), which requires some sort of gatekeeping, whether that's explicitly through a paywall or implicitly through status markers, such as displaying the number of likes, friends, or retweets. Craigslist doesn't use profiles, so users can't display markers of social status. On the employer side, ads are ranked by date and there's no option for boosting visibility, meaning that all ads are basically equal. In a social-media landscape driven by likes, visible social networks, and selfie displays of consumer status, craigslist can feel too much like an unfiltered free-for-all.

Craigslist embraces a free-for-all approach to content and access, in keeping with early web values. The problem is that the web around craigslist has moved away from openness and toward curated displays of status. Craigslist's competitors offer gatekeeping functions that sort and filter ads, in addition to verifying and reviewing workers. Craigslist prioritizes a level playing field over a system ranked by sponsorship and payment. While apps like OfferUp and Letgo have visible profiles or social networks, craigslist users have to rely on the content of their ads to appeal to buyers or employees. Beaver saw craigslist's come-one-come-all policy as a form of egalitarian accessibility:

> When you have advertisements, and when you have paid spots in like Google and other adware, it's much easier for people to get their ad not even looked at. So this gives you kind of an opportunity and an equal playing field that anyone can kind of partake in this. It does not necessarily rate you as higher or lower, based on how much money you've put in.

In contrast to platforms with sponsored posts or advertising, (most) craigslist ads are free to post and all are ranked solely by date. Rather than opaque algorithmic sorting or fee-based ranking, craigslist ads can only get boosted visibility through reposting, which is discouraged by the site. Even though competition for visibility endures, craigslist's functioning is straightforward and the playing field is level.

When it comes to dealing with perceptions of class-based stigma, craigslist's reputation problems resonate with earlier battles for status and attention among social-media platforms. Reputation is a self-fulfilling prophecy—as people begin to feel a site isn't "for them," they migrate to platforms with more elite reputations, as was the case in a transition of popularity between Myspace and Facebook. By looking at media hype and reputation currency of Myspace, we get a clearer picture of the consequences for craigslist in being labeled a "low-caliber" platform in "the poor-people's internet."

Craigslist, Myspace, and a Gentrifying Internet

Craigslist's position in the online gig economy specifically and the wider web broadly has a parallel in the early days of social media, when Myspace went from being number one to a punch line about scams, sexual deviance, and technological obsolescence (Bercovici 2012; Kelleher 2010). Although any number of factors contributed to Myspace's decline in popularity, researcher danah boyd (2013) noted that class politics played a key role. Because of Facebook's Ivy League roots, the platform has always had an imprint of upper-class values, which have been diluted but not altogether removed as membership opened up beyond elite colleges to all US colleges (in 2004) and then high schools (in 2005), and eventually the general public (in 2006). In contrast, Myspace's early adopters included indie bands and hipsters, but over time the site gained a reputation for appealing to teens and young people who were of color and working class.

Myspace got its start in 2003, and at its peak was the most popular social-media platform around, with over 110 million active users per month (Marwick 2008). As other social-media platforms, particularly Facebook, emerged, Myspace saw a steep decline in numbers and was hovering around 50 million users in 2015 (C. Smith 2019). Part of the reason for Myspace's decline had to do with its reputation as messy, dangerous, and only of interest to poor youth of color. As boyd theorized, the division between teen preferences in Facebook and Myspace "can be seen through the lens of taste and aesthetics, two value-laden elements that are deeply entwined with race and class" (2013, 204). By comparing Myspace and craigslist, we gain a clearer picture of how class is negotiated online, and the consequences for a platform in being labeled "lower class."

One of boyd's (2013) arguments about the class politics of Myspace versus Facebook involves the latter's minimalism as an antidote to the messiness of Myspace pages, which could be tweaked and altered by users. Facebook was cleaner and sleeker when it came to profiles, which are identical in structure, although not in content. It wasn't just that Myspace and Facebook looked different from each other, it was that their differences were coded along lines or race and class. As boyd noted, "to some, bling and flashy MySpace profiles are beautiful and creative; to others, these styles are garish. While style preference is not inherently about race and class, the specific styles referenced have racial overtones and socio-economic implications" (214). According to the teens that boyd interviewed, Facebook was viewed as an elite platform for upper- and middle-class white and Asian kids, while Myspace came to be thought of as the preferred platform for working-class teens, particularly black and Latinx youth. Rather than making these connections overtly, teens categorized the sites in terms of their aesthetic appeal.

If Myspace's problem was the messiness of its interface, the parallel for craigslist is its lack of functionality. Where Facebook seemed sophisticated because of its minimalism, to many users craigslist seems backward because of its straightforward design and lack of features. When I surveyed craigslist users about what they would change about craigslist, they almost always talked about its lack of features and outdated aesthetics. To give a few examples:

I would change the format, it is dated.

I would change the aesthetic of the site to make it more pleasing to look at.

I would make an official app and update the [user interface] of the website because it is stuck in the early 2000s.

Although craigslist employs a number of web developers to maintain and make small changes to the platform's features, it looks and feels much like it did in the 1990s. Meanwhile, tech companies have worked deliberately to instill in users an expectation of continual upgrades and updates (Chun 2016), which means that many people expect platforms to keep up with new trends in aesthetics and features. Myspace didn't anticipate a collective change in mainstream taste for how a social-media platform should look and feel. Over a much longer period of time and seemingly with a lot more intentionality, craigslist's reputation for being "low caliber" is partly about the refusal to update its appearance or add features that are increasingly standard across peer platforms.

Problems with spam, scams, and safety are the clearest parallel between Myspace and craigslist, with both platforms struggling to adapt to concerns about online crime. Just as many craigslist users see the platform as too hands-off when it comes to content moderation, "MySpace failed to address the problems presented by spammers and scammers and their accounts started getting hacked due to security flaws introduced when users started copying and pasting layout code into profile forms" (boyd 2013, 217). As Myspace grew more popular, spam and fraud contributed to the site's reputation for sexual predators, a reputation that was out of step with facts. As Alice Marwick (2008) explained in a careful analysis of the moral panic around Myspace, there's no reason to assume that a platform with more than one hundred million accounts would be crime-free, but mainstream accounts of social-media use emphasized a risk for sexual violence and scams, particularly for kids and teens. It's important to remember that when Facebook and Myspace were competing for users, social-media use was much less intergenerational, meaning that kids, teens, and young people were on social media but parents, grandparents, and most people over thirty were not.

Without personal experience of social-media use, parents were particularly susceptible to media narratives of lost privacy and sexual deviance.

In the next chapter, I'll address craigslist's policies on content moderation, but comparing Myspace and craigslist helps clarify the consequences of not updating features, and of slowly or inadequately dealing with spam. A platform's initial success will always generate competition, and one way for platforms to carve out space in a crowded field is to cast existing sites as outdated and unsafe. For Myspace and craigslist, this process unfolded largely through media panics that tapped into narratives of race and class.

boyd (2013) used the framework of white flight to describe the decline in Myspace users, arguing that teens came to see the platform as not just dangerous but lower class, and left for the safer, more elite connections promised by Facebook. While white flight helps describe some of the reputation problems and moral panics around craigslist, I think gentrification offers a clearer metaphor of craigslist's class politics. When people connect gentrification to digital media, it is almost always in the context of the tech industry's role in reshaping neighborhoods in and around company headquarters (Bort 2015; Goldman 2013; Howard 2016; Rodenbeck 2013). Within academic literature, a more popular metaphor for space, power, and digital platforms has been colonialization. In the late 1990s, when online access depended on phone lines and modems, much of this literature concentrated on the links between colonial powers and infrastructure (e.g., Ebo 2001; M. Hall 1999; Salter 2005). But as a debate about safety, messiness, and class, gentrification offers a more useful vocabulary for thinking about craigslist's class politics.

Gentrification names a complex process of neighborhood change, where a small group of insiders move into an urban space, and over time shift existing business and social networks (Lee, Slater, and Wyly 2010; Zukin 1987, 2009). In the United States, gentrification is a deeply raced—and often racist—process that involves newcomers (usually young, affluent white people) displacing longtime residents, who are usually people of color with fewer financial resources. Tensions around gentrification include financial concerns, as long-standing businesses like bodegas, barber shops, and nail salons are displaced by coffee shops, bistros, and yoga studios. Having more affluent neighbors raises home values and property taxes, rendering previously affordable neighborhoods out of reach for families who may have lived there for generations, breaking social ties and weakening community cohesion. An irony of gentrification is that many newcomers seek out urban zones that have a strong sense of community and culture, only to upend the very characteristics that first drew them to the neighborhood.

Drawing on language of gentrification, we might think of craigslist as a long-standing internet resident watching itself become more obsolete and more othered as its incoming online neighbors establish new aesthetic (and political) norms.[4] A perverse cruelty of gentrification is a shifting of otherness from newcomers to old-timers. Take the "Gigs" and "Jobs" sections as an illustrative case: In the early days of craigslist, job ads signaled craigslist's interests in the tech sector, a fairly elite segment of the job market. As new sites emerged with more features and a prettier aesthetic, craigslist began to seem shabbier and shadier. Even as it continued to provide the same services, from the standpoint of reputation and narrative, craigslist was backward and outdated. For craigslist, like Myspace, the gap between old and new is narrated through a lens of messiness, safety, and class.

Conclusions

How can craigslist's class problems help us reflect on the politics of the gig economy? Is it a problem if craigslist is seen as the poor-people's internet? What would be lost if craigslist tried to (re)join the ranks of the elite? To close out this chapter, I'll consider how craigslist's aesthetics and platform politics relate to class. Thinking about work means thinking about the politics of companies and employers, and assumptions about what a workday should look like. In the context of the gig economy, thinking about work also means asking about the role of technology in finding employment, the opportunities and constraints of platform-based job seeking.

Craigslist looks the way it does on purpose. In my conversations with Newmark and from reading interviews with Buckmaster, it's clear that craigslist has no plans for major upgrades to its appearance. More than stubborn nostalgia, this decision seems like a commitment to a particular set of platform politics. As tech journalist Justin Peters told me in an interview:

> Part of why craigslist looks the way it is, is because Craig Newmark is the way he is and because the people with whom he surrounds himself for so long are as contrary as they are. And they have had this fixation with keeping the site almost like a tribute to the web they remember, like, in the mid-nineties.

In my work on countercultural communities (Lingel 2017a), I have argued that when platforms support communities that are in some way marginalized, major design updates risk alienating long-standing users. Unless changes come from and are designed by users, platforms can lose their sense of authenticity, by which I mean the ability for everyday users to see them-selves in the technologies they use. One of the main reasons for studying craigslist and writing this book is the platform's unusual resistance to the kind of default updating I've critiqued. When there are sexier and more sophisticated ways to be an online marketplace for jobs, what is won and lost from deliberately staying behind?

One way of thinking about craigslist's reputation is as an unintended outcome of its commitment to accessibility. To understand craigslist's invest-ment in accessibility, we have to go back to the socio-technical norms of the 1990s. Although openness and access drove a lot of Web 1.0 rhetoric, in the early days, internet access required expensive equipment and significant expertise. Over time, internet access became cheaper and more accessible. Schools began teaching digital literacy, and social-media sites integrated content-publication tools into their platforms, meaning people no longer had to learn mark-up or coding in order to get their text, photos, and vid-eos online. Whereas in the 1990s getting online took technical skills, in the 2000s it became easier to get online but harder to know who to trust or pay attention to. Craigslist's reputation illustrates these trade-offs in access and status. Over time, the meaning of access has changed from openness as a positive form of inclusion to openness as a negative lack of safety. Moreover, increased access to platforms makes it harder to get content seen or heard, which is partly why users on a number of platforms are willing to pay to promote themselves. Put another way, in the 1990s, elitism required techni-cal skill, but on the contemporary web, elitism means a display of status or the ability to pay for promoted content. The flipping of accessibility from positive to problematic signals a shift in platform values away from demo-cratic norms of equal access to more corporate norms of self-promotion. For craigslist, the lack of vetting systems and promoted content has contributed to its reputation as a resource for working-class people, a far cry from its origins in elite tech work.

Another facet of craigslist's blue-collar associations has to do with per-ceptions of the employment opportunities available. One lesson gained from thinking about craigslist and the gig economy is the attention to privilege within as well as between platforms. As Graham, Hjorth, and Lehdonvirta have pointed out, despite techno-optimism of digital technologies overcom-ing structural inequalities, "not everyone can compete equally on digital platforms" (2017, 137). While gig work is often hyped as an opportunity for advancement, digital labor platforms can reproduce rather than renegotiate differences in privilege:

If we accept that practices of work in the capitalist world system have always been characterized by exploitation and power imbalances between labor and capital, then it seems odd to think that there was even a suggestion that digital mediations of work would do anything other than amplify those processes. (153)

Part of the discomfort around craigslist is a broader uncertainty and cynicism about the gap between the careers promised by the tech industry versus the gigs that have been delivered. While elite tech jobs are certainly still available, the newest innovations around work and big tech promise microtasks and a string of gigs rather than employment that is rewarding beyond the ability to pay bills.

If craigslist is indeed part of the poor-people's internet, should it change? In a way, the question is moot because the company's leadership seems committed to it staying as it is. But we should also pause at the idea that a site that works for the working class needs to change. Writing about Facebook and Myspace, boyd noted, "The idea that working-class individuals should adopt middle-class norms is fundamentally a middle-class notion" (2013, 212). Perhaps it is a similarly middle-class assumption that craigslist's class politics are a problem. In an increasingly gentrified internet, craigslist may become even more important for its accessibility and holdout politics. The class claims that people make about craigslist when they describe it as blue-collar or the poor-people's internet reflect a growing discomfort with a lack of gatekeeping, which over time has morphed from a sign of inclusion to one of danger. Critiques of craigslist as messy, dangerous, and lower class demonstrate the political gap between the web as accessible and open versus the web as closed and commercialized.

6

People Seeking People

CRAIGSLIST, ONLINE DATING, AND SOCIAL STIGMA

"Recklessly Seeking Sex on craigslist" (Quenqua 2009). "Not all single people are looking to settle down, and the ones who aren't have finally found their heaven: the Casual Encounters page of online bulletin board craigslist" (Sohn 2003). "Every day, a handful of people with no experience working a street corner and no prior ambition to pursue the world's oldest profession sign on to craigslist's New York site and post an ad to sell sex—or something like it" (Werde 2003). If you only read the headlines and ledes of tech journalism in the early 2000s, you could easily think that craigslist personals existed solely for kinky freaks and sex workers. Whether they're published in print or online, personal ads have always been sensationalized and stigmatized as a tool for the desperate or deviant (Cocks 2009). This chapter reflects on the stigma surrounding craigslist personals, which I read as the social cost of the platform's commitment to early-web politics. By keeping the platform anonymous and public, and by welcoming non-mainstream users like sex workers, people interested in kink, and the queer community, craigslist promoted Web 1.0 values of access and tolerance. But these politics came with a cost, opening the platform to criticisms of supporting scams, human trafficking, and risky sex.

For many people I interviewed, the personals were described as the most dangerous or suspicious part of craigslist. As Denny explained:

I've got to say that when I think about the people I bought things off [on craigslist], no problem. When I think about the people who are giving me gigs and rides, no problem. So, I can't help but notice it's when you put yourself out there [for dating] that it gets weird.

In Denny's experience, buying and selling and finding gigs and ride shares were reasonably free of problems and drama, but using the personals section was asking for trouble. Many craigslist users felt that the personals brought down the credibility of the entire platform. As a survey respondent complained in February 2018, "If I could change one thing about [craigslist], I would remove the personals section because it just isn't safe and gives craigslist a bad name." A few weeks later, craigslist personals would be gone.

The personals were removed from craigslist sites across the United States and Canada in March 2018, in response to legislation passed in the US Congress. FOSTA was hailed as a victory by people who saw platforms like craigslist as responsible for violence against women and children forced into sex work. For others, FOSTA meant the end of an era, a sudden erasure of personal ads that had for two decades provided a source of hookups, friendship, and entertainment. I briefly described FOSTA in chapter 2 in my discussion of craigslist's legal battles. In this chapter, I come back to FOSTA as a jumping-off point for talking about craigslist personal ads, platform politics, and stigma.

What is the big deal with craigslist personals? Why does this section amplify the platform's reputation for scams, fraud, and danger? How are craigslist personals different from other online dating sites and why do they matter in conversations about platform politics? The subject of stigma came up in chapter 5's discussion of the class politics of craigslist jobs. But experiences of shame and judgment are heightened when it comes to personal ads, which introduce issues of sex and sexuality. After putting craigslist personals in the context of stigma about online dating, I walk through the basics of posting personal ads. From there, I describe how people reacted to the end of the craigslist personals, interpretations of FOSTA, and key features that separate craigslist from other online dating platforms. Within the world of small-p politics, online dating raises a slew of questions around sexuality, gender roles, privacy, and trust. Big-p politics drove the shutdown of craigslist personals, in that craigslist was responding to FOSTA, a piece of federal legislation. Unpacking craigslist's response to FOSTA helps us see what was distinctive about the platform's personals section, as well as the power struggles between users, platforms, and legislators.

In addition to a small number ($n = 7$) of interviews conducted with people who used craigslist personals, I rely on a Reddit forum dedicated to the topic of craigslist to think through the politics around online dating ads. The self-proclaimed "front page of the internet," Reddit is an online platform where users share photos and trade memes and talk about current events, hobbies, and interests. The platform is divided into sub-Reddits, each devoted to an issue or interest, from manga porn to academia to particle physics. The craigslist forum on Reddit is largely about suspicious ads and interactions—the top thread is called "Is It a Scam?" where users ask for input on identifying and dealing with suspected scams. After FOSTA passed, Redditors created a thread titled "craigslist Just Took Down All Personals Sections :(" to debate the bill's consequences. Like posts on craigslist, Reddit comments are anonymous, providing a frank discussion of craigslist's distinctive technical features and social value.[1] The thread generated over seven hundred comments in just two days, which I scraped and analyzed to understand how people on the web made sense of FOSTA and the end of craigslist personals. (For additional details on interview and Reddit analysis, see the methods appendix.) More than any other section, the personals demonstrate a Web 1.0 vision of social connection, where experimentation and risk were valued over trust infrastructure. Craigslist's politics of openness and inclusion were contested most fiercely when it came to sex and dating, demonstrated by legislation like FOSTA as well as the tendency to stigmatize craigslist personals and the people who use them. Like newspaper classified ads of the past, craigslist personals were often viewed suspiciously by the general public, sensationally by the media, and as a gateway to the margins by academics. By being so open and accessible, craigslist invited spectators and voyeurs, as well as critics. Stigma here emerges as a response to the gap between social expectations of sex and dating and the messy, shady, serendipitous reality of the web.

Stigmatized Desires: Social Norms Surrounding Mediated Dating

People can be judgmental about online dating, and even more so when it comes to craigslist. While it's impossible to know the exact ratio of vanilla to kinky content in the personals, the platform has claimed that millions of successful relationships have started on craigslist (Reynolds, 2017), many of which are very conventional. These stories are overshadowed by sensational accounts of queer experimentation, kinky fetishes, and sex work, like those that opened this chapter. There is a substantial body of research on mediated dating, which includes dating via print and online media (Deaux and Hanna 1984; Epel et al. 1996; Gonzales and Meyers 1993; Goode 1996; Harrison and Saeed 1977; Hatala and Prehodka 1996; Linlin 1993; Lynn and Bolig 1985; Sitton and Rippee 1986). Regardless of the media format, research skews toward marginalized practices and communities. For example, digital-media researchers studying online dating often focus on men who have sex with men and health risks associated with casual sex (Frederick and Perrone 2014; Grov 2012; Grov and Crowe 2012; Moskowitz and Seal 2010; Rostow 2005; Savin-Williams 2017; J. Ward 2007, 2015).

For academics as well as journalists, the tendency to focus on marginalized people carried over to research on craigslist. In her analysis of how the mainstream press has covered craigslist, Chelsea Reynolds noted that, "Almost all of the scholarship about craigslist focuses on public health interventions and HIV/AIDS. While this is an important area of investigation, it continues to stigmatize craigslist users as vectors for infectious disease" (2015, 219). A similar pattern of connecting craigslist to gay men, HIV, and AIDS played out in the popular press (see Browning 2015; Holley 2015). Left out of these articles and investigations are the millions of completely unsensational relationships that got their start on craigslist, day after day and post after post.

While portrayals of craigslist as inherently queer or kinky are skewed, it is true that digital technologies have been crucial for queer communities since the early web, when early chatrooms and message boards were dedicated to queer users and topics (A. Cooper 1998; Finlon 2002; Greenblatt 1998). Craigslist was part of the early web's constellation of queer online resources that were used for hooking up as well as community building. With its roots in San Francisco, a city well known for its progressive politics and LGBT friendliness, craigslist wanted to be inclusive when it came to online dating (Sohn 2003). Craigslist also welcomed sex workers in the personals section, made clear by the company's long-standing battles with state officials over its "Adult Services" ads (Lindenberger 2010). By taking these stances, craigslist effectively welcomed a certain degree of stigma, in that mainstream culture was bound to push back on the platform's support for groups on the margins.

Many forms of stigma are wrapped up in popular coverage of craigslist personals: queer sex, risky sex, extramarital affairs. For sociologist Irving Goffman, stigma refers to a specific gap between the reality of society—"the actual"—and the ideal version of society—"the virtual" (1963, 5). Stigma comes from a failure to live up to social expectations, where the discrepancy between the actual and the virtual "has the effect of cutting [a person] off from society and from himself so that he stands a discredited person facing an unaccepting world [*sic*]" (19). Stigma is not just a social problem, it's a communication problem, where the gap between the actual and the virtual has to be explained. In other words, stigma names the distance between normal and abnormal, with people on both sides pushing narratives to justify or attempt to reduce the gap. When it comes to craigslist personals, accounts from academics and journalists can be read as attempts to fill in gaps of understanding between mainstream norms of sex and dating and the sensational content that could be found on craigslist. Stigma operates in a cycle for craigslist, with quirky, kinky, or queer desires getting significant attention, reinforcing craigslist's reputation as a hub for sensational ads and deviant people.

The Basics: Posting a Personal Ad

Before the section was taken down, posting a personal ad on craigslist was very similar to posting other ads on the platform. Users started with the "post to classifieds" link in the upper right-hand corner, then selected the "Personals" section. From there, users could pick from a range of relationship types. Six categories dealt with dating, romance, or casual sex: the four "seeking" categories (women seeking women [WFW], women seeking men [WFM], men seeking women [MFW], and men seeking men [MFM]) were geared toward conventional expectations of dating. In contrast, users posted to "Misc Romance" for kinky or fetish relationships, while "Casual Encounters" was used by people looking for "no-strings-attached" (NSA) and "friends-with-benefits" (FWB) hookups. In addition to categories for finding dates, users could post to the "Strictly Platonic" section to find activity partners and nonromantic social connections. These categories mattered for signaling the kinds of relationships that craigslist invited, but also because, as *CNET* editor Jasmine France (2010) noted in a column, "Nothing will get your ad flagged for removal faster than posting in the wrong category." The fact that ads could be flagged for miscategorization didn't entirely prevent slippage. Some people described multiple relationship types in their ads, while others might claim to be interested in platonic relationships only to ask for more in later communications.

To write a personal ad, users came up with a title and described their desired relationship, partner, or encounter. Finally, they added their e-mail address and age. As of 2002, users could upload photos along with their ads, although previously photos could be included with some basic HTML skills. The "Personals" category was also the home for "Missed Connections," where people could post ads about strangers they found attractive in the hopes that a later meeting could be arranged.[2] "Missed Connections" has prompted art projects, fictional satire, and dating-site knock-offs (Beale 2007; Paviour 2015; Refsal 2012; Waller n.d.; Wortham 2009), and it's the only personals section to survive FOSTA—it lives on under the "Community" category.

Although many types of craigslist ads prompted online guides and tutorials, the "Personals" section produced an impressive amount of advice on how to write a successful ad. As part of the stigmatizing narrative about craigslist, some journalists advised against using craigslist personals, arguing that the platform was linked to STDs (Browning 2015), child sex trafficking (Phillips 2017), and violence (Friedman 2014). But others saw advantages to using craigslist personals, and offered advice for writing and responding to online ads. Diane Mapes (2008), a Seattle-based freelance writer, doled out the following advice:

> If you want to stand out on craigslist—or any online dating site—keep away from the canned corn. Don't tell people that you "love to laugh and have fun" (who doesn't?) or that you're "looking for a real man/woman" (as opposed to what, a Blade Runner-style replicant?). Resist the urge to air dirty dating laundry with headlines like "Tired of women who play games" or "Prove to me all men are not dogs!" That kind of stuff only makes you seem bitter. And unoriginal, as about 3,000 other people have posted the same thing. Today. (para. 6)

Mainstream-newspaper advice columns were one source of advice about craigslist, but suggestions were also posted on the platform itself in the form of personal ads. Advice ads suggested best practices for using craigslist to find dates, friends, and partners, such as encouraging the use of photos: "If you do not have a picture to exchange, then you have no right to be up in here emailing chicas and trying to hook up. Please! This is 2002!" (Anonymous 2002, para. 3).

Other posts were less about giving advice than calling out bad behavior. Another MFW how-to advice giver warned, "To the person trying to pay $6K for a girlfriend for the summer: WOW! Already you have a strike against you" (Anonymous 2006). Craigslist users gave suggestions about seeking out queer and trans partners, while sex workers exchanged tips and advice about craigslist's pros and cons (Quan 2009). Across the different efforts from journalists, bloggers, and users to explain how to write personal ads, we can tease out a struggle between an optimistic faith in online connection and a fearful suspicion that to use a site like craigslist was to invite danger and welcome stigma.

Remembering, Debating, Replacing: Reddit Reactions to the End of craigslist Personals

On a normal day, the craigslist sub-Reddit is fairly mellow, with a handful of posts about scams, perhaps a heated debate about controversial practices like selling (versus adopting) animals. But March 22, 2018, was not an ordinary day when it came to the topic of craigslist, because as of that date, users trying to access craigslist personals ads were greeted by this notice:

> US Congress just passed HR 1865, "FOSTA," seeking to subject websites to criminal and civil liability when third parties (users) misuse online personals unlawfully. Any tool or service can be misused. We can't take such risk without jeopardizing all our other services, so we are regretfully taking craigslist personals offline. Hopefully we can bring them back some day. To the millions of spouses, partners, and couples who met through craigslist, we wish you every happiness!

As people learned that craigslist personals were shut down, Reddit became a meeting point to commiserate, complain, and suggest alternative platforms for online dating. Analyzing Reddit conversations about FOSTA and craigslist gives us a window into popular debates around digital culture, social stigma, and regulating technology.

As Redditors came online to debate the news about FOSTA and share experiences about craigslist, the primary reaction was one of shock and sadness:

> Still so weird to think of it as something that doesn't exist anymore. So sad.

> Commenting just to sympathize.

> What a bummer.

> It sure is sad to see the personals gone.

In many Reddit posts, feelings of sadness were quickly followed by justifications for why they used craigslist. Posters often used a kind of disclaimer that acknowledged craigslist's seedy reputation while insisting that positive experiences were possible. For example, one poster noted, "Not everyone uses it to meet hookers, a lot to people actually ended up getting real relationships from this site." Another poster explained, "I know people think CL personals is the bottom of the barrel. I've had more success meeting people on there than traditional dating sites. It sucks. I just found out." The extent of craigslist's stigmatized narrative becomes clear in the repeat claims of Redditors who felt obligated to separate their personal experiences of success from a dominant narrative of scams, sleaze, and violence.

Part of mourning the end of craigslist personals involved remembering an earlier moment when the section was (allegedly) more reliable and less sleazy. These accounts describe FOSTA as an inevitable response to the platform's battle against scammers, bots, and sex workers. During an interview, Gillian (who met her long-term partner on craigslist) gave an illustrative description of a deteriorating "Personals" section:

> It's hard for me to give an exact date but personals on craigslist got really shitty. Which is something you will probably hear from anybody who had been using it consistently. By really shitty I mean, people figured out how to game the system in various ways. They got rife with prostitution ads [and] trolling.

Many Redditors agreed, noting "the quality had absolutely **BOMBED** in the past 4 or 5 years," "[Casual Encounters] had become way trashier," and "a fabulous service has been destroyed by spammers, scammers, bots, and yes, criminals." On craigslist, bots repost the same content over and over in order to appear at the top of the page. Bots were frequently blamed on scam artists and sex workers, people willing to spend more time and resources keeping their ads visible.

Complaints about sex workers on craigslist bring up a different problem around legitimacy and stigma. Some users felt that sex work was an inappropriate use of the platform, in keeping with general disapproval of sex workers (Hoang 2010; Scambler 2007). Others were fine with sex workers on moral grounds, but felt that they'd overtaken certain sections, like "Casual Encounters." One Reddit poster complained, "because of craigslist's trash spam filter, sex workers' ads started overtaking that section. It was a dumpster fire." In addition to the number of ads, others complained about sex workers writing misleading ads. As Gillian explained, "sex workers had a lot of nefarious tactics to trick people into thinking they were legitimate ads." In the next chapter, I'll get into craigslist's efforts to combat scams and fraud, but in the context of personals, longtime users often lamented the platform's inability to cope with either the scale or the tactics of sex workers using the personals to find new clients.

Overall, two things emerge from Redditors' complaints about craigslist's deterioration. First, concerns about bots and prostitution can be a way of distancing oneself from ads (and people) that are deviant or abnormal. Like defensive disclaimers about craigslist's reputation, complaints about the site's declining quality help manage the idea of using a platform with a reputation problem. Second, debates about legitimate versus illegitimate use of the personals give a clearer sense of what exactly triggers stigma when it comes to craigslist personals. Of the many complaints voiced on Reddit about craigslist personals, the sharpest criticisms tended to land on sex workers rather than, for example, married men stepping out on their wives.

In addition to mourning the end of the personals, Redditors wondered about pragmatic outcomes of craigslist's decision and debated the political motivations behind FOSTA. Discussing alternative platforms was the most common category of posting in the Reddit thread, with over eighty posts either suggesting or critiquing platforms that could replace craigslist personals. A representative comment warned, "Prepare for the transcendent relocation of all the collective craigslist fucksquatches to Grinder, Tinder, Fetlife, and miscellaneous personals boards." Questions about platform alternatives often acknowledged the user groups most associated with craigslist personals: men who have sex with men, trans people, and sex workers. One poster asked, "now that craigslist personals are gone, what website can men go to for random and anon hookups??" Another noted, "This is a travesty for the LGBT community, especially those of us who aren't out." While some alternative sites were suggested in particular cities or for particular groups (like gay men), Doublelist was the most common suggestion for a general-audience online dating platform. A Reddit poster described Doublelist as "just like craigslist casual encounters. Give it a go. It's new and growing but it works like craigslist so you won't see any spam or bait and switch marketing. It's essentially the exact same interface." Although posts described a variety of alternatives, most commenters seemed resigned to a replacement that wouldn't have the same levels of popularity: "We need something better, but even if we get it, it will take forever for it to get as big as craigslist."

Reddit posters also worked to unpack the political dimensions of FOSTA. Coming on the heels of anti-net-neutrality decisions by the Federal Communications Commission in 2017 (for more on net neutrality, see Meinrath and Pickard [2008]; Nunziato [2009]), some commenters connected FOSTA to a general climate of deregulation that prioritized corporate control over individual freedom. As one commenter noted, "RIP Section 230, and much more of the internet than just craigslist." Another stated, "Feels like the internet is really starting to clamp down." A Republican-appointed Federal Communication Commission commissioner Ajit Pai was largely responsible for overturning net-neutrality protections in 2017, and people commonly assumed that FOSTA was motivated by Republicans who disapproved of casual sex and hookups: "Fucking spineless politicians. I really hate [Republicans]. Stupid and ineffective. Now, child trafficking will go on as usual, but it will be more difficult for the rest of us to find casual sex online with other consenting adults."

Although many posters blamed Republicans, who controlled both the House and Senate at the time the bill passed, others pointed out that FOSTA enjoyed significant bipartisan support, with all but two senators, Ron Wyden and Rand Paul, voting to approve it. Given the near unanimous support for the bill in Congress, Republican moralizing wasn't really to blame for FOSTA. But Redditors were right to wonder how much the pro-FOSTA camp drew strength from anti-sex-work rhetoric. Pro-FOSTA activists relied on stigmatized narratives about craigslist personals, without acknowledging the platform's efforts at fighting human trafficking or the relatively small number of crimes versus the millions of users who found nontrafficked dates, hookups, and partners. Noted one Reddit post:

> [Politicians] hear shit like pedophile, human trafficking, terrorist, blah blah blah and just assume "this bill has to be good, it stops bad guys." When really it legislates morality. I've dated with success and I've successfully hooked up online multiple times. This law is only going to hinder civil liberties.

FOSTA supporters mobilized against pervasive and brutal crimes around human trafficking and forced sex work (McGloin 2018). But the messy reality is that some sex work is voluntary, and claiming opposition to human trafficking can mask a moral distaste for sex work or other stigmatized relationships and identities. On a practical level, shutting down sites like craigslist personals can backfire: as I noted in chapter 3, researchers have found that retiring online platforms that support sex work can actually lead to increased levels of violence against sex workers (Cunningham and Kendall 2011).

In debating the political motivations behind FOSTA, Redditors took aim at partisan agendas from Republicans and voiced suspicions that the bill was a cover for disliking casual sex, extramarital hookups, and kink. More than a specific political agenda, FOSTA tapped into a broader public sentiment against stigmatized forms of sex and desire. With its long-standing support of queer users and sex workers, craigslist had run up against conservative social norms for decades. While craigslist saw its support for LGBT users and sex workers as progressive and feminist, many journalists, lawmakers, and researchers saw the same politics as promoting health crises and violence against women. FOSTA represented federal regulations that solidified long-standing suspicions that craigslist users weren't just kinky or quirky but dangerous and criminal.

Iconic Affordances: Anonymity and Blank Slates

Sensational coverage of craigslist personals helped label the platform as stigmatized, but also positioned craigslist personals as iconic. Many Redditors viewed the end of craigslist personals as a defining moment in digital culture. For these posters, FOSTA was responsible for ending a major piece of internet history:

> Feels like a huge part of the internet just vanished.

> Wow, the craigslist personals were iconic!

> End of an Era.

> As crude as it was, it was a cornerstone of the internet.

What made craigslist personals so iconic? People who analyze technological devices and platforms sometimes use the word "affordances" to describe the features that can push or pull users toward certain behaviors (see Davis and Chouinard 2016; Postigo 2016). Affordances shape the practices that emerge around a platform—the tags, captions, and titles on Flickr encourage users to treat photos like pieces of art (Marshall 2009), while the sharing mechanisms, privacy controls, and multiple-account rules on Tumblr support its use by queer and trans users (Renninger 2015; Tiidenberg 2016). Two key affordances made craigslist personals distinctive when it comes to online dating: anonymity and a blank-slate format. Thinking about the affordances of craigslist personals helps to pin down what exactly was lost with their abrupt demise.

Like traditional newspaper personal ads, craigslist personals were anonymous, often containing highly personal disclosures about dating interests and sexual preferences, but not identifying information like a name or contact details. Being able to post anonymously meant that users could describe themselves intimately without fear of judgment or harassment. Yet anonymity also opened the door to shady behavior. While one poster noted, "There is nothing resembling CL personals and I don't know what we are going to do now to safely, conveniently, and discretely find friends," others saw anonymity as enabling "a huge amount of games, fakes, and flakes." In the next chapter, I unpack anonymity as part of craigslist's philosophy of user privacy. But as far as online dating, anonymity acted as an encouraging pull to disclose nonmainstream interests or desires, and at the same time pushed a signal of suspicious behavior.

Anonymity and stigma operated in a cycle on craigslist. Being able to use the platform anonymously meant that users could express desires with a reduced fear of backlash, while the public nature of posts confirmed that the site was used by people with marginalized sexual interests. Of course, the site was also used by people with very mainstream sexual interests, but publicly expressing sexuality, even heteronormative sexuality, is still a violation of Western social norms. Anonymity also meant a lack of any additional context information that could balance out stigmatized interests. Admitting to an interest in foot worship might seem less outrageous alongside contextual information like one's profession, age, or education level, all of which are encouraged or required metadata fields on dating platforms like OkCupid and eHarmony. But on craigslist, personal ads could consist of solely extreme interests, without any additional information to soften or manage a stigmatized narrative.

Because craigslist personals were anonymous, users could also be fluid in the desires they expressed. Without a stable, persistent profile, people could experiment with their self-descriptions, try on new personas, and suggest new arrangements. Bobbi described a "trial and error" process of learning how to write effective ads: "It wasn't really easy because . . . Sometimes I would get ghosted by those who responded, and then other times I would get rejections. Then I would have to revise my post over and over." In contrast to one-off ads, profiles encourage a static set of interests and self-descriptors (Hogan 2010). While people can change their self-descriptions or create multiple profiles on platforms like eHarmony and Tinder, profiles tend to be pretty stable and most platforms have rules about using only one account. In keeping with progressive politics around sexual freedom, craigslist users could be much more fluid, acting on whims or experimenting with their sexuality.

Anonymity applied to writing personal ads, and also to reading them. Popular attention to craigslist is in part due to how accessible the platform is, and personal ads became a source of entertainment because they could be browsed anonymously. On many dating sites, when people visit one another's pages, their activity is logged and visible to other users. For example, browsing anonymously on OkCupid requires a more expensive level of site membership, making anonymity a privilege rather than a default. On craigslist, posting and reading classifieds doesn't require a login, and there's no way for users to track who reads their ads. Several posters on Reddit noted the entertainment value of craigslist personals as part of their reaction to FOSTA:

> I liked to poke around when I was bored at work just to see what people were doing in my area.

> I don't meet people on cl but I browse the section a lot when I'm bored.

> lmfao thats where i went to when i had nothing to do. Always great to lol at.

Personal ads are entertaining to the reading public for the same reason that they're useful for academics: ads are a public display of highly personalized interests and desires.

Craigslist personals opened up a window into the dating lives of strangers, and, while the desires themselves weren't new, they had never been so publicly accessible. Although Bella used craigslist personals to find dates, she more frequently used them as a form of entertainment: "I'm very voyeuristic. . . . So I would read all the x-rated personals, and especially the Missed Connections. It's just people screaming into the universe. . . . The armchair psychologist, anthropologist in me necessarily has to engage in voyeurism in order to do the anthropology, right?" With no fees for accessing content and no public log of page visits, people could read one another's ads without any financial or social cost. Whether people used craigslist for dating or solely for amusement, anonymity mattered as an affordance that allowed anyone to read or post ads.

A second affordance that separates craigslist from other online dating platforms is the blank-slate approach to ads. Over time, online dating (like mainstream social-media platforms generally) became increasingly structured. Mainstream dating platforms typically ask users to fill out extensive profile information, take personality quizzes, and provide multiple photos

(Toma, Hancock, and Ellison 2008). In contrast, craigslist kept things simple—personal ads consisted of two main text boxes—one for a title, one for the body of the ad—which users could fill in however they wanted. Rather than taking personality quizzes so that the platform can suggest matches, or creating a profile based on a list of prompts, craigslist personals were almost entirely unscripted. While some ads were brief and to the point, others were lengthy, idiosyncratic, and deeply personal. As Gillian described:

> The thing that I liked about craigslist that was different from Nerve and Match.com . . . is that it was a lot less contrived. You just went and typed up whatever you wanted to say, whether that was like, "I need to get fucked up the ass today," or some 5,000 word manifesto about yourself. There were those extremes and you could just do it.

Gillian's reference to five-thousand-word manifestos was only just barely hyperbole: while newspaper classified ads discouraged lengthy ads by charging customers per character, craigslist personals cost the same amount—nothing—to post, no matter the length. Other than requiring users to categorize the relationship they sought (e.g., a "Casual-Encounters" hookup or FWB arrangement), craigslist provided very little guidance on how to use the personals section, giving users a blank canvas on which to project their personalities and interests.

Writing and responding to craigslist ads took work. Without a preset format to guide what info should be shared, people had to decide what to post, and the ensuing free-for-all pushed the work of matchmaking from the platform to users. Bella argued that this kind of work was an important, and even pleasurable, part of the dating process, while she saw more recent apps like Tinder as too transactional and sanitized:

> The whole thing [with Tinder] is completely weird to me, that you just like swipe on humans, right? You do no work, you do no human work. It's just this gross platform, with literally trays of humans being served to you. . . . It's completely transactional—there's no kind of romantic work being done.

Online dating sites that came after craigslist designed their platforms to include trust mechanisms like requiring photos and suggesting matches. By stubbornly refusing to update either the design or policies, craigslist essentially required its users to undertake the work of screening for safety and sorting for matches. While many saw this design as outdated and untrustworthy, users like Bella saw advantages of developing social and technical literacy in the work of reading and matching.

As part of the freedom to choose how to write a personal ad, many craigslist users valued the platform's emphasis on text over photos. Going back to OkCupid as a contrast, users are not only required to post at least one photo, the profile image must be identifying because "just as you wouldn't wear a ski mask hiding your face at a singles bar . . . anonymous profiles are not appropriate on OkCupid" (OkCupid 2019). Photos were never required on craigslist, and personal ads continued to be very text heavy, even after the platform began supporting photos in 2002. Relying mainly on text rather than photos shifted the matchmaking emphasis from physical appearance to expressing one's personality, sexual preferences, or fantasies. As one Reddit commenter explained:

> Instead of a degrading "why has no one swiped right on me" process like tinder . . . [craigslist used] a cool email function where you could tell people anonymously what you wanted to try out, what you were looking for, and say way more about yourself to others online. . . . So much easier when you can get to know a person AND their sexuality/interests without having to judge their looks right away. . . . Even people with really unique fetishes or freaky kinks, or straight up fucking *strange* personalities, tendencies, looks, and/or habits? They *could* still really find a worthwhile relationship, experiment, or meet some cute ass people, or finally fulfill their fantasies.

While anonymity is part of craigslist's reputation for danger and the blank-slate format feeds the reputation for zany quirkiness, these features can be advantages for people who want to do their own matching and sorting, or who prioritize individual interests and desires over physical appearance.

As affordances, anonymity and a blank-slate format are neither wholly good nor wholly bad. Any technical feature can be experienced as a benefit for some but a disadvantage for others. Craigslist became iconic partly because of how accessible ads were, and also because of how open it allowed people to be about themselves, their interests, and their desires. But openness also meant that people's intimate information was freely available to be read and judged by strangers, many of whom were more interested in entertainment than starting a relationship. Craigslist personals got started before online dating had stabilized with norms that encouraged visibility through photos and the use of "real" names. Like the rest of craigslist, the personals weren't updated to match shifting online norms. Over time, the gap between craigslist and mainstream platforms became more pronounced—and more stigmatized. The profiles, quizzes, and personality matches of contemporary online dating platforms are intended as forms of convenience, as well as trust building. Being able to see someone's face and social networks can afford more accountability and less harassment (Norcie, De Cristofaro, and Bellotti 2013). At the same time, dating platforms that emphasize photos for matching can lead to racist, classist, and femme-phobic discrimination (McGlotten 2013). For people with quirky, offbeat, or queer desires, craigslist's blank slate met the need for openness and creativity, as opposed to the constraining push of pop-psychology quizzes and algorithmic matching.

In Goffman's (1963) classic account of stigma, communication is key to coping with social disapproval. Whether the source is addiction, physical disfigurement, or being part of a marginalized group, stigmatized people have to figure out when and how to reveal details about their otherness. In terms of online dating, researchers have argued that managing stigma is wrapped up in how personal decisions are narrated: "one variable that may affect . . . stigma is the way in which their stigmatized status is communicated to . . . family and friends. Because communication has the power to modify context, the way in which a stigma is communicated may impact how one feels about that stigma" (Wildermuth 2004, 74). The easy and anonymous access to craigslist personal ads came with a lack of control over how and by whom ads were read. According to Goffman, "a very widely employed strategy of the discreditable person is to handle his risks by dividing the world into a large group to whom he tells nothing, and a small group to whom he tells all and upon whose help he then relies [*sic*]" (1963, 95). Part of the fascination with craigslist personals is the collapse of this tidy divide of information management. Feelings or desires that would previously have been divulged to only a select few are now shared publicly, which is a big part of what made craigslist useful, and also what made it so sensational.

Craigslist's decisions about the personals section reflect a set of politics about the web. In terms of design as well as user policies, craigslist pushed a vision of autonomy, encouraging users to be open about their interests, personalities, and wants, without the sanitizing filter of quizzes and personality tests. At the same time, these features supported a narrative of craigslist as a breeding ground of kink and deviance, with easily sensationalized ads overshadowing the millions of mainstream, vanilla, and downright boring ads posted every day. To be clear, there's plenty of kink on mainstream dating sites like OkCupid and Match (Mosthof 2016), but features like logins, filters, and personality quizzes make stigmatized interests less obvious and more contextualized. With its Web 1.0 emphasis on accessibility and experimentation, craigslist made itself appealing to people on the margins, but it also supplied fuel for thinking of craigslist as dangerous, kinky, and immoral.

Conclusions

Part of the web's appeal has always been the ability to find something—or someone—that would be difficult or impossible to find offline. Whether people are looking for local information, antique furniture, or a fetish partner, platforms like craigslist connect users across distances and divides, helping them find things, people, and places. For craigslist, helping people search means being as open and accessible as possible. More than just a design feature, craigslist's openness has a political dimension in its support for queer people and sex workers. Taking a pro-queer, pro-fetish, and pro-sex-work stance in the personals came with a cost, because helping people find partners in a niche sex community is more politically charged than helping someone find an unusual job or a rare collectible item. Rather than a narrative of finding community or love, or developing a sense of self, much of the attention from academics, journalists, and policy makers to craigslist focused on the extremes of sexual experimentation and identity. In this view, craigslist made things and people *too* easy to find. Just as craigslist gigs were viewed as low caliber because the section was so open and unfiltered, craigslist personals were stigmatized because the section's affordances made personal desires too accessible and revealing.

As of 2013, approximately one-third of married couples had first met online (Cacioppo et al. 2013) and it's harder to sustain a narrative of stigma as more people use online dating to find dates, friends, and partners. But not all online dating sites are the same when it comes to reputation and values. eHarmony and Christian Mingle push conservative values and relationship norms, demonstrated in disputes over how the platforms handle sexual orientation and gender identity (Ng 2016; Rao 2008). On the other side of the spectrum, craigslist's leadership expressed support of queer people as well as tolerance for kink, fetish, and sex work. In the uneven distribution of lingering stigma against online dating, craigslist was targeted for its casual acceptance of weirdness and kink, as well as its inability to eliminate bots and scams.

Craigslist personals became political on two levels—the big-*P* politics of federal legislation and the small-*p* politics of interpersonal judgments about sex. When Congress passed FOSTA, its goal was to hold platforms like craigslist and Backpage accountable for their role in human trafficking and sex work. On Reddit, many suspected that this rhetoric shielded a simple dislike of casual hookups or sexual experimentation. It's too soon to tell if FOSTA has made a dent in human trafficking, or whether the bill will survive legal challenges in court (Levy 2018). But the bill represents an important intervention around online technologies and sexual behavior, a political response to long-standing fears about the capacity of the web to facilitate fraud and violence.

When it comes to interpersonal politics and social stigma, craigslist opened up debates over social norms for sex and dating. With its aversion to censorship and support for sexual minorities, craigslist was willing to sub-vert norms around talking publicly about not just sex, but queer and kinky sex. Interviewed about the CE section in 2003, Newmark noted, "A lot of people are a lot more interested in something casual than I ever imagined, and that's okay with me as long as no one gets hurt. Unless they want to be" (quoted in Sohn 2003). While craigslist's leadership deliberately welcomed queer people, sex workers, and people seeking nonnormative relationships, the company struggled to deal with the fallout of its politics. Craigslist's pro-gressive values came with consequences, including the increased difficulty of battling bots and the risk of facilitating human trafficking. Craigslist pre-ferred to emphasize the millions of average users who met and formed ties via the personals, just as the company protested the level of popular attention around rare but extreme cases of violence (discussed in chapter 3). Overall, craigslist struggled to produce an effective counternarrative that could shift or soften its reputation for facilitating seedy and risky behavior. The same affordances that make craigslist appealing—anonymity and a blank-slate format—contributed to the sensationalism, suspicion, and stigma of using an online dating platform that was so open and uncensored.

The people who lose out with the end of craigslist personals are the same groups who often lose out in battles over legitimate versus stigmatized online politics: people on the margins. Mainstream online dating platforms tend to discriminate against black women and Asian men (Papamarko 2017), as well as sex workers (Dewey 2014) and people with disabilities (S. Williams 2016). For these groups, the anonymity and openness of craigslist offered impor-tant advantages, but for a more general public these same features signaled something more sensational and suspect. Looking at craigslist personals and the attached narrative of stigma helps to explain a key rule of technologi-cal design—that no feature is universally good or bad, and that all have the capacity to be political.

7

Craigslist's People Problems

POLITICS AND FAILURES OF TRUST

Whether buying or selling, finding work, or finding dates, craigslist exchanges involve trust. Even brief craigslist interactions come with expectations and norms, with implicit and explicit rules of engagement. Users have to decide if an ad is genuine or fraudulent, a process that starts with sorting through posts and extends to meeting up in person. If users come across an ad that they find suspicious, they can either leave it be or try to take action, which could be on their own, with the platform, or with law enforcement. There is no one set of norms for dealing with people problems on the web. Platforms may encounter similar people problems, but deal with them in ways that reflect their specific politics and values. What do trust and trust failures look like on craigslist? On a platform with minimal intervention from admins, what are the rules of participation? What tools and policies does craigslist rely on to keep users safe? When someone breaks the rules, how do users hold one another accountable?

In the last three chapters, I have walked us through the practices and politics of selling used goods, finding work, and using the personals, looking at how craigslist is used in everyday-life peer-to-peer exchange and job seeking. This chapter takes a bit of a swivel, looking across craigslist's different sections to think about how trust operates. I start with descriptions of the main problems that emerged from interviews with craigslist users—flaking, scams, and personal safety. Across the board, people expressed exasperation with interactions that fail because someone flakes, or makes them feel unsafe. Having identified key problems, I turn to users' perceptions of bad actors and craigslist's attempts to solve issues of scams and keeping users safe. Although descriptions of problems were pretty cohesive, differences surfaced around who was ultimately responsible for bad behavior. Who do we blame for scams and harassment—people, platforms, or law enforcement? Given craigslist's main responses to these concerns—flagging and anonymity—how and for whom are these efforts effective?

In this chapter (as in the prior three), I rely on interviews conducted with craigslist users between 2017 and 2018. I also conducted interviews with law-enforcement and industry experts who work specifically on issues of fraud connected to craigslist. In addition, this section includes an analysis of posts to craigslist's help forum. With my collaborators Jonathan Pace and Matt O'Donnell, I scraped craigslist's help forum for references to scams, cons, and fraud. Between 2010 and 2017, we found 2,281 threads containing the words *fraud*, *scam*, *con*, and *trick* (and their variants). Reading over comments from the help forum, we saw people looking to understand craigslist's policies on community moderation. Craigslist doesn't provide statistics on crime and, in general, online scams are underreported because of embarrassment or uncertainty about how to document the problem (O'Donnell 2019). Although we don't know exactly how often craigslist users are scammed or how bad the problem is relative to other platforms, we do know what tools the platform offers to try to keep people safe: flagging suspicious ads and keeping users anonymous. In this chapter, I unpack the politics around these tools of managing trust on craigslist, arguing that the safety that comes from flagging has a lot to do with gender, race, and privilege. Trust isn't distributed evenly across the web. Users' gender, race, or class background can shape their expectations of a platform and the people who use it. Craigslist is committed to keeping users anonymous, but its vision of online safety works better for some users than others. I will argue that in conversations about community moderation, safety, and privacy what's needed is a more nuanced framework around platform politics, particularly when it comes to anonymity.

Problems: Flakes, Scammers, and Safety

If you imagine a spectrum of problems on craigslist, with irritating missteps on one side and criminal activity on the other, you begin to get a sense of the range of social issues that emerge when strangers come together online. It starts with flaking. Almost everyone I spoke with about craigslist expressed frustration around flaky behavior, whether that meant long delays during e-mail and text exchanges or people failing to show up at agreed-upon meeting times. As Jax noted, "craigslist people are very flaky. My biggest pet peeve is people who will not cement a time. It drives me nuts." Lou agreed, saying, "craigslist is full of flakes," although at the same time, she noted that she herself tends to flake on craigslist exchanges, and this was common among participants.

Although participants complained of tardiness and no-shows on craigslist, these issues were also pervasive on similar sites and apps like Facebook Marketplace, Letgo, and OfferUp, and some participants wondered if flaking was a side effect of internet culture as a whole. For example, Flo noted, "Flaking is part of the human condition. And the internet just makes that easier." For Flo, flaking becomes more likely with digital communication, part of a larger set of social transitions provoked by the internet. Trust failures start with flaking, opening the door to a wider set of disappointments and failures when people come together on platforms.[1] Complaints about flakiness assign blame to individuals rather than individual websites, reducing trust in people rather than platforms. Exasperating rather than scary, flakiness wastes other users' time, but it doesn't really threaten their privacy or safety. When it comes to financial and physical security, however, the stakes are higher and people look to platforms and law enforcement to intervene.

Everyone I interviewed saw online scams as a problem, but unlike flaking fewer people had personal experiences of being scammed. Micah described scams as a serious and continual problem online, particularly for "people who aren't Internet savvy, who haven't really been around the Internet to really see or understand the signs of a scam. . . . I actually went along with [a scam] just to see what would happen. I ended up [printing out our correspondence and] framing it, actually." Micah went on to describe attempting to sell a car on craigslist, and getting a response from someone who wanted to send a money order for twice the asking price. The scam involved asking Micah to deposit the money order and then return the extra amount by check: "I got the checks, but I knew it was a scam. I just kept them because I wanted the actual checks to frame." There is a performative dimension in Micah's account that anticipates some of the blame narratives that we will see in the next section. At the same time, part of the work and expertise required to use craigslist involves figuring out whether an ad is genuine or fake, which means that users themselves shoulder responsibility for keeping themselves safe.

For people using craigslist to find short-term jobs and gigs, the most common issue that participants described involved check fraud and data fishing. Shelly shared a scam that she had encountered more than once: "Sometimes in the gigs section you'll send somebody a resume and think it's a reputable job . . . but it's remote. And they'll send you a check in the mail, I've gotten checks in the mail that are fraudulent checks. And they'll ask you to cash it." This scam involves sending fake checks in exchange for services or used goods—scam victims complete work or send goods only to find out that the check is fake. John had experience with check fraud as well as requests for personal information, or data fishing:

> Sometimes you get the people that like to scam stuff. They want you to send all of your information. And then a couple of times I've been sent a fake check. I know what a check looks like and there were no seals, there was nothing, it was just really fake. I didn't even, like, take it to the bank or anything.

Some craigslist users consult websites or friends to figure out if an ad is fake or fraudulent. But many handle problems on their own, learning which ads to trust and which ones are suspect.

People I interviewed were annoyed by flakiness and worried about scams, but the biggest concern involved physical safety and the threat of violence during in-person craigslist exchanges. Participants had even less experience with violence than scams, although many of them had heard of bad encounters from friends, friends of friends, or on the news. An exception was Zara, who shared a scary account of a craigslist exchange gone wrong. Like a number of women I spoke with, Zara always insisted on meeting craigslist buyers and sellers in public spaces rather than her home, and, for good measure, she brought her dog with her whenever possible. Despite these precautions, Zara described how meeting someone to buy a used amp turned into a violent encounter:

> ZARA: Well, this guy was being really aggressive. [My dog] Mojave was barking like crazy, which was super unusual, he has never done that. I always bring him with me on things like that. I am glad that I did. It was actually really scary, because the guy had a knife. I thought he was going to stab my dog.
> INTERVIEWER: Wow, so walk me through what happened.
> ZARA: I just met him in a WaWa parking lot. I was buying something, so he knew I had, like, $200 in my pocket. He just got in my face

and showed me this knife on his side. Mojave jumped out of the window of my car and jumped up and bit him in the face. He was bleeding and then he just walked away.

INTERVIEWER: Whoa. He was trying to sell you something? Right?

ZARA: Yeah. He was selling this vintage Fender Amp for, like, $50. It was really, like, a $700 amp. I think it was a situation where on the way there, people made him way higher offers. He was mad because I was going to buy it for $50 when people were like, "That's way too low."

Incredibly, Zara actually completed the transaction, demanding and then receiving the amp for the original price. Zara was unusual in that she had a first-hand encounter with a violent craigslist user. But many of the preventative tactics she described—meeting in public and bringing a dog—were listed repeatedly as safety tips by many of the women (and some of the men) that I interviewed.

Concerns about safety were heightened for women, who often felt that they were more at risk when it came to meeting strangers from the internet. The anonymous nature of craigslist exchanges was tied to anxiety around in-person meet ups. As one participant, Flo, explained:

craigslist is anonymous, which sucks for women under patriarchy, femmes under patriarchy. Anonymity does not guarantee my safety. It actually makes me more vulnerable because I don't know who the fuck I'm going to meet up with and there's no recourse other than this anonymous fucking trail of interactions on an email exchange.

The discomfort that women reported parallels long-standing narratives of women, danger, and public space. Statistically speaking, women are much more likely to be attacked in their homes and by someone they know rather than in public by a stranger: According to 2014 statistics, 80 percent of rapes against women in the United States are committed by people known to the victim (Sinozich and Langton 2014). But discourses of strangers targeting women in public space are powerful, boosted by common experiences of street harassment. On the whole, women expressed safety concerns more often, and described taking more precautions when making exchanges, than men did. Many men I interviewed also acknowledged that even if they didn't have safety concerns for themselves, they understood the need for women to treat craigslist exchanges differently.

Flaking, scamming, physical violence—each represents a failure of trust on craigslist, with stakes that range from an inconvenient lack of communication to threatening, violent encounters. Trust failures demand a response, which starts with assigning blame for encounters that go wrong. The work of dealing with trust failures is doled out across people, platforms, and the authorities. In the next section I look at the different stakeholders held responsible for bad actors: users, law enforcement, and craigslist.

Assigning Blame for Bad Behavior: People, Law, Platform

The craigslist help forum contains thousands of reports of transactions gone wrong, a collective archive of scams, fraud, and deception. Looking across these various threads, three different categories emerged in terms of whom users held responsible for scams and cons: individual buyers and sellers, law enforcement, and craigslist as a platform. In the first category, some participants felt that spam and scams were simply too ingrained into human nature to be eradicated, and, beyond using common sense, there wasn't much to be done. Others pointed to law enforcement as ultimately responsible, and a third group demanded more action from craigslist (see table 7.1). Separating users' viewpoints on platform responsibility into neat categories suggests a clear division of accountability. In reality, dealing with trust failures often involves a combination of users, platforms, and law enforcement, each with different stakes in fraud prevention. After briefly describing how people in the help forum see accountability as a problem for individual users or law enforcement, I'll dig into how craigslist as a platform responds to trust failures through two policies: flagging and anonymity.

A common belief in the craigslist help forum is that individual users are responsible for keeping themselves safe. As one user succinctly stated, "You can't be scammed unless you cooperate." In this view, scams involve a dupe as well as a scammer, and people who fall prey to fraud are to blame for their lack of savvy. Another common theme among people who hold one another (rather than the platform or the police) responsible for managing scams was a somewhat rueful belief that, after its early days of good behavior, craigslist was currently overrun by scams and spam:

> The community-moderation plan does not work. There are simply too many spam/scam ads for flagging to make a difference. . . . And there are not enough of us who do understand, appreciate, and respect the craigslist paradigm to effectively fill the community moderation role. The barbarians have crashed the gates and sacked the virtual civilization that was once craigslist. craigslist has degenerated into the free-for-all flea market for the mindless and criminal elements of the internet.

TABLE 7.1. Responsibility for Scams and Cons

Responsible Party	Help Forum User Comment
Individuals	"Cheaters and thieves will continue to operate until suckers stop making it profitable for them. Try not to be a sucker."
Law enforcement	"People, it's not craigslist's fault, it's your lazy incompetent government law enforcement agencies! They harass craigslist about the erotic services section, which is typically two consenting adults, but when it comes to an outright thief, they sit on their lazy asses and don't do shit!"
Platform	"Craigslist should hire a few people per state to go through and remove scams. . . . Craigslist has the money and the resources to hire people to manage these things better. . . . Hiring more people and training them could really help with scammers."

Themes of deterioration suggest a now-and-then view of craigslist, where early craigslist users believed in a "paradigm" of trust and respect, while current users care only about making a profit.

In the help forum, references to law enforcement were far less common than blaming individual users or the platform. Narratives about the police also tended to be vague, as in suggestions that users "call the police," rather than pointing to particular agencies or programs designed to combat online fraud. A commenter from Florence, Italy, responded to a scammed user, "It looks like you've been scammed. It's a common scam. You will need to pursue this in the 'real world.' With cops and such." In interviews, participants sometimes talked about meeting in front of police stations to make exchanges, but the only person who described actively reaching out to legal entities in the fight against scams was Shelly. When I asked how she handled scam content, Shelly replied, "I would get these emails from scammers, and I'd be like, I'm sending your number to the government! I'm flagging you." At first, I assumed that Shelly misunderstood what happened when users flag content, and thought that flagging content resulted in a report to law enforcement. Later in the interview, Shelly clarified that she preferred using a government reporting website over craigslist's flagging tool: "No, I don't have time to flag it. I'll flag it in my email and send it. You know, the email you send it to? It's a government email, I just copy it in there. I just send them right off to the government spam site." For Shelly, using craigslist's flagging mechanism was a waste of time because she saw asking a platform to police itself as ineffective and it was law enforcement, rather than craigslist, that was responsible for putting an end to scams. For most people on the craigslist help forum, however, craigslist was ultimately accountable for keeping users safe, data private, and scams to a minimum.

Preventing Trust Failures: Flags and Anonymity

Questions of how platforms should handle bad behavior stretch as far back as the internet itself. Early online communities developed rules of interaction in response to disruptive user behavior (Baym 1995; Dibbel 1993; Keleman and Smith 2001; Komito 2001; Smith, McLaughlin, and Osborne 1998). Some platforms deal with bad actors on a mostly technical level, such as algorithmic filters to detect junk content (Brunton 2012). Other platforms create online mechanisms that rely on user labor, like Wikipedia's system of public discussion boards and edit logs (Forte, Larco, and Bruckman, 2009). Facebook has experimented with a range of moderation policies, currently using a combination of flags and content moderators to manage interpersonal harassment, extremist views, and violent material (Gillespie 2018a). Craigslist's approach is both reactive and proactive, relying on flags to respond to suspicious ads and keeping users anonymous as a form of protecting privacy. Neither of these approaches prevents fraud or keeps users safe completely, and both come with trade-offs in terms of platform politics.

The Messy Democracy of Flags

Flagging has become a staple of online community moderation, whether for reporting graphic content on YouTube or hate speech on Facebook. As Gillespie writes in his book on community moderation, "most platforms now invite users to 'flag' problematic content and behavior, generating a queue of complaints that can be fed to the platform moderators—typically, to its army of crowdworkers first—to adjudicate" (2018a, 128).

Craigslist relies on flagging as a tool of community moderation, tasking users with reporting ads that are miscategorized or contain prohibited content. On the "Flags and Community Moderation" page, craigslist (n.d.[b]) explains the role of flagging:

> craigslist users self-publish tens of millions of free postings each month, subject to the CL terms of use (TOU). CL users flag postings they find to be in violation via the "prohibited" link at the top of each posting. Free classified ads sufficiently flagged are subject to automated removal. Postings may also be flagged for removal by CL staff or CL automated systems. Millions of ads are removed by flagging monthly, nearly all of which violate the CL terms of use. Of course no moderation system is perfect, and a small percentage of ads removed are compliant.

In this explanation of flagging, craigslist emphasizes the scale of the problem ("tens of millions of free postings") and the range of approaches to flagging: users, craigslist staff, and algorithms. Craigslist provides no details on the breakdown of how flagging happens—meaning how many ads are flagged by users versus employees versus craigslist bots—and users I interviewed assumed it was up to them to flag inappropriate content.

To flag an ad, users click on a "prohibited" checkbox toward the upper left-hand corner of the screen. Hovering a mouse over the box brings up the explanation "flag as prohibited/spam/miscategorized." Doing so then "hides" the ad, meaning that the user who flagged the ad sees the title in strikethrough. As one participant, Rob, described it, the strikethrough has the effect of streamlining the search process: "flagging will remove the listing from your view and then it will stay removed as long as you're using the same computer. That way I could just clean up my search and save myself the browsing. And then also theoretically contribute to data integrity." Rob's process involves a lot of work, flagging ads first to get a list of legitimate ads to skim. Craigslist has a one-size-fits-all approach to flagging, where the same flag marks something as prohibited, spam, and miscategorized, rather than having separate flags for each form of inappropriate content.

There isn't a lot of clarity around what happens once a user flags a craigslist ad—users don't know how many flags are required to remove an ad and they aren't able to suggest a new category for an ad if it has been mislisted.[2] In interviews, participants mostly saw craigslist's hands-off approach as part of the platform's overall minimalism and a "whatever goes" attitude toward content. As a result, the work of moderation is pushed almost entirely to users, as Denny explained: "There's not much management, there's not much oversight. . . . It's not like a discussion board where you have moderators or anything. So . . . you're not going to have someone working at craigslist or something and flagging your shit. It's really a community based platform."

It's unclear how effective flagging is, partly because (like most platforms) craigslist doesn't release data on the number of ads flagged or users punished. In addition, criminals and scammers have developed tools to evade flagging. I talked to Allen Atamer, a software developer and online-fraud expert, who saw flagging as an outdated approach to protecting users:

Craigslist has a mechanism called flagging that users can click to report certain abuses like ads for weapons or human body parts. In the first 10 years, it was used reasonably well, but then bad guys learned how to circumvent flagging, using things like bots and ad minions. They can force feed those ads onto the craigslist and there's nothing anyone can really do to stop them. So as a result, the "work from home" and "cheap concert tickets," scams of the day, and product sold "out of the back of the (virtual) truck" abound on Craigslist. (Interview with author, June 19, 2018)

Fraud is a cat-and-mouse game of developing tools for responding to scammers, and while flags are easy to use, they offer a thin layer of protection against a persistent problem.

Flagging is the one active tool baked into craigslist's interface for dealing with spam or scam ads, but as well as vigilant mutual aid it can be used for petty vindictiveness. John said that he flagged content "all the time" because:

> Even in the talent section I see a lot, creepy posts out there, be like, "I'm looking for a person that sits there. Has to be this model-type girl and I'd like to flirt with her." I just be like, "Nobody wants to see that." And if I see repeated posts that sound too good to be true . . . it's fake.

As a photographer who sometimes used craigslist to find models, John saw "scammy" ads as a threat to legitimate attempts to recruit talent online. Denny also saw "pervert" ads as particularly offensive:

> I flag all kinds of stuff. Sometimes I'll see the scammy kind of crap that I'll flag just because I've seen it every single day, and I know they're just trying to screw people over. But the one that I do most often is the fucking craigslist perverts. Like the ones that are looking for "housekeeper down for casual relationship and big tits." I'm literally just shocked because they're always just blatantly soliciting prostitution. . . . I know that flagging isn't an instant thing. You don't get taken down after one flag. I have a bunch of devices, so if I really feeling kind of strong about it, I'll kind of go on all of them and just flag it until it's gone.

Denny's account of flagging offers two key insights: First, as someone who spends a lot of time on craigslist, Denny expressed a sense of responsibility to other users, not unlike interviewees who talked about reaching out to users who had mispriced an item, discussed in chapter 4. Second, because flagging lacks transparency, users like Denny develop their own theories to explain the behind-the-scenes process of removing ads.

Flagging comes with many of the same selling points and frustrations as running a meeting by consensus. Everyone gets a say, which means that *everyone* gets a say. As a journalist in *Wired* explained in 2009:

An ad can be flagged off [craigslist] for any reason. Reject too many people for a job opening and they may flag your ad in spite every time they see it—and every new ad you post, too. Describe yourself as incredibly handsome and cynical date-seekers may flag you as a favor to the innocent. The claim that craigslist, used by millions of strangers, is somehow a democracy begins to be believable exactly here, in the crotchets, irritations, prejudices, and minor forms of harassment that characterize life in a small town where any proposal you make is subject to the judgment of everybody. (Wired staff 2009)

Craigslist users share a platform that has a spam problem, and flagging is a key mechanism of dealing with rule breakers, interlopers, and scam artists. But because flagging is anonymous and lacks transparency, it has the potential for misuse.

In her discussion of craigslist personal ads and user moderation, White (2012, 204) argued that being able to flag ads as inappropriate opened up opportunities for bias and discrimination. In particular, she argued that when women posted personal ads that mentioned nonnormative sexual or romantic interests, they were likely to be quashed by overly judgmental flaggers. While participants like John and Denny described their flagging as motivated by a desire to protect others from ads they saw as clearly fraudulent, their judgments also contain normalized values about gender and sexuality. When I interviewed Gillian about her use of craigslist personal ads, she described having her legitimate ads flagged out of heteronormative misogyny:

> The women's side of the personals, especially the women's straight side of the personals, got over run with prostitution ads. The backlash of that was extremely anti-woman. In that, if you were a woman who was posting the assumption was that you were a prostitute. Which meant that I got a lot of people writing to me either assuming that I was a prostitute or flagging me because they thought I was a prostitute.

Gillian's experiences demonstrate the potential for flagging to be skewed, turning an allegedly neutral tool for preventing spam into a biased mode of censorship.

White (2012) used a textual-analysis approach in her discussion of craigslist posts, and she didn't offer data to support the claim that women's ads are disproportionately flagged by other users. Without talking to actual users, it's impossible to have any firm data on flagged posts written by women versus men, making White's arguments more speculative than empirical. While it's clear from accounts like Gillian's that ads have undoubtedly operated as yet another venue for policing sexuality, it's worth considering alternative readings.

For White, flagging is a dangerous tool of censorship and enforcing sexual conformity. But for sex workers, flagging can be a tool of community care and protection. As one sex worker described in a 2010 blog post:

> After the introduction of post screening in "Adult Services," most suspect ads were rejected and the community itself was, by most accounts, rather vigilant in flagging ads for removal that were inappropriate. Legitimate advertisers would even complain about hypersensitive watchdogs who'd flag EVERY ad on general principle. . . . There was a very responsible community of women and men who relied on the site for money who are being closely affected by its removal. I took the position of "This is where I work and I want to be sure no one's doing anything bad here." I flagged ads I thought were suspicious and I know I wasn't the only one doing that. (Trixie the Anonymous Domme 2010)

This account sees flagging as a form of expert judgment, where members of a particular community—in this case, sex workers—are able to identify legitimate versus illegitimate ads. When it comes to flagging, different motivations, from discrimination to community protection, are expressed through the same tool.

Flagging may be democratic, but it's not very transparent. As Crawford and Gillespie noted in their account of online content moderation, flagging "may harken to other democratic and governance processes, but [it does] not operate within a transparent or representative system" (2016, 411). Once a user flags something, it is not at all obvious what happens to the ad or the user who posted it because "Platforms do not report how many users flag, what percentage of those who do flag provide the most flags, [or] how often platform moderators remove or retain flagged content" (Gillespie 2018a, 130). Flagging matters on craigslist because other means of discouraging bad actors—like public shaming—aren't easily available on a platform with anonymous users and temporary posts. On e-mail lists, message boards, and social-media platforms, people can call one another out, block one another, or leverage personal connections to intervene. How does anonymity play into problems between people? As an effort to manage online trust, what problems does anonymity solve and what problems does it introduce?

The Double-Edged Sword of Anonymity by Default

Anonymity is a defining feature of craigslist, the key factor that separates it from competing sites like Thumbtack, Nextdoor, Indeed, and VarageSale. Broadly speaking, online norms around naming have shifted from pseudonymity and anonymity to using one's "real" name, meaning the name on one's state-issued ID. Facebook has been a key player in the shift from pseudonyms to real names, dating back to its origins at Harvard. When it first launched in 2004, Facebook was available only to Harvard students, meaning that people had to prove their institutional affiliation to join. Later, Facebook opened up to other elite universities, then all US universities, then everyone over fourteen years of age, but it kept the policy of authenticating user identity. Important precursors to Facebook also required "real" names, like the Whole Earth 'Lectronic Link (the WELL, which Craig Newmark has described as a key influence in building craigslist). But for the most part, early web users chose pseudonyms for their email addresses and profile names, while later platforms like Facebook and LinkedIn insisted on verified names and identities.[3]

On craigslist, users are anonymous by default. Although some people opt to include identifying information like a phone number or home address in their ads, most don't, leaving e-mail as the main mode of contact. Initially, craigslist allowed people to e-mail one another directly, but in 2013 the site implemented a two-way e-mail relay system to cloak users' real e-mail addresses with dummy addresses (for example, converting lingel@upenn .edu to rcc9la26d7534400a6a03514c34f9200@reply.craigslist.org). The change was meant to provide additional security, allowing people to use the site without revealing personal contact information.

Anonymity has historically been a feature of classified ads, particularly personal ads. In a way, the two-way e-mail relay system mimics the middleman system of early personals ads, with a newspaper publisher acting as a go-between for ad authors and respondents, effectively cloaking their identities until they chose to de-anonymize themselves (Bader 2005; Cocks 2004). Trade-offs in safety take shape here, with increased privacy for people posting, but no ability to vet information. In an interview, Gillian described how the e-mail relay system changed her perceptions of craigslist personals and online safety:

> I started to think about the re-mailer as not safe. So, you send a picture on the re-mailer, I don't know where that picture goes. I don't know . . . how long they keep their data. I have no idea. So, then there started to

be a little bit of a split between people who felt like the re-mailer was protecting them and people who felt like the re-mailer was a black box that eroded their control over their information.

Technically, even if I have an e-mail address (rather than a relay address) for another craigslist user, I still don't have assurances that she won't repost content somewhere else, but Gillian's point is that the relay system removed even the minimal identifying information of a personal e-mail address. The relay system reflected a balancing act of anonymity, pitting privacy against accountability. Jasmine put this trade-off succinctly: "I think [anonymity is] bad because you really don't know who this person is and what they really want. But on the other side, then they're not getting any personal information from you." Craigslist restricts user information to the post itself, where people can choose to disclose personal information, but there's no external means of fact-finding or verification.

We can contrast this to one of its most recent competitors, VarageSale. The app-based company got its start in 2015, the brainchild of Tami Zuckerman, a soon-to-be-mom and kindergarten teacher at the time she started brainstorming a peer-to-peer exchange service that would emphasize safety and local community. While anonymity is the default on craigslist, Varage-Sale has many mechanisms of visibility. Users must have a Facebook account, which displays their profile and network to VarageSale users. In addition, VarageSale uses community leaders to moderate content and as a first line of defense in moderating user disputes. VarageSale's marketing frequently emphasizes safety without explicitly mentioning craigslist, but others make the comparison pretty clear. For example, YouTuber Matthew Brian Brown, who reviews apps and provides tips for online self-promotion, claims:

> The easiest way to compare [VarageSale] to any other technology that exists right now is to look at something like craigslist, but remove the rape and stuff. craigslist can be a very scary place and that's because it's entirely anonymous. But what VarageSale has done is made this far more personal by allowing people to connect their Facebooks as well as restricting people and users to the local communities. By doing this they are effectively removing a lot of spam, as well as making it more of a local-driven, personal community. (Brown 2016, 0:21)

For Brown, VarageSale is the anti-craigslist, a safer, more trustworthy platform, largely because he puts faith in Facebook as a screening mechanism for freaks or would-be fraudsters.

What does it mean to leverage Facebook as a vetting tool for participation? According to its cofounder and CEO Carl Mercier, VarageSale requires users to log in via Facebook because it is the "closest thing to real identity on the Internet" (quoted in Serebrin 2015). Mercier also states that the use of real names creates a "safe, trusted environment," and that "People love interacting with real people." Across the web, a range of platforms are adopting this logic, using a process called bootstrapping. Bootstrap logins link platform accounts, as when sites like VarageSale require users to have an account on Facebook. Typically sold to users as a form of convenience, bootstrapping has important consequences for data and privacy. Beyond the fact that this system excludes people not on Facebook (or whichever platform bootstrapping requires), cross-platform logins create tangles of identifying information that make it difficult for users to retain a sense of control over their own data. Unsurprisingly, these concerns do not surface in VarageSale's explanations for the decision to require a Facebook account.

In assessing the value of outside platforms as tools of authentication, many users echo the views of VarageSale administrators. When I asked what made people more nervous about craigslist than Facebook groups like Internet Yardsale or Free Your Stuff, most pointed to having a visible social network as a form of accountability. Flo argued that bootstrapping acts as a deterrent against scams: "Just the accountability of having a profile and being able to be contacted [means] there's nobody trying to pull a fast one." For Flo, Facebook makes people visible, giving her access to contact information and photos of potential buyers and sellers. Molly, a very active member of Philadelphia's Free Your Stuff, agreed. Like Gillian, she pointed to the cloaked e-mail feature as a form of danger rather than a feature of safety:

> Part of what I liked about Free Your Stuff [is that it avoids the] anonymity on craigslist, [anonymity] becomes something of a liability with free stuff, because so many people flake and you never know who's coming to your house. You're emailing, it's not even their email address, it's randomized usually. The description of Free Your Stuff is basically, "craigslist sucks, let's actually talk to each other. craigslist is a bunch of tire kickers, close talkers," that was the description . . . and I'm like, "Yes! I hate craigslist. I hate being afraid."

For Molly, Facebook acts as a vetting mechanism, a way to authenticate someone's identity, and avoid the fear of dealing with anonymous craigslist users.

In contrast to thinking of visibility on social-media platforms as providing a sense of trust, other participants shared exactly the opposite view. For example, Agnes described a reluctance to post on Facebook because of the link between an ad and her social network:

> The main thing is that you're anonymous on craigslist and you're not on Facebook, obviously. So that makes me feel a lot more hesitant to post [certain things]. . . . I'm not gonna post something that maybe I would be embarrassed for other people to see. Versus on craigslist, whatever, I don't care. And you don't really need to be as polite when you're anonymous. Not that I'm trying to be rude to people. On Facebook, when you message someone, there's a lot more, "Oh, hello!" pleasantries, and craigslist it's like "Is it available?"

To Agnes, anonymity provides privacy and can make exchanges more direct. But drawing a clear line between measures of safety and privacy is tricky. Put another way, the same mechanism of online vetting that can help people feel more confident about buying and selling safely can also lead to bias and discrimination.

An increasing number of platforms require "real" names to provide more visibility and deter bad actors, but the policy isn't foolproof. Airbnb is sometimes described as a safer version of craigslist for finding local housing, with the logic that it's safer because of the accountability of reviews and profiles. Yet the visibility of user profiles can also lead to discrimination. In a well-publicized 2017 incident, an Asian-American Airbnb user had her reservation cancelled by a host minutes before her scheduled check-in, with the explanation: "I wouldn't rent it to u if u were the last person on earth," and "One word says it all. Asian" (Solon 2017). The problem of bias on Airbnb is extensive enough that it spawned a competing site, Innclusive, which markets itself as a bias-free travel site: "Discrimination happens on Airbnb and other platforms primarily through folks seeing the names and photos of guests before accepting the booking. On our platform we remove this opportunity for discrimination by introducing the photo only after the booking is confirmed" (Innclusive, n.d.). The same mechanism that Airbnb, Facebook, and VarageSale hold up as a guarantor of community can thus also be a gateway for bias and racism.

In my interviews with craigslist users, I noticed differences on the topic of safety that tracked along race and gender.[4] While the middle-class white women I spoke with usually saw craigslist's policy on anonymity as a loss of personal safety, many of the black women I interviewed felt differently, where concerns for physical safety were balanced by an interest in retaining privacy. For example, Shayla, a twenty-two-year-old black woman, explained:

> I think [anonymity is] a good thing. It could be a bad thing in certain situations but overall I think that's a good thing. I think it's just protecting people's privacy. See, if I'm selling stuff I wouldn't want people to see me—people out here that might need it might want to come get me for it. Yeah. I would just rather be anonymous until I decide that I want to give that person [information about] my identity.

For Shayla, anonymity provided a form of safety, in contrast to posting an ad that exposed her to risk. Gillian, a black woman in her late thirties, also saw anonymity as a form of protection rather than danger:

> I think about [anonymity] more in terms of protection. Because, my concern in meeting someone shady is not like, I'm gonna meet somebody, we're gonna go to a bar, they're gonna seem like a really nice guy and then I'm gonna go back to his place and he's gonna rape me. No, it's more like I'm gonna think this person is okay, I'm gonna meet them, I'm gonna get a bad sense and then they're gonna know who I am, and they're gonna steal my shit.

Complex negotiations of patriarchy and racism come into play here, because women have legitimate reasons for thinking about physical safety and agency in public space. At the same time, women's relationships to danger and risk are inflected in complicated ways by race and class. In the United States, concerns about women's safety are often limited to white women's safety (Osucha 2009). In my interviews with craigslist users, white women most often associated anonymity with fear, frustration, and anger. In contrast, I noticed that black women's views of anonymity were more complex and revealed a greater concern for personal privacy.

Tensions raised by women of color resonate with other groups of people with heightened concerns about safety. During the 2009 controversy about adult services (discussed in chapter 3), a number of sex workers described craigslist's anonymity policy as a form of safety. Journalist and former sex worker Melissa Gira Grant (2009) argued that craigslist provided more control and agency for sex workers in conducting their work and retaining information: "People talk about a transition from the red-light district to the online red-light district, and the way the internet allows sex workers to operate their own businesses, without having to have a third party, and to share information anonymously." Other sex workers agreed that the ability to control information and maintain anonymity provided a form of safety. According to a 2010 blog post by Trixie the Anonymous Domme:

> The beauty of Adult Services, compared to other listing sites such as Backpage or CityVibe, was that a provider was in total control over how much information she wanted to share. The anonymous email feature and automatic expiration specific to CL ads meant that posters could communicate with prospective clients without giving away information that would make them vulnerable to stalking—or allow their temporary choice to haunt them on the Internet for eternity.

For sex workers, anonymity affords many kinds of protection. In the short term, it provides distance during e-mail exchanges while determining whether or not a prospective client seems trustworthy, and keeps personal information out of the hands of stalkers. In the long term, defaulting to anonymity means that there's no online profile to document one's history as a sex worker. Sex work is extremely dangerous, making sex workers experts on safety in public space. Listening to their views on the affordances of anonymity should matter precisely on questions of women, technology, and risk taking.

Because it has stayed so stable, craigslist helps us reflect on major shifts in anonymity online. Writing about the sharing economy, Sundararajan saw craigslist as a relic that hadn't changed with the times, failing to give users mechanisms for building trust. For Sundararajan, a general faith in others online involves systems of reviewing and vetting, which he referred to as a "digital trust infrastructure" (2016, 60). When people I interviewed contrasted peer-to-peer platforms as trustworthy or untrustworthy, they tended to point to the kind of digital trust infrastructure that Sundararajan suggests, meaning verified ID, review systems, and a visible set of social connections. But it's worth pointing out that not everyone puts their faith in the digital trust infrastructure, because it works better for some groups than others. As becomes clear in the nuanced comments from women of color, the emergence of platforms like Innclusive, and experiences of sex workers, the mechanisms that Sundararajan (like Facebook, Airbnb, VarageSale, and many other social-media platforms) sees as "digital trust infrastructure" can end up enabling racism and discrimination rather than building trust.

Conclusions

Like every online platform, craigslist struggles to keep up with problems of deception and harassment. The company cooperates with law enforcement to track down bad actors, and relies heavily on its users to take precautions and flag suspicious content. But as Gillespie has argued of community moderation on mainstream social-media sites, "there is an inherent paradox in looking to a community to police itself. The user population of Facebook or YouTube is enormous and heterogeneous. . . . These platforms are home to many communities, and some disagree . . . in their understanding of the platform and what it is for" (2018a, 93). Gillespie's point is that from the platform's perspective, community moderation assumes a shared vision of what a platform is for, requiring users to embrace a single set of practices, rules, and punishments, rather than asserting individual values and politics. When online publics are more diverse, it becomes harder to get users to buy into and enforce a shared set of rules.

Of course, expecting a diverse group of people to come to terms with their differences and somehow navigate social conflict is not new to the internet—it's a process familiar to most countercultural communities, neighborhood associations, and activist groups, whose members rarely embrace all of the rules and norms of the communities and publics they join. On craigslist, some of the norms that help manage people problems come from the platform, as in tools like flagging and design decisions like anonymity, and others surface organically from users, like attempts at vigilante justice against scammers. There is a political dimension to the ways that people and platforms try to manage bad actors, and in the context of craigslist, I want to end this chapter by thinking about the politics of anonymity as a tool for managing people problems versus anonymity as a problematic way of being online. What gets lost when we hear "anonymity" and assume bad behavior?

Like its design and business model, craigslist is a holdout when it comes to anonymity. Users are anonymous by default, a policy that has come to seem backward as social-media companies increasingly insist on (and find ways to monetize) verified identification of users. While craigslist is far from the only platform that defaults to anonymity, the company goes against the grain of most of its competitors, like eBay, Nextdoor, and VarageSale. Pushing users to identify themselves may be marketed as a form of safety or convenience, but it's also a crucial part of how most platforms make money. As Wendy Chun noted in her account of technological design norms: "Ever since the internet emerged as a mass medium in the mid 1990s, corporations have framed securing users' identities as crucial to securing trust. Two assumptions drive this argument: one, that the worst dangers come from anonymous strangers rather than friends; and two, that transparency guarantees better actions" (2016, 109). The commercial logic that Chun identified conflates anonymity with problematic behavior and links verification to trustworthy behavior. Yet intersections of identity and the internet are far more complicated than a black-and-white binary of anonymity/bad, visibility/good. What's needed is a more nuanced account of anonymity, which can alternately be read as a feature that provides privacy and an affordance that encourages bad behavior.

In her highly influential text *Life Online* (1998), Annette Markham examined metaphors of using the web, which she characterized alternately as a place, tool, and way of being. Grafting Markham's framework onto different mechanisms of anonymity can help clarify some of the tensions around privacy, visibility, and safety. When it comes to online marketplaces, craigslist sees anonymity as a *tool* of safety and privacy, while companies like VarageSale and Airbnb see anonymity as a threatening *way of being* online. Craigslist's anonymity policy is intended to protect privacy and prevent harassment. As a tool, anonymity can be used to provide security or protect against discrimination. Mainstream web companies delegitimize anonymity as a way of being online, holding up visibility as a safer way of being. Part of the confusion around anonymity comes from failing to separate *tools* of privacy and security from harmful *ways of being* and interacting online.

From early internet bulletin board systems to Reddit and 4chan, there have always been sites that function with pseudonymity and anonymity. But anonymity is more than a technical feature—it requires a degree of collective buy-in and social acceptance. Rather than allowing anonymity and pseudonymity to coexist with platforms that encourage or require identification, we've seen a long-standing campaign against anonymous behavior. In this context, craigslist's view of anonymity as a tool feels increasingly out of step with the mainstream web's continual push for authenticating users and publishing personal information.

Writing about a rare but well-publicized incident of murder facilitated by craigslist, a journalist for *GQ* noted, "Trust is how craigslist works in the first place. The shocking thing isn't that the occasional bad actor on craigslist shows up and takes advantage of that trust. The shocking thing about craigslist is that it almost never happens" (Friedman 2014). Craigslist's digital trust infrastructure is limited, partly because the platform sees anonymity as a tool for protecting privacy rather than a threatening way of being on the internet. To return to my earlier question of what gets lost when we think of anonymity and assume malicious intent, the answer is that what we lose is an entire history of assuming that users would want to be anonymous online as a way of protecting their privacy, or simply because there was no need (and no push from platforms) to divulge personal information. Having a counterexample of a long-standing, popular, and profitable platform pushes users toward anonymity matters as a way of legitimizing early-web politics. While major tech players insist that privacy is dead, craigslist insists that privacy is normal and trust can be enforced by anonymous people working to solve online problems.

Conclusion

THE CASE FOR KEEPING
THE INTERNET WEIRD

A new cynicism has taken hold in conversations about the web. Journalists have documented increasing levels of digital harassment (Hess 2014), lawmakers have investigated online forms of election interference (A. Ward 2018), and researchers have linked depression and anxiety to extended social-media use (King 2018). With so many alarm bells going off, it's almost hard to recall the exuberance and optimism around digital technologies as tools of connectivity, tolerance, and democracy—key themes surrounding the web for the past quarter century.

It's important to think through the ways that digital technologies have failed to live up to our expectations and to document the uneven distributions of power and profit that characterize the contemporary web. A small number of players control a growing portion of the web, and calling out the inequalities in Google searches (Noble 2018) or the political influence of Facebook (Vaidhyanathan 2018) is vital for informed discussions about digital culture. But it's also important to think about whether the optimistic possibilities of the internet's early days have been eclipsed completely, or whether it is still possible to find meaningful experiences of democracy, diversity, and tolerance online. This book argues that craigslist is an imperfect but important success story for the internet, and more specifically, a story of how to keep the internet ungentrified.

The two parts of this book have worked through craigslist's politics in different ways. In part I, I described how craigslist became a company, the transition from print to digital classifieds, and key court cases that put the platform's politics to the test. Craigslist grew up during a period of intense excitement about digital technologies, when the politics and norms of online publics were very much up for grabs. Over time, craigslist's policies and aesthetics remained stable, while all around it new norms took shape, along with different business models and relationships between users and platforms. Craigslist's model of charging a small fee for certain services came from its media predecessor, the classified ad. The two formats also share an emphasis on local connections and anonymous communication. Decisions about user fees, a local focus, and anonymity made sense in the context of 1990s digital culture, but eventually provoked criticism—and, occasionally, lawsuits. For internet activists, legal precedents based on craigslist cases are a mixed bag—on the one hand, craigslist advocated fiercely for platform-neutrality laws like CDA 230. On the other hand, craigslist has responded aggressively when people attempted to use the platform's data to build new tools or make art. By shifting from different lenses of craigslist's history—in the tech industry, its media history, and legal criticism—we get a clearer picture of craigslist's role in the wider world of digital platforms, and a more thorough understanding of its politics, which emphasize simple design, accessibility, and anonymity as a tool of privacy. Over time, craigslist has refused to update either its design or its policies, reminding us of just how much the mainstream web and its politics have changed.

In part II, I dove into the everyday politics of using craigslist to buy and sell, find jobs, find dates, and deal with people problems. Craigslist is many things to many people, but some themes stretched across accounts of using the platform's different sections. Looking for work and hookups on craigslist brought up negative labels like "the poor-people's internet" and "bottom of the barrel." Stigmatizing craigslist as a tool for the desperate points to the platform's struggle to overcome bots and scam artists, and also to the cultural cost of refusing to update aesthetics and upgrade features. By holding on to norms from the early web, craigslist can feel like a part of the internet that's been left behind, but this is also what makes craigslist accessible, both in the sense that using the platform doesn't require a smartphone, and in the sense that it keeps upgrades to a minimum, meaning there's rarely a new learning curve.

Another tension that surfaced across chapters is the conflicted role of anonymity. For much of the web, being anonymous signals dark or criminal intentions, and many craigslist users I interviewed connected anonymity to the platform's problems with scams and cons. At the same time, anonymity allowed people writing personal ads to be open about their interests, and provided privacy for users who didn't want to give up personal information when buying or selling used goods. Anonymity sets craigslist apart from many of its peer sites and points to complicated questions about safety, privacy, and responsibility, which surfaced in different accounts of using and thinking about craigslist in everyday life. Craigslist feels safe to some people more than others. While a small degree of risk is the price of entry for using craigslist, a benefit is increased privacy, which can be particularly important for people on the margins.

Craigslist looks and feels like an older version of the web, and that's on purpose—the result of a commitment by Craig Newmark and Jim Buckmaster to hold the line on a particular vision of platform politics. For Newmark and Buckmaster, the web is at its best when it is easy to use, geared toward the local and the practical, and nonhierarchical in terms of who gets to use it. Craigslist was also designed with a high tolerance for quirks, kink, and weirdness, in keeping with a Web 1.0 belief in diversity and open expression. While craigslist has always welcomed people on the margins, as a consequence the platform has become increasingly marginalized, both in its reputation for problems and for being behind the times compared with the mainstream web. Paying attention to the gaps between craigslist and its peers can help point us toward a more democratic, less gentrified internet. To build a case for keeping the internet weird and democratic, I focus on two distinctive features of craigslist's platform politics: making users anonymous and a transparent approach to monetizing user activity. Gentrifying the internet isn't just about how things look, it's also about social norms and business models. By keeping users anonymous and its monetization direct, craigslist issues a challenge to core assumptions about ways of being online and how tech companies make money.

In Defense of Anonymity

Anonymity is one of the things that makes craigslist craigslist. From the melancholy of "Missed Connections" to the suspense around in-person meet-ups, doing everyday things on craigslist involves uncertainty because of the platform's commitment to anonymity. Unlike much of the web, craigslist doesn't provide "digital trust infrastructure" like reviews or profiles (Sundararajan 2016), and as a result, the platform pushes security work back on the users. When people describe craigslist as taking a lot of work, as we saw in accounts of buying and selling, finding gigs, and the personals, they're talking about the labor required to figure out if an ad is fake or real, if a user is legitimate or dangerous. A lack of digital trust infrastructure is part of what keeps craigslist open, meaning that anyone can use the platform without logging into an external site like Facebook or Google, but also what makes it risky and weird.

Anonymity can be good or bad, which comes through in the academic research on online anonymity and pseudonymity. Some have argued that being anonymous online can help people open up when it comes to difficult topics (Ma, Hancock, and Naaman 2016). Others connect anonymity to free speech and open dialogue.[1] For example, business journalist Steve Cooper (2013) argued that anonymity has benefits for public discourse: "Too many times people refrain from speaking their mind (or even the truth) because they fear the repercussions or judgment. Maintaining anonymity is often the first step in broaching tough topics" (see also Akdeniz 2002). More than helping to protect people with minority views, anonymity can help people on the margins to share their experiences and ideas without fear of push back or harassment (see Allen 2010; Ekstrand 2003).

For some, anonymity is valuable because it allows people to voice unpopular or fringe views. But arguments about anonymity and free speech can feel tone deaf when it comes to online harassment and extremist content. As Alison Herman argued in a piece about widespread harassment of women journalists, a troubling paradox emerges around women's options to participate in the public sphere after being targeted by trolls online:

> For those unable or unwilling to jump through hoops in order to protect their personal safety (and again, no one should be expected or required to), few options are left but to stop the activity that made them vulnerable in the first place. . . . What's left is an online landscape that looks a whole lot like the rest of the world, where women and other marginalized groups are underrepresented, their voices shunted to the sidelines in favor of those who can generally speak up without fear. (2014, para. 4)

For Cooper (2013), anonymity benefits free speech because it allows people to speak openly and voice unpopular views. But for Herman, anonymity is what encourages an audience to react violently to content it doesn't like, effectively restricting free speech through fear. People targeted by hackers and trolls suffer psychologically from constant threats of violence, as well as financially and socially when threats keep them from leaving the house or going to work (Hess 2014). Less directly, online harassment can reshape online publics by deterring dialogue, conversation, and participation.

The internet is too big and too diverse to have a single policy either for or against anonymity. Making the right decision, whether from a parenting, platform, or policy-maker perspective, will always be context dependent. If we look at the pros and cons of craigslist's policy on anonymity, two arguments surface. First, we need more precision around different kinds of anonymity. In chapter 7, I argued that when it comes to tensions around online anonymity and safety, we need to separate anonymity as a tool of privacy from anonymity as a harmful way of being online. If we focus only on the latter, we eliminate the protections of the former. Having a more robust understanding of anonymity means acknowledging the ways that anonymity can bring important benefits, particularly for people on the margins. Second, the solution to problems of online fraud and harassment cannot be an outright restriction on anonymity. The stigma against being anonymous online has roots in legitimate concerns about safety, but we must also acknowledge the ways that anonymity threatens core business models of dominant web platforms like Facebook and Google. We are rapidly reaching a point when it may take significant effort and skill to remain anonymous online (Greenberg 2014; Villas-Boas 2015). An internet where everyone has to be visible, all of the time, is not an internet of transparency, it's an internet of control. Craigslist is an important (and increasingly lonely) reminder that online anonymity can work, even if it requires us to take on more responsibility for determining trust, instead of pushing that work onto the platform.

Transparent Monetization

I argued above that forcing people to use their "real" names online is not a liberating form of transparency—it's a problematic display of power. But there are kinds of transparency that can create more equitable relationships between users and companies. In chapter 1, I pointed out some of the things that make craigslist an unusual platform. As a privately held company, craigslist's leadership has the freedom to prioritize users over shareholders, which is key to understanding craigslist's look, feel, and politics. In a time when legal experts and the tech elite are advocating the breakup of megacompanies like Google, Amazon, and Facebook (Ehrlich 2017; Wu 2018), craigslist is stubbornly small. And in contrast to opaque mechanisms of repackaging user data to sell to advertisers, craigslist makes money in a straightforward and transparent way. Differences in craigslist's corporate structure and the transparency of its business model matter in terms of protecting its vision of platform politics.

Among people agitating for change in the tech industry, transparency is a familiar rallying cry. Many functions of the tech sector are targeted in demands for transparency, from algorithms (Hosanagar and Jair 2018) to hiring practices (Omens 2018) to advertising (Susman 2017). Transparency only makes a difference, however, if what's being revealed is legible or actionable. For example, calls to make algorithms public seems sensible as far as wanting to understand search-engine results, but just revealing the algorithm will not be meaningful to people without training in computer science or machine learning. Increasing transparency around hiring practices can reveal important discrepancies in who gets hired, but doesn't matter if companies don't feel pressure to change their HR strategies. There is a troubling way in which companies can reveal data in the name of transparency, knowing full well that the published information has little power or impact. As Gillespie (2018b) has observed, "transparency, even in its candor, is a performance, leaving as much unseen as seen." All of these concerns should make us hesitate when it comes to demands for transparency. Nonetheless, I would argue that when it comes to how platforms make money, transparency is vital for a clear understanding of the relationships between people and technology.

Comparing craigslist's business model with the approach of a mainstream platform helps us see the political consequences of making monetization visible. I use Facebook as an example of online politics because it's the most popular online platform, meaning that its policies set the norm for its competitors. Put another way, Facebook's politics of monetizing users matters precisely because it is so popular and profitable. Facebook is free to use, but the company tracks user behavior in order to sell advertising that can be tailored to specific demographics. This process is entirely invisible to users, many of whom have no idea how their news feed is organized or who is promoting content. In contrast, craigslist's sole revenue stream is the small fee collected from users who post certain kinds of ads, like job or real-estate listings. When Facebook users are unclear on how the platform makes money from services that appear free, it's because the process of analyzing data and selling ads is deliberately opaque. When craigslist users are unclear on how the platform makes money, it's because they're part of the user group that is not charged the small fees that keep the site alive and profitable.

In Facebook's vision of transparency, people should be as visible and readable as possible, while the platform should be opaque and invisible. We see this in its business model, as well as privacy settings that maximize content sharing as a default, cryptic TOS agreements, and the constant shift of features and upgrades. Craigslist's vision of transparency is a what-you-see-is-what-you-get minimalism. A small number of services cost a small amount to use, and the rest of the platform is free—not just as a matter of cost to use but also free from advertising. It is unclear which data craigslist tracks about its users but, on a fundamental level, the lack of banner ads means that people aren't turned into products to be repackaged for third parties. The slow pace of upgrades can frustrate users who expect new features, but it keeps the platform familiar and legible. Craigslist ads can be weird or kinky or fake, but the underlying relationship between users and the company is straightforward. Platforms like Facebook have prettier interfaces, new features, and digital trust infrastructure, but they conceal a complicated web of data and marketing that is deliberately hard for users to see, let alone protest. Craigslist demonstrates a successful business model that doesn't maximize profits at the expense of user privacy or agency. Like its policy on anonymity, craigslist's business model reflects a commitment to Web 1.0 ethics, where the refusal to update is more than a stubborn nostalgia for 1990s digital culture—it's a set of values about how online publics should function.

Update Minimalism and Platform Refusal

Most of us use platforms, devices, and products without knowing much about the politics of the companies who create them. Yet the decisions we make about how to spend time online are political, just like the decisions we make about what to buy and where to shop. Insisting on ideological consumption has been an activist strategy for some time, where consumers are urged to think of buying products and services as an implicit form of supporting a company's political agenda (see Banet-Weiser and Lapsanky 2008). Craigslist's politics can be summed up as a form of platform refusal, meaning a rejection of certain norms and values that have become normalized on the mainstream web.

Media refusal typically refers to an individual's decision to disengage from some or all social-media platforms as part of a personal or collective politics (see Light 2014). In one of the first academic pieces on the topic, Laura Portwood-Stacer argued that "refusal can be understood as a tactic of critique, which manifests the objections and dissatisfactions people feel toward media products, or even media and consumer culture more broadly" (2013, 1044). In craigslist I see a platform version of media refusal, and specifically a refusal to participate in what Wendy Chun (2016) and Acker and Beaton (2016) have separately described as habitual updating, or "update unrest." Both concepts describe constant changes to a platform's features and design, reflecting a power dynamic where platforms can change at will and without warning. Meanwhile, users are expected to adapt to new design features or policies, typically without having been asked for their preferences or input. While there are high-profile examples of updates gone awry (like Snapchat's disastrous 2018 redesign), on the whole updating has come to feel inevitable. Yet the cycle of continual upgrades has consequences that are cultural as well as environmental. Update culture normalizes a constant cycle of technological change and further entrenches a dynamic where platforms have significantly more power than users. Meanwhile, the emphasis on new technologies and features pushes people to buy new devices, creating a rapid cycle of replacement called "technological obsolescence." The constant consumption of new products strains environmental resources and helps justify unfair labor practices (Gehl 2014).

Craigslist sticks to what might be called update minimalism. As participants pointed out over and over, using craigslist can feel like using an old-fashioned, stripped down, or backward version of the web, feelings that were connected to the site's policies on anonymity as well as its extremely stable design. The platform's refusal to update is why craigslist feels outdated, or what I have called *ungentrified*. In an interview, Gillian used metaphors of gentrification to describe craigslist's relationship to the broader web:

> It's like when you have a neighborhood that you love, and it gets super gentrified, and there's that one coffee shop that still holds on. . . . It's this one outpost. . . . It's like craigslist is the historic building of the internet, right? And on the internet there is no such thing as a historical preservation society that says this thing has value simply because it existed. . . . That's another piece of evidence of the sort of overbearing commercial imperatives of the internet. Which is that, you know, once that moment comes and it's no longer sustainable, it's just gonna go.

Craigslist defies many of the most basic assumptions about how to be a successful tech company. It's small, privately held, and conservative in its growth. It doesn't update its appearance or its policies but still turns a profit, although the leadership is okay with making less money than it could. Craigslist is weird not just because of the kooky, kinky content that people post to the site but also because it adheres to old-school notions of the web, while staying useful to millions of users.

Throughout this book, I have described craigslist as a holdout of 1990s digital culture. Being a holdout doesn't mean that craigslist has done everything right, but it does mean that the platform can help us gauge how the internet has changed over time. In comparison to the web around it, craigslist can feel uncomfortable or inconvenient because the platform is out of step with other online publics, largely because major players in the tech industry have worked to normalize certain experiences of safety and convenience (Draper and Turow 2019). Rather than letting mainstream companies erase the history of platforms that came before, we can use holdouts like craigslist to question assumptions about platform politics that seem unassailable. Craigslist helps us see that online anonymity comes with increased work and risk, but can provide safety and privacy. The platform also offers proof of concept for transparent business models that don't force users to surrender privacy for services. Craigslist demonstrates that platforms can refuse to update and still be usable, and that sometimes, for some people, messy serendipity is preferable to slick predictability.

There is a lot that we can learn from craigslist about transparency, anonymity, and platform politics of refusal. And there's a lot to lose if craigslist disappears. The future of craigslist is uncertain. It seems unlikely that the company will ever reclaim the same level of popularity that it had in the early 2000s. Over the past decade, craigslist's ranking dipped from eighth in 2009 to tenth in 2014, and down to eighteenth in 2019. Closing down the personals is partly to blame, as is increasing competition from platforms like Nextdoor, Thumbtack, and Facebook Marketplace. It's likely that craigslist's popularity will continue to wane, although it may hold strong in densely packed cities like New York and Los Angeles, as well as its home base, San Francisco. While its ranking may be slipping, craigslist still makes money. Because the company is privately held, it is impossible to know how much, but even if its popularity continues to decline, for many people craigslist will be difficult to dislodge as a go-to resource. And as long as Buckmaster is in charge, I predict that craigslist's update minimalism will continue, in keeping with Newmark's original vision of platform politics.

For some of the people I interviewed in this book, the end of craigslist would make the web safer, removing an outlier website that's overrun with bots and scams. But for others, shutting down craigslist would feel like a real loss, not just because they find it to be a convenient way of doing everyday things, but because it preserves a certain way of being online. Telling the story of craigslist is a way of telling a story about the internet and how it has changed over time. If or when craigslist shuts down for good, we'll be losing more than a place to sell old couches or hire a man with a van. We'll be losing a piece of digital culture, one of the few platforms that has been online all along and still feels familiar, helping us to do everyday things in our neighborhoods, and holding on to an early vision of how the web should be.

METHODS APPENDIX

I am a longtime craigslist user, well known among my family and friends for using it to sell everything from bike baskets to cat carriers, and for finding apartments, roommates, and jobs. Despite many years of using the platform, when I started writing this book there was a lot I didn't know about craigslist, like its history in the tech industry, its politics, or why it seemed to hold on to the look and feel of the web in the 1990s. As an internet-studies researcher, I saw craigslist as a signpost for tracking changes in digital culture, and knew that I would need multiple lines of inquiry to tell an adequately rich story. What it means to study a platform is still an open question, and my goal with this methods appendix is to explain my path in telling craigslist's story. I decided to approach the site in layers, working through different facets of its history, and from there develop key arguments about platform politics. Essentially, I saw the first part of the book as a very extended and multi-layered literature review, which could help me identify the concepts and tensions to pursue in the second part of the book.

After reading the limited research on craigslist, I decided to situate craigslist in a broader history of media and law. No technology emerges without a past—whether a website, software application, or device, technologies have predecessors that they seek to challenge, improve, and replace. Craigslist's print predecessor is the classified ad, and initially I thought of doing a comparative project analyzing content of craigslist ads against historical classifieds. Eventually, I realized that my research questions weren't about how people expressed themselves in classified ads, but the socio-technical politics underlying craigslist as a platform. In that sense, it became important to think of craigslist as having a media history that partly echoed and partly upended classified ads. One of the biggest criticisms of craigslist is that its free ads killed local newspapers, and any full accounting of the platform's politics should account for its relationship to the newspaper industry. My analysis largely relied on secondary sources, reading the (fairly small) number of monographs on classified ads as well as press coverage of craigslist's connection to newspaper ads.

Court cases offered another path for thinking about craigslist's politics, and more specifically what happens when craigslist's politics are contested. Given my lack of legal training, I relied on instructive texts on critical legal analysis (Streeter 1990) to help me structure my approach. Craigslist has been involved in a number of lawsuits, and I decided to focus on the *Dart* and *3taps* cases as a result of talking both formally and informally to legal experts, by reviewing law blogs and doing a LexisNexis search about craigslist and lawsuits. My process of analysis started by reading the legal decisions and then reviewing related law-journal articles and blog posts. Reading legal decisions had the unexpected (but in hindsight, obvious) benefit of learning about some of craigslist's inner workings and financial structure. As a privately held company, legal proceedings provided some of the only glimpses into craigslist's finances and boardroom decisions.

After I'd laid out craigslist's history as a company, as a media artifact, and in the courtroom, I had a robust account of the platform's roots and politics. In part II, I wanted to figure out how people use craigslist in everyday life. I cycled through a number of frameworks before landing on the marketplace, gig work, the personals, and moderation. To get there, I leaned on the idea of craigslist's politics as manifest in the tasks that most often brought people to the platform. By focusing on how users accomplish everyday tasks, I could develop a holistic account of craigslist's platform politics as they emerge in accounts of ordinary users doing ordinary things online.

Interviews

Interviews form the bulk of data in this book. Throughout the text, I draw on interviews with insiders and experts to provide context on the company's history and politics. In addition, I conducted interviews with ordinary users to understand how craigslist is used on a daily basis. I interviewed insiders and experts to gain a sense of craigslist's history and asked for permission to use their names in the book. For everyday craigslist users, I asked participants to choose pseudonyms.

Experts and Insiders

In a lot of ways, the first interview I did for this book was also the most important. After leveraging some personal contacts to put me in touch, I first sat down to interview Craig Newmark in May 2017. From media coverage, I knew that journalists had more than once ambushed Newmark with unexpected questions (or accusations); for example, bringing up sex trafficking when they'd promised to cover Newmark's philanthropy. I wanted to convey to Newmark that my goal was an academic account of craigslist that recognized its contributions to internet history while also acknowledging the platform's flaws and missed opportunities. Our first interview lasted about forty-five minutes and covered craigslist's early days, Newmark's view of the tech industry, and key changes in digital culture. Newmark has given many interviews, and having reviewed a number of these conversations prior to our first meeting, I was struck by how often I heard echoes of earlier interviews. Maybe I'm stretching the comparison, but it reminded me of software engineers who cut and paste code from one script to another when they need to repeat a function.

Over the next year, I spoke periodically with Newmark, occasionally over the phone but more often by e-mail. Newmark put me in touch with Anthony Batt and Christina Murphy, who had been involved with craigslist in its early days. Because Newmark put me in touch with them, I knew that Batt and Murphy were likely to be supportive of the website, so finding other experts with different views (described below) was key to striking a balanced perspective. In December 2017, I met Newmark at craigslist's San Francisco office, where he gave me a brief tour and sat down with me for another extended interview. In all of our conversations, Newmark was careful to distinguish between background and on-the-record information. Unlike all the other interviews in this book, I took extensive notes during our conversations, rather than audio recording them. Prior to publication, I confirmed all of Newmark's quotes. On the whole, I found him to be warm, unassuming, and enthusiastic, particularly when it came to the different charitable causes and nonprofits he supports. I'm grateful to Newmark for the time he gave for interviews and hope he finds my analysis fair and well rounded.

In addition to talking to people about the early days of craigslist, I reached out to a number of experts to learn about different facets of the site's history or social implications. Newmark put me in touch with Prentice Danner, a public-affairs specialist for the San Francisco division of the FBI. We spoke in the summer of 2017 about craigslist's cooperation with the bureau's efforts to stop human trafficking. Additional expert interviews included Allen Atamer, Andrew Bridges, Justin Peters, and Eric Oglander, all of whom I contacted individually to set up interviews. I sought out people with different forms of expertise and perspectives on craigslist, the tech industry, and digital culture to provide a well-rounded account of the platform. These interviews tended to be shorter and more focused than the semistructured interviews I conducted with craigslist users.

Craigslist Users

My interviews with craigslist users started by focusing on people who use online secondary markets. I conducted these interviews with my collaborator Jen Ayres. Jen's doctoral work focused on secondary markets, particularly around thrifting and vintage. Although Jen had spent years moderating and participating in online message boards, none of this research had made it into her dissertation. With shared interests in how online platforms intervened in secondary markets, we decided to start with these online groups, recruiting for interviews people who bought and sold used goods online. These groups included Queer Exchange, Facebook Marketplace, and OfferUp. In total, we interviewed seventeen people, all interviews conducted in person and in Philadelphia (see table A.1).

Starting in February 2018, I began recruiting for interviews people who used craigslist to find work. I posted an ad to Philadelphia's Gigs section, identifying myself as an assistant professor at the University of Pennsylvania who studied digital culture. The ad gave two options for participation—an in-person interview or filling out a short online survey. I recruited nine participants this way, interviewing eight of them in person in Philadelphia and one by Skype. With the survey, I hoped to gather some basic statistics about craigslist use. Doing so confirmed my sense that most people used craigslist for used goods and for jobs, and very few people used it for events or the forums. As a qualitative researcher, this was actually my first survey—perhaps unsurprisingly, it was a very open-ended survey, asking participants to contrast positive and negative interactions on craigslist, what they liked about the site and what could be improved. I posted the ad in seven cities (Philadelphia, Chicago, Toronto, Denver, Atlanta, Los Angeles, Houston), chosen to represent a range of geographic locations across the United States and Canada. Completing the survey entered participants in a prize draw to win a $100 gift card, and in total I received just over one hundred responses.

Recruiting participants with experience using craigslist personals was one of the biggest challenges of this book, and I learned a lot about the stigma surrounding craigslist personals in my struggle to find people to interview. I was able to recruit a small number of participants through my personal network, but the closure of the personals in March 2018 made locating additional interviewees more difficult. I turned to the online survey

TABLE A.1. Craigslist User Interviews: Participant Details

Interview Category	Participant Pseudonym	Age	Years Using craigslist
Personals	Beaver	23	5
	Bella	37	20
	Bobbi	31	1
	Cathy	44	12
	Gillian	40	13
	Janae	26	10
	Rhonda	26	7
Gigs	Agnes	24	6
	David	28	12
	Denny	25	9
	Jasmine	22	2
	John	28	6
	Micah	36	22
	Nathaniel	41	8
	Rob	41	15
	Seb	35	20
	Shayla	20	4
	Shelly	24	6
Buying and Selling	Arkansas	35	27
	Botgrinder	36	17
	Cleo	34	7
	Deena	30	10
	Flo	40	1
	Jax	38	21
	Lou	30	6
	Mimi	35	7
	Molly	46	10
	Nikki	30	9
	Opal	35	8
	Phoebe	26	6
	Renee	25	2
	Smish	24	5
	Sophia	22	6
	Yma	27	7
	Zara	25	3

I conducted via the Gigs section to extend recruitment: the survey asked people to list all of the craigslist categories they'd used, and I contacted everyone who reported using the personals. I was able to interview an additional six participants, all over the phone or by video chat. As difficult as recruitment was, getting participants to open up about craigslist personals was equally challenging. In general, I prefer conducting interviews in person, but I found that these conversations felt a little bit easier because of the distance built into phone and video communication.

All interviews were transcribed and coded in NVIVO, a software package for qualitative data analysis. I used a combination of thematic (Braun, Clarke, and Terry 2014) and open (Strauss and Corbin 1990) coding. I began with high-level themes around the secondary marketplace, gigs, dating, and moderation strategies. I coded all of the interviews in one NVIVO file, which in some ways made things tricky. I had wanted the different groups of interviews to speak to one another, drawing on my previous approach for comparing countercultural communities (Lingel, 2017a, b). But this book looks within rather than between platforms, and I sometimes felt that I was losing precision in my coding by combining gig workers' views of work with buyers and sellers, for example. NVIVO does allow for grouping texts (interviews) so I was able to analyze sets of interviews; however, I found my codebook getting increasingly unwieldy as I tried to update it with new reflections from different interview groups. Typically, I develop a codebook after doing a small number of interviews. While it grows and shifts over time, it's meant to keep me consistent over the course of coding a large number of interviews. In this case, I think it actually might have made more sense to write the codebook after all of the interviews had been coded, as a way of reflecting on shared characteristics within a theme across interview sets. Instead, much of this reflection came out in the process of writing. I like to think that the analytical outcome was the same, but the process felt messier and more cumbersome.

Textual Analysis

In addition to interviews, I analyzed a number of primary sources. Some of these sources, like craigslist TV and the mash-up texts, were meant to help me understand how craigslist operates in pop culture. I watched every episode of craigslist TV, which comprises four seasons of short episodes dedicated to craigslist ads, published on YouTube between 2010 and 2012. This analysis didn't make it into the book, although I briefly discuss the show in

Lingel (2018). With help from Eric Forbush, I analyzed a collection of blogs, Tumblrs, YouTube channels, and Twitter feeds that referenced craigslist in the title, making notes on the number of posts, publication dates, and key themes. At certain points in this project, it became clear that interviews couldn't provide everything I wanted to know about craigslist, which led me to three key sources of data: the craigslist blog, the craigslist Reddit forum, and the craigslist help forum.

Craigslist Blog

I was disappointed not to be able to interview Jim Buckmaster, despite my best efforts. Newmark agreed to reach out on my behalf and I repeatedly attempted to contact Buckmaster on my own, but I received no response. As the company's longtime CEO, Buckmaster's firsthand comments would have been distinctly valuable in understanding the site's politics and design values. As a way of incorporating Buckmaster's views without direct contact, I searched for and read numerous interviews with Buckmaster, many of which are incorporated into chapter 1. I also read the more than three hundred blog posts that he has penned on the craigslist blog since 2000 and coded them in NVIVO software. I used an open coding approach (Strauss and Corbin 1990), looking to track the different themes that were most common in the company's public-facing blog.

Reddit's craigslist Thread

As I noted earlier, recruiting participants who used craigslist personals was difficult. I had learned about Reddit's craigslist forum previously, and I saw the extended discussion on FOSTA as a rich source of information about the role of craigslist personals in digital culture, and ordinary web users' interpretations of FOSTA. With help from Rich Cardona, John Garber, and Vladimir Gordynskiy, I scraped the Reddit forum into a csv file, which I uploaded and analyzed in NVIVO. As I noted in chapter 6, the anonymous and temporary nature of Reddit accounts makes it difficult to obtain consent, and researchers are split on the ethics of citing public comments without permission (Zimmer 2010). Reddit comments are public and the anonymous nature means that comments cannot easily be traced back to individual people, but it's clear that comments were not made with the intent of having them incorporated into academic research. It's impossible for me to anonymize the thread itself, so following Markham (2012) and Hine (2015, 187), I have opted to modify the language of individual Reddit comments, while preserving their style, tone, and overall message. Like the craigslist blog posts, I kept the Reddit analysis in a separate NVIVO file from the interviews.

Craigslist Help Forum

In order to analyze themes of fraud and scams, I decided to investigate craigslist's help forum. Collaborating with Matthew O'Donnell and Jonathan Pace, I ran a custom script utilizing Beautiful Soup, a Python library that pulls data out of HTML files and renders the data in manageable parse trees. Our script located every thread in the craigslist help forum containing the following terms and their semantic variations: *fraud*, *scam*, *con*, and *trick*. This criterion sample included 2,281 relevant threads, posted between 2010 and 2017. Given that thread conversations follow a comment-response cycle, we designed the script to render whole threads rather than singular posts, allowing us to capture the ebb and flow of naturally occurring web discourse (Denzin 1999). All posts were read and analyzed for key themes, using an open coding approach (Strauss and Corbin 1990).

Although the posts we gathered are sensitive in that many of them refer to moments of anger and confusion, they are anonymous and posted in a public forum. Public access does not provide carte-blanche permission for researchers to utilize data in their studies (Markham and Bride 2006; Zimmer 2016); however, these posts cannot be traced back to individual users, and posts can't be searched directly, providing a very high level of anonymity (Markham and Buchanan 2012). As a whole, I felt that the public-facing nature of these posts and the high degree of anonymity provided adequate justification for their use.

This is the first book-length, academic treatment of craigslist, which is both exciting and something of a burden. Writing this book was incredibly fun. I learned new methods and I felt that, at the very least, I was making internet-studies scholarship a little more complete by contributing a study of a long-standing, well-used website. But I also felt a certain amount of pressure to present craigslist in a balanced way, without the benefit of a previous academic text to argue against or agree with. Craigslist has a lot of problems but it has also been made a scapegoat—by journalists, other platforms, policy makers, ordinary users, and law enforcement. I wanted to take craigslist as a serious object of inquiry, which meant attending to serious criticisms but attempting to put them in a broader context. Although I have struggled at times to bundle all of the different methods, criticisms, quirks, and histories together in this book, I also see my overarching approach as one of trying to manage a messy platform. As a longtime craigslist user, I wanted to preserve the quirkiness and serendipity of craigslist, to point to the ways that its goals are mundane and its outcomes usually successful, sometimes silly, and, on rare occasion, scary. I wanted to acknowledge the ways that craigslist has changed, while mostly talking about what it preserves—an early-web ethic of access and platform responsibility that can help us challenge mainstream norms of commercialization and exclusivity.

NOTES

Introduction

1. The preferred spelling of craigslist is with a lowercase "c," a preference I observe in this book, except where it begins a sentence.

Chapter 1

1. West (2010) described Buckmaster and Newmark as "extortionists" in their demand for payment from eBay. In an e-mail to craigslist's outside counsel, Newmark remarked that he was "definitely not interested in seeing the dumb guy [Knowlton] get" money from eBay without receiving similar consideration.

2. *eBay Domestic Holdings, Inc. v. Newmark*, 16 A.3d 1, 4 (Del. Ch. 2010).

3. *eBay*, 16 A.3d at 7.

Chapter 2

1. T. Baekdal, (@baekdal), "So blaming Craigslist," Twitter, October 17, 2018, comment on "It's funny how little they ended up using from me. The total email exchange was 5 emails (3500+ words), in which I explained why we are misleading ourselves," https://twitter.com/baekdal/status/1052561645950533632.

2. I'm grateful to Joe Turow for sharing this example with me.

Chapter 3

1. 519 F.3d 666 (7th Cir. 2008).

2. *Dart v. Craigslist, Inc.*, 665 F. Supp. 2d 961, 963 (N.D. Ill. 2009).

3. Markoff committed suicide before the case went to trial, so I use the term "alleged" throughout my brief description of the events.

4. Brisman's 2009 murder wouldn't be the last plotted via craigslist. See Dewey (2016) for a (somewhat sensationalized) account of crimes linked to craigslist.

5. The suit with 3taps is not the only time craigslist has gone to court on this issue. Another example is *craigslist Inc. v. Naturemarket Inc.*, 694 F. Supp. 2d 1039 (N.D. Cal. 2010). I've opted to concentrate on this particular legal battle because it's the case that focuses most specifically on the question of access versus use, as opposed to a case like *Naturemarket*, where a number of other legal issues were also being decided. I'm grateful to Cassie Barnum for her help reviewing craigslist's legal cases to make this determination.

6. *craigslist Inc. v. 3taps Inc.*, 942 F. Supp. 2d 1178, 1185 (N.D. Cal. 2013).

7. *3taps*, 942 F.Supp.2d at 1189.

8. Brief for the EFF as amicus curiae, p. 1182, *3taps*, 942 F. Supp. 2d.

Chapter 4

1. In cultural studies, *subculture* often is used to refer to any group of people who have practices that are outside (but not necessarily in opposition to) the mainstream. In this definition, subcultures can refer to college fraternities and bowling leagues as much as fetish clubs and animal-rights activists. The word *counterculture*, in contrast, has been used to refer to subcultures that intentionally oppose mainstream norms and values (see R. Williams 1973).

Chapter 5

1. As one participant, Shelly, explained: "[craigslist is] a useful tool in society because first of all that money doesn't get taxed, screw the government. Donald Trump doesn't pay taxes, I'm not paying taxes okay? . . . I hate him. He doesn't pay taxes and he has millions of dollars, I don't wanna pay taxes. I don't pay taxes on any of my money right now."

2. For an important exception see Ames et al. (2011). Given the intertwining of race and class in the United States, we might also consider research on Black Twitter as contributing scholarship on the internet and class (Brock 2012; Ramsey 2015; Sharma 2013), but even then, this work is rarely framed explicitly in terms of class.

3. I use the terms "working class," "blue collar," and "working poor" somewhat interchangeably in this discussion, although each has certain connotations. For a review of how class has been conceptualized in the social sciences, see Savage et al. (2013). Although participants all talked about work and most brought up class politics, I did not ask about income during interviews or whether they self-identified as working class, partly because it was only during analysis that I began to see how important class narratives were to craigslist's role in the gig economy. It's also likely that I was simply uncomfortable asking about class, which is a tricky subject in the United States, made trickier by my affiliation with an elite institution, the University of Pennsylvania. If I could redo interviews with themes from this chapter in mind, I would ask participants to define terms like "working class" and "blue collar" and whether they identified with any of those labels.

4. Using gentrification as a lens is not meant to minimize the serious economic implications tied to urban gentrification. While many urban planners, policy makers, and theorists insist that gentrification is a driver of economic opportunity, I align my views with academics and activists who see gentrification as reproducing structural inequalities of race and class. I find the concept of gentrification helpful because it names a complex web of socioeconomic tensions, which are also taking shape in online publics. Neither set of problems has easy solutions.

Chapter 6

1. The anonymous and temporary nature of Reddit accounts makes it very difficult to obtain consent for reproducing posts in academic work, and researchers are split on the ethics of citing public comments without permission (Zimmer 2010). Although Reddit comments are public and the anonymous nature means that comments cannot easily be traced back to individual people, it is clear that comments were not made with the intention of having them incorporated into academic research. It's impossible for me to anonymize the thread itself, so following Markham (2012) and Hine (2015, 187), I have opted to modify the language of individual Reddit comments, while preserving their style, tone, and overall message.

2. In a 2004 interview, Newmark explained that he created "Missed Connections" as a romantic gesture toward missed opportunities: "Sometimes you meet someone and don't do anything assertive and wind up being very pissed off with yourself. . . . I'm a bit of a romantic" (quoted in Cormier 2004). Based on many casual conversations over the course of writing this book, readers may be disappointed that I do not provide more analysis of "Missed Connections." For these readers, I can only point to the range of popular texts dedicated to this section on craigslist: Blackall (2011), Feurer (2017), and Wertz (2009).

Chapter 7

1. I am grateful to Tarleton Gillespie for pushing my thinking on flaking as a kind of trust failure.

2. The most thorough account of craigslist's approach to community moderation is the "Flag Help Forum." Posts explain the flagging process and offer advice on how to post ads that will avoid getting flagged. The flag forum has approximately 40,000 posts, almost entirely from anonymous users rather than craigslist administrators.

3. Policies on using "real" names have significant consequences for trans users (Haimson and Hayes 2017), drag queens (Lingel and Golub 2015), indigenous people (Holpuch 2015), and many others. Moreover, the fact that Facebook's official policy demands authenticity doesn't mean that all its users comply. There are numerous cases of fraudulent, deceptive, and ironic uses of Facebook profiles. In 2012, Facebook admitted that 8.7 percent of its accounts were fakes or duplicates (Kelly 2012). In 2017, *USA Today* asked the FBI to investigate a wave of fake Facebook accounts, which accounted for half of the newspaper's following on the social-media platform (Weise and Heath 2017).

4. I do not have the kind of data that allow me to make generalizable claims about how entire groups of craigslist users experience anonymity, privacy, and safety. But my data do allow me to note salient patterns that emerge in the process of analyzing interview data, which can inform a broader set of arguments about race, gender, and privilege in the context of data and visibility.

Conclusion

1. In a US political context, anonymity is typically associated with free speech and free association. Regarding the former, in 2016 the American Civil Liberties Union won a suit protecting online anonymity (Eidelman 2016) for an academic website providing anonymous peer review. One of the most famous court cases on this issue dates back to 1958, when Alabama's attorney general sued the National Association for the Advancement of Colored People to reveal its membership. Regarding the latter, in 1995 the Supreme Court decided that the ability to publish anonymously is guaranteed under the First Amendment (*McIntyre v. Ohio Elections Commission*, 514 U.S. 334 [1995]).

BIBLIOGRAPHY

Acker, A., and B. Beaton. 2016. "Software Update Unrest: The Recent Happenings around Tinder and Tesla." In *System Sciences (HICSS), 2016 49th Hawaii International Conference on Social Systems*, edited by T. Bui and R. Sprague, 1891–1900. Washington, DC: IEEE.

Akdeniz, Y. 2002. "Anonymity, Democracy, and Cyberspace." *Social Research* 69, no. 1: 223–37.

Alexa. n.d. "Craigslist.org Competitive Analysis, Marketing Mix and Traffic." Accessed February 28, 2019. https://www.alexa.com/siteinfo/craigslist.org.

Allen, D. 2010. "Anonymous: On Silence and the Public Sphere." In *Speech and Silence in American Law*, edited by A. Sarat, 106–33. Cambridge: Cambridge University Press.

Alt, D. 2018. "Students' Wellbeing, Fear of Missing Out, and Social Media Engagement for Leisure in Higher Education Learning Environments." *Current Psychology* 37, no. 1: 128–38.

Ames, M. 2014. "Documents Show How eBay's Meg Whitman and Pierre Omidyar Conspired to Steal craigslist's Secrets." Pando. December 1, 2014. https://pando.com/2014/12/01/whitman-omidyar-craigslist-eBay/.

Ames, M. 2015. "Pierre Omidyar's Corporate Spying Scandal Buried for Good as eBay Sells craigslist Stake." Pando. June 19, 2015. https://pando.com/2015/06/19/pierre-omidyars-corporate-spying-scandal-buried-for-good-as-eBay-sells-craigslist-stake/.

Ames, M. G., J. Go, J. J. Kaye, and M. Spasojevic. 2011. "Understanding Technology Choices and Values through Social Class." In *Proceedings of the ACM 2011 Conference on Computer Supported Cooperative Work*, edited by J. Bardram and N. Ducheneaut, 55–64. New York: ACM.

Ankerson, M. S. 2012. "Writing Web Histories with an Eye on the Analog Past." *New Media and Society* 14, no. 3: 384–400.

Ankerson, M. S. 2018. *Dot-Com Design: The Rise of a Usable, Social, Commercial Web*. Vol. 15. New York: New York University Press.

Anonymous. 2002. "Personals Ads Tips for Men from a CL Woman." *craigslist*. Accessed July 12, 2019. https://www.craigslist.org/about/best/sfo/5806986.html?lang=en&cc=us.

Anonymous. 2006. "Guidelines for Writing a Good Craigslist Personal Ad . . . Advice for Men." July 12, 2019. http://lostinthemuse.blogspot.com/2006/06/guidelines-for-writing-good-craigslist.html.

Associated Press. 2010. "State Attorneys General: Craigslist Should Drop Adult Services." *Oregon Live*. Last updated August 24, 2010. https://www.oregonlive.com/politics/index.ssf/2010/08/state_attorneys_general_craigs.html.

Bader, S. 2005. *Strange Red Cow: And Other Curious Classified Ads from the Past*. New York: Clarkson Potter.

Banet-Weiser, S., and C. Lapsansky. 2008. "RED Is the New Black: Brand Culture, Consumer Citizenship and Political Possibility." *International Journal of Communication* 2: 21.

Barbrook, R., and A. Cameron. 1996. "The Californian Ideology." *Science as Culture* 6, no. 1: 44–72.

Baym, N. K. 1995. "The Emergence of Community in Computer-Mediated Communication." In *CyberSociety: Computer-Mediated Communication and Community*, edited by S. G. Jones, 138–63. Thousand Oaks, CA: Sage.

Beale, S. 2007. "I Saw You, Craigslist Missed Connections Comics." Laughing Squid. March 31, 2007. https://laughingsquid.com/i-saw-you-craigslist-missed-connections-comics/.

Bellafante, G. 2018. "Uber and the False Hopes of the Sharing Economy." *New York Times.* August 9, 2018. https://www.nytimes.com/2018/08/09/nyregion/uber-nyc-vote-drivers-ride-sharing.html.

Benilde, M. 2010. "The End of Newspapers?" *New York Times.* March 16, 2010. http://www.nytimes.com/2010/03/17/opinion/17iht-edbenilde.html.

Bensinger, G. 2015. "eBay Divests Craigslist Stake, Ends Litigation." *Wall Street Journal.* Last updated June 19, 2015. https://www.wsj.com/articles/eBay-sells-craigslist-stake-back-to-craigslist-1434730678.

Bensinger, G. 2017. "Uber Gears Up to Block Bid to Form a Union in Seattle." *Wall Street Journal.* Last updated March 11, 2017. https://www.wsj.com/articles/uber-gears-up-to-block-bid-to-form-a-union-in-seattle-1489237201.

Bercovici, J. 2012. "First Facebook Killed MySpace, Now It's Saving It." *Forbes.* February 13, 2012. https://www.forbes.com/sites/jeffbercovici/2012/02/13/first-Facebook-killed-MySpace-now-its-saving-it/#46c2b70746a2.

Bereznak, A. 2017. "Craig from Craigslist's Second Act." *Ringer.* June 1, 2017. https://www.theringer.com/2017/6/1/16042734/craig-newmark-interview-craigslist-journalism-421c50020179.

Bernard, Z. 2017. "Here's the Story behind How Silicon Valley Got Its Name." *Business Insider.* December 9, 2017. http://www.businessinsider.com/how-silicon-valley-got-its-name-2017-12.

Blackall, S. 2011. *Missed Connections: Love Lost and Found.* New York: Workman.

Blitstein, R. 2005. "Craig$list.com." *SF Weekly.* November 30, 2005. https://archives.sfweekly.com/sanfrancisco/craiglistcom/Content?oid=2158444.

Blodget, H. 2008a. "Craigslist Kills the Newspaper Industry." *Business Insider.* March 6, 2008. http://www.businessinsider.com/2008/3/craigslist-kills-the-newspaper-industry.

Blodget, H. 2008b. "Craigslist Valuation: $80 Million in 2008 Revenue, Worth $5 Billion." *Business Insider.* April 3, 2008. http://www.businessinsider.com/2008/4/craigslist-valuation-80-million-in-2008-revenue-worth-5-billion.

Bloomberg. n.d. "Craig Newmark." Bloomberg. Accessed February 28, 2019. https://www.bloomberg.com/profiles/people/3387607-craig-a-newmark.

Bort, R. 2015. "The Tech Industry Is Stripping San Francisco of Its Culture, and Your City Could Be Next." *Newsweek.* October 1, 2015. http://www.newsweek.com/san-francisco-tech-industry-gentrification-documentary-378628.

boyd, d. 2013. "White Flight in Networked Publics: How Race and Class Shaped American Teen Engagement with MySpace and Facebook." In *Race after the Internet*, edited by L. Nakamura and P. A. Chow-White, 203–22. New York: Routledge.

boyd, d., and N. B. Ellison. 2007. "Social Network Sites: Definition, History, and Scholarship." *Journal of Computer-Mediated Communication* 13, no. 1: 210–30.

Braun, V., V. Clarke, and G. Terry. 2014. "Thematic Analysis." *Qualitative Research in Clinical Health Psychology* 24: 95–114.

Breslow, J. M. 2013. "The State of America's Middle Class in Eight Charts." *Frontline.* July 9, 2013. https://www.pbs.org/wgbh/frontline/article/the-state-of-americas-middle-class-in-eight-charts/.

Brock, A. 2012. "From the Blackhand Side: Twitter as a Cultural Conversation." *Journal of Broadcasting and Electronic Media* 56, no. 4: 529–49.

Brown, M. B. 2016. "Safer than Craigslist—VarageSale App Review—Virtual Garage Sale." YouTube. March 14, 2016. https://www.youtube.com/watch?v=5ZurZTOe9Oo.

Browning, D. 2015. "What's Behind a Rise in HIV? Craigslist Hookups, U Prof Finds." *Star Tribune.* January 30, 2015. http://www.startribune.com/what-s-behind-a-rise-in-hiv-craigslist-hookups-u-prof-finds/290400001/.

Brunton, F. 2012. *Spam: A Shadow History of the Internet*. Cambridge, MA: MIT Press.

Bruthiaux, P. 1996. *The Discourse of Classified Advertising: Exploring the Nature of Linguistic Simplicity*. New York: Oxford University Press.

Buckmaster, J. 2008a. "Green Machine." *Craigslist blog*. March 31, 2008. http://blog.craigslist .org/2008/03/31/green-machine/.

Buckmaster, J. 2008b. "Joint Statement with Attorneys General, NCMEC." *Craigslist blog*. November 6, 2008. http://blog.craigslist.org/2008/11/06/joint-statement-with-attorneys-general-ncmec/.

Buckmaster, J. 2009. "CL Collaboration with AGs, NCMEC Early Results." *Craigslist blog*. March 9, 2009. http://blog.craigslist.org/2009/03/09/cl-collaboration-with-ags-ncmec-early-results/.

Buckmaster, J. 2010. For Amber Lyon, CNN." *Craigslist blog*. August 30, 2010. http://blog.craigslist .org/2010/08/30/for-amber-lyon-cnn/.

Buelow, S. 2013. *Quick Web Sales!: A Beginner's Guide to Selling Your Stuff on Craigslist*. Appleton, WI: New Media Jet.

Burrell, J. 2012. *Invisible Users: Youth in the Internet Cafes of Urban Ghana*. Cambridge, MA: MIT Press.

Cacioppo, J. T., S. Cacioppo, G. C. Gonzaga, E. L. Ogburn, and T. J. VanderWeele. 2013. "Marital Satisfaction and Break-Ups Differ across On-Line and Off-Line Meeting Venues." *Proceedings of the National Academy of Sciences of the USA* 110, no. 25: 10135–40.

Cali, B. E., J. M. Coleman, and C. Campbell. 2013. "Stranger Danger? Women's Self-Protection Intent and the Continuing Stigma of Online Dating." *Cyberpsychology, Behavior, and Social Networking* 16, no. 12: 853–57.

Castells, M. 1997. *The Power of Identity*. Vol. 2 of *The Information Age: Economy, Society, and Culture*. London: Blackwell.

Catalano, F. 2018. "From Rhapsody to Napster: How This Pioneering Music Service Coulda Been Spotify—and Why It Isn't." *GeekWire*. April 14, 2018. https://www.geekwire.com/2018 /rhapsody-napster-pioneering-music-service-coulda-spotify-isnt/.

Chávez, A. 2018. "The House Passed an Anti-Sex-Trafficking Bill that Could Restrict Online Speech and Endanger Sex Workers." *Intercept*. March 1, 2018. https://theintercept.com/2018/03/01 /sex-trafficking-bill-free-speech/.

Christensen, C., M. Raynor, and R. McDonald. 2015. "What Is Disruptive Innovation?" *Harvard Business Review*. December 2015. https://hbr.org/2015/12/what-is-disruptive-innovation.

Christensen, K. 2017. "LA Community Newspaper Editor Sentenced in Illegal Firearms Ads." *Los Angeles Times*. May 26, 2017. https://www.latimes.com/local/lanow/la-me-ln-newspaper -editor-guns-20170526-story.html.

Chun, W.H.K. 2008. *Control and Freedom: Power and Paranoia in the Age of Fiber Optics*. Cambridge, MA: MIT Press.

Chun, W.H.K. 2016. *Updating to Remain the Same: Habitual New Media*. Cambridge, MA: MIT Press.

Clucas, D. 2004. "Simple Does the Trick for Classified Ad Web Site." *Boulder County Business Report*. January 23, 2004. https://www.craigslist.org/about/press/simpletrick.

Cocks, H. G. 2004. "Peril in the Personals: The Dangers and Pleasures of Classified Advertising in Early Twentieth-Century Britain." *Media History* 10: 3–16.

Cocks, H. G. 2009. *Classified: The Secret History of the Personal Column*. New York: Random House.

Cooper, A. 1998. "Sexuality and the Internet: Surfing into the New Millennium." *CyberPsychology and Behavior* 1, no. 2: 187–93.

Cooper, S. 2013. "Trolls Not Allowed: Rise of Quality Online Comments." *Forbes*. September 27, 2013. https://www.forbes.com/sites/stevecooper/2013/09/27/trolls-not-allowed-rise-of -quality-online-comments/#257cb32d375c.

Corbin, K. 2009. "More Heat for Craigslist over Erotic Services Ads." *Internet News*. April 27, 2009. http://www.internetnews.com/webcontent/article.php/3817456/More+Heat+for +craigslist+Over+Erotic+Services+Ads.htm.

Cormier, R. 2004. "The Day We (Almost) Met." *Spark Weekly*. January 28, 2004. https://www.craigslist.org/about/press/almostmet.

craigslist. n.d.[a]. "Craigslist Is Hiring!" About. Accessed February 28, 2019. craigslist.org/about/craigslist_is_hiring.

craigslist. n.d.[b]. "Flags and Community Moderation." About. Accessed February 28, 2019. https://www.craigslist.org/about/help/flags_and_community_moderation.

craigslist. n.d.[c]. "Jim Buckmaster." About. Accessed February 28, 2019. https://www.craigslist.org/about/jim_buckmaster.

Crawford, K., and T. Gillespie. 2016. "What Is a Flag For?: Social Media Reporting Tools and the Vocabulary of Complaint." *New Media and Society* 18, no. 3: 410–28.

Crunchbase. n.d. "Craigslist." Accessed February 28, 2019. https://www.crunchbase.com/organization/craigslist.

Cullen, R. 2001. "Addressing the Digital Divide." *Online Information Review* 25, no. 5: 311–20.

Cunningham, S., and T. D. Kendall. 2011. "Prostitution 2.0: The Changing Face of Sex Work." *Journal of Urban Economics* 69, no. 3: 273–87.

Cyriax, O. 2009. *The Encyclopedia of Crime*. London: Andre Deutsch.

Dalbello, M. 2004. "Institutional Shaping of Cultural Memory: Digital Library as Environment for Textual Transmission." *Library Quarterly* 74, no. 3: 265–98.

Dalton, G. 1982. "Barter." *Journal of Economic Issues* 16, no. 1: 181–90.

Dave, P. 2012. "Craigslist Backs Off Exclusive Rights to Ads." *SFGate* (blog). August 12, 2012. http://blog.sfgate.com/techchron/2012/08/10/craigslist-backs-off-exclusive-rights-to-ads/.

Davis, J. L., and J. B. Chouinard. 2016. "Theorizing Affordances: From Request to Refuse." *Bulletin of Science, Technology and Society* 36, no. 4: 241–48.

Dean, J. 2005. "Communicative Capitalism: Circulation and the Foreclosure of Politics." *Cultural Politics* 1, no. 1: 51–74.

Deaux, K., and R. Hanna. 1984. "Courtship in the Personals Column: The Influence of Gender and Sexual Orientation." *Sex Roles* 11: 363–75.

Denzin, N. 1999. "Cybertalk and the Method of Instances." In *Doing Internet Research: Critical Issues and Methods for Examining the Net*, edited by Steve Jones, 107–25. Thousand Oaks, CA: Sage.

Dewey, C. 2014. "Do Dating Apps Have a Prostitution Problem?" *Washington Post*. July 21, 2014. https://www.washingtonpost.com/news/the-intersect/wp/2014/07/21/do-dating-apps-have-a-prostitution-problem/?noredirect=onandutm_term=.6628e4d4d1a1.

Dewey, C. 2016. "Think Twice before Answering that Ad: 101 Murders Have Been Linked to Craigslist." *Washington Post*. January 11, 2016. https://www.washingtonpost.com/news/the-intersect/wp/2016/01/11/think-twice-before-answering-that-ad-101-killers-have-found-victims-on-craigslist/.

Dibbell, J. 1999. *My Tiny Life: Crime and Passion in a Virtual World*. London: Fourth Estate.

Douglas, N. 2006. "SXSW: Craig Gets a Makeover." *Gawker*. Accessed March 13, 2016. http://gawker.com/160270/sxsw-craig-gets-a-makeover.

Draper, N. A., and J. Turow. 2019. "The Corporate Cultivation of Digital Resignation." *New Media and Society*. doi:10.1177/1461444819833331.

Driscoll, K. E. 2014. "Hobbyist Inter-networking and the Popular Internet Imaginary: Forgotten Histories of Networked Personal Computing, 1978–1998." Unpublished doctoral dissertation, University of Southern California.

Duffy, B. 2015. "Amateur, Autonomous, and Collaborative: Myths of Aspiring Female Cultural Producers in Web 2.0." *Critical Studies in Media Communication* 32, no. 1: 48–64.

Ebo, B. L., ed. 2001. *Cyberimperialism?: Global Relations in the New Electronic Frontier*. Westport, CT: Greenwood.

Ehrlich, E. 2017. "Time to Break Up the Google-Facebook-Amazon Monopoly." *USA Today*. October 19, 2017. https://www.usatoday.com/story/opinion/2017/10/19/google-Facebook -amazon-time-to-break-up-web-trusts-ev-ehrlich-column/759803001/.

Eidelman, V. 2016. "ACLU Wins Case Protecting Identity of Anonymous Online Critics." *ACLU* (blog). Accessed July 12, 2019. https://www.aclu.org/blog/free-speech/internet-speech /aclu-wins-case-protecting-identity-anonymous-online-critics.

Ekstrand, V. S. 2003. "Unmasking Jane and John Doe: Online Anonymity and the First Amendment." *Communication Law and Policy* 8, no. 4: 405–27.

Electronic Frontier Foundation. 2006. "EFF Honors Craigslist, Gigi Sohn, and Jimmy Wales with Pioneer Awards." April 27, 2006. https://www.eff.org/press/archives/2006/04/27.

Elizabeth. 2017. "Thank You Craig Newmark and Craigslist Charitable Fund." Palomacy. March 17, 2017. http://www.pigeonrescue.org/2017/03/17/thank-you-craig-newmark -craigslist-charitable-fund/.

Epel, E. S., S. Spanakos, J. Kasl-Godley, and K. D. Brownell. 1996. "Body Shape Ideals across Gender, Sexual Orientation, Socioeconomic Status, Race, and Age in Personal Advertisements." *International Journal of Eating Disorders* 19, no. 3: 264–73.

Farivar, C. 2015. "3taps to Pay Craigslist $1 Million to End Lengthy Lawsuit, Will Shut Down." *Ars Technica*. June 29, 2015. https://arstechnica.com/tech-policy/2015/06/3taps-to-pay -craigslist-1-million-to-end-lengthy-lawsuit-will-shut-down/.

Ferrari, E. 2019. "The Technological Imaginaries of Social Movements: The Discursive Dimension of Communication Technology and the Fight for Social Justice." Doctoral dissertation, University of Pennsylvania.

Feurer, A. 2017. *I Hope You Find Me: The Love Poems of Craigslist's Missed Connections*. Los Angeles: Knock Knock.

Finlon, C. 2002. "Internet Resources." *Journal of Gay and Lesbian Social Services* 14, no. 1: 99–107.

Ford, H. 2015. "Fact Factories: Wikipedia and the Power to Represent." Unpublished doctoral dissertation, University of Oxford.

Forte, A., V. Larco, and A. Bruckman. 2009. "Decentralization in Wikipedia Governance." *Journal of Management Information Systems* 26, no. 1: 49–72.

France, J. 2010. "Romancing the Craigslist—Jasmine's Tech Dos and Don'ts." *CNET*. August 12, 2010. https://www.cnet.com/news/romancing-the-craigslist-jasmines-tech-dos-donts.

Franzoni, C., and H. Sauermann. 2014. "Crowd Science: The Organization of Scientific Research in Open Collaborative Projects." *Research Policy* 43, no. 1: 1–20.

Frederick, B. J., and D. Perrone. 2014. "'Party N Play' on the Internet: Subcultural Formation, Craigslist, and Escaping from Stigma." *Deviant Behavior* 35, no. 11: 859–84.

Friedman, D. 2014. "The Craigslist Killers." *GQ*. July 14, 2014. https://www.gq.com/story/craigslist -killers.

Führer, K. C. 2012. "Contradicting Nazi Propaganda: Classified Advertisements as Documents of Jewish Life in Nazi Germany, 1933–1938." *Media History* 18, no. 1: 65–76.

Gammelgaard, K. 2010. "Czech Classified Advertising under Stalinism: Transformation of a Genre." *Slavonica* 16, no. 2: 79–95.

Garrett, J. 2016. "The Weird and Wonderful Things Reflected in Mirrors on Craigslist." *Wired*. March 29, 2016. https://www.wired.com/2016/03/eric-oglander-craigslist-mirrors/.

Gehl, R. W. 2014. *Reverse Engineering Social Media: Software, Culture, and Political Economy in New Media Capitalism*. Philadelphia, PA: Temple University Press.

Gillespie, T. 2010. "The Politics of 'Platforms.'" *New Media and Society* 12, no. 3: 347–64.

Gillespie, T. 2018a. *Custodians of the Internet: Platforms, Content Moderation, and the Hidden Decisions that Shape Social Media*. New Haven, CT: Yale University Press.

Gillespie, T. 2018b. "Facebook and YouTube Just Got More Transparent. What Do We See?" *NiemanLab*. May 3, 2018. http://www.niemanlab.org/2018/05/Facebook-and-youtube-just-got-more-transparent-what-do-we-see/.

Gillespie, T. 2018c. "Platforms Are Not Intermediaries." *Georgetown Law Technology Review* 2, no. 2: 198–216.

Gira Grant, M. 2009. "The Craigslist Sex Panic." *Slate*. May 27, 2009. http://www.slate.com/articles/technology/webhead/2009/05/the_craigslist_sex_panic.html.

Glave, J. 1999. "The Delisting of Craig's List." *Wired*. October 1, 1999. https://www.wired.com/1999/10/the-delisting-of-craigs-list/.

Goffman, E. 1963. *Stigma: Notes on the Management of Spoiled Identity*. Englewood Cliffs, NJ: Prentice-Hall.

Goldman, A. 2013. "The 'Google Shuttle Effect': Gentrification and San Francisco's Dot Com Boom 2.0." Unpublished doctoral dissertation, University of California, Berkeley.

Gonzales, M. H., and S. A. Meyers. 1993. "Your Mother Would Like Me": Self-Presentation in the Personals Ads of Heterosexual and Homosexual Men and Women." *Personality and Social Psychology Bulletin* 19, no. 2: 131–42.

Goode, E. 1996. "Gender and Courtship Entitlement: Responses to Personal Ads." *Sex Roles* 34, no. 3–4: 141–70.

Graham, M., I. Hjorth, and V. Lehdonvirta. 2017. "Digital Labour and Development: Impacts of Global Digital Labour Platforms and the Gig Economy on Worker Livelihoods." *Transfer: European Review of Labour and Research* 23, no. 2: 135–62.

Gray, M. L. 2009. *Out in the Country: Youth, Media, and Queer Visibility in Rural America*. New York: New York University Press.

Gray, M. L., S. Suri, S. S. Ali, and D. Kulkarni. 2016. "The Crowd Is a Collaborative Network." In *Proceedings of the 19th ACM Conference on Computer-Supported Cooperative Work and Social Computing*, edited by P. Bjørn and J. Konstan, 134–47. New York: ACM.

Greenberg, A. 2014. "How to Anonymize Everything You Do Online." *Wired*. June 17, 2014. https://www.wired.com/2014/06/be-anonymous-online/.

Greenblatt, E. 1998. "Lesbian Resources on the Web." *Feminist Collections* 19, no. 2: 24.

Gregg, M. 2013. *Work's Intimacy*. New York: John Wiley and Sons.

Gregson, N., and L. Crewe. 2003. *Secondhand Cultures*. Oxford: Berg.

Grov, C. 2012. "HIV Risk and Substance Use in Men Who Have Sex with Men Surveyed in Bathhouses, Bars/Clubs, and on Craigslist.org: Venue of Recruitment Matters." *AIDS Behavior* 16: 807–17.

Grov, C., L. Agyemang, A. Ventuneac, and A. S. Breslow. 2013. "Navigating Condom Use and HIV Status Disclosure with Partners Met Online: A Qualitative Pilot Study with Gay and Bisexual Men from Craigslist.org." *AIDS Education and Prevention* 25, no. 1: 72–85.

Grov, C., and T. Crow. 2012. "Attitudes about and HIV Risk Related to the 'Most Common Place' MSM Meet Their Sex Partners: Comparing Men from Bathhouses, Bars/Clubs, and Craigslist .org." *AIDS Education and Prevention* 24, no. 2: 102–16.

Haimson, O. L., and G. R. Hayes. 2017. "Changes in Social Media Affect, Disclosure, and Sociality for a Sample of Transgender Americans in 2016's Political Climate." In *Proceedings of the Eleventh International AAAI Conference on Web and Social Media*, edited by D. Ruths, 72–81. Menlo Park, CA: AAAI.

Hall, G. 2016. *The Uberfication of the University*. Minneapolis: University of Minnesota Press.

Hall, M. 1999. "Virtual Colonization." *Journal of Material Culture* 4, no. 1: 39–55.

Harrison, A. A., and L. Saeed. 1977. "Let's Make a Deal: An Analysis of Revelations and Stipulations in Lonely Hearts Advertisements." *Journal of Personality and Social Psychology* 35, no. 4: 257–64.

Hatala, M. N., and J. Prehodka. 1996. "Content Analysis of Gay Male and Lesbian Personal Advertisements." *Psychological Reports* 78: 371–74.

Hazen, D. 2010. "Scapegoating Craigslist Is Not Going to Solve the Problem of Underage Prostitution." *Alternet*. June 4, 2010. https://web.archive.org/web/20100608141603/http://www.alternet.org/story/147100/scapegoating_craigslist_is_not_going_to_solve_the_problem_of_underage_prostitution/.

Helmond, A. 2015. "The Platformization of the Web: Making Web Data Platform Ready." *Social Media + Society* 1, no. 2: 1–11.

Hempel, J. 2004. "A Talk with Craigslist's Keeper." *Business Week*. September 8, 2004. https://www.craigslist.org/about/press/craigslist.keeper.

Herman, A. 2014. "Online Harassment and the Cruel Paradox of Being a Woman on Social Media." *Flavorwire*. January 7, 2014. http://flavorwire.com/432313/online-harassment-and-the-cruel-paradox-of-being-a-woman-on-social-media.

Hess, A. 2014. "Why Women Aren't Welcome on the Internet." *Pacific Standard*. Accessed July 12, 2019. https://psmag.com/social-justice/women-arent-welcome-internet-72170.

Hine, C. 2015. *Ethnography for the Internet*. London: Bloomsbury.

Hirschman, E. C. 1987. "People as Products: Analysis of a Complex Marketing Exchange." *Journal of Marketing* 51, no. 1: 98–108.

Hoang, K. 2010. "Economies of Emotion, Familiarity, Fantasy, and Desire: Emotional Labor in Ho Chi Minh City's Sex Industry." *Sexualities* 13, no. 2: 255–72.

Hogan, B. 2010. "The Presentation of Self in the Age of Social Media: Distinguishing Performances and Exhibitions Online." *Bulletin of Science, Technology and Society* 30, no. 6: 377–86.

Holley, P. 2015. "When Craigslist Comes to Town, HIV Infections Go Up, Study Says." *Washington Post*. February 2, 2015. https://www.washingtonpost.com/news/morning-mix/wp/2015/02/02/when-craigslist-comes-to-town-hiv-infections-go-up-study-says/?noredirect=on&utm_term=.ba7769d52029.

Holpuch, A. 2015. "Facebook Still Suspending Native American Accounts over Real Name Policy." *Guardian*. February 16, 2015. https://www.theguardian.com/technology/2015/feb/16/facebook-real-name-policy-suspends-native-americans.

Hosanagar, V., and K. Jair. 2018. "We Need Transparency in Algorithms but Too Much Can Backfire." *Harvard Business Review*. July 23, 2018; last updated July 25, 2018. https://hbr.org/2018/07/we-need-transparency-in-algorithms-but-too-much-can-backfire.

Howard, P. 2016. "Is Social Media Killing Democracy?" *Policy & Internet* (blog), Oxford Internet Institute. November 15, 2016. https://www.oii.ox.ac.uk/blog/is-social-media-killing-democracy/.

Hu, Y., J. F. Wood, V. Smith, and N. Westbrook. 2004. "Friendships through IM: Examining the Relationship between Instant Messaging and Intimacy." *Journal of Computer-Mediated Communication* 10, no. 1: JCMC10111. https://academic.oup.com/jcmc/article/10/1/JCMC10111/4614464.

Innclusive. n.d. "How Innclusive Addresses Issues of Discrimination." Accessed February 28, 2019. https://www.innclusive.com/why-innclusive.

Irani, L. 2015. "Difference and Dependence among Digital Workers: The Case of Amazon Mechanical Turk." *South Atlantic Quarterly* 114, no. 1: 225–34.

Irani, L. C., and M. Silberman. 2013. "Turkopticon: Interrupting Worker Invisibility in Amazon Mechanical Turk." In *Proceedings of the SIGCHI Conference on Human Factors in Computing Systems*, edited by S. Brewster and S. Bødker, 611–20. New York: ACM.

Isaacson, W. 2014. *The Innovators: How a Group of Inventors, Hackers, Geniuses and Geeks Created the Digital Revolution*. New York: Simon and Schuster.

Ivanova, I. 2018. "Worker Wages Drop while Companies Spend Billions to Boost Stocks." *CBS News*. July 11, 2018. https://www.cbsnews.com/news/worker-wages-drop-while-companies -spend-billions-to-boost-stocks/.

Jackson, S. J. 2016. "(Re) Imagining Intersectional Democracy from Black Feminism to Hashtag Activism." *Women's Studies in Communication* 39, no. 4: 375–79.

Jenkins, H. 2006. *Convergence Culture: Where Old and New Media Collide*. New York: New York University Press.

John, N. A. 2017. *The Age of Sharing*. New York: John Wiley and Sons.

Johnson, L. 2018. "'Let's Not Forget that Craigslist Destroyed Local Journalism': Not Everyone Is Happy with the Founder of Craigslist Getting a School Named for Him after Making a Huge Donation." *Business Insider*. June 11, 2018. https://www.businessinsider.com/not-everyone -is-happy-with-the-founder-of-craigslist-2018-6?r=US&IR=T.

Johnson, M. 2007. *The Dead Beat: Lost Souls, Lucky Stiffs, and the Perverse Pleasures of Obituaries*. New York: HarperCollins.

Johnsville News. 2005. "Bio of Craig Newmark: Founder of Craigslist." *Johnsville News Blogspot*. August 26, 2005. https://johnsville.blogspot.com/2005/08/bio-of-craig-newmark-founder -of.html.

Jones, S. 2009. "Online Classifieds." Pew Research Center, Internet and Technology. May 22, 2009. http://www.pewinternet.org/2009/05/22/online-classifieds/.

Keleman, M., and W. Smith. 2001. "Community and Its 'Virtual' Promises: A Critique of Cyber-libertarian Rhetoric." *Information, Communication and Society* 4, no. 3: 370–87.

Kelleher, K. 2010. "How Facebook Learned from MySpace's Mistakes." *Fortune*. November 19, 2010. http://fortune.com/2010/11/19/how-Facebook-learned-from-MySpaces-mistakes/.

Kelly, H. 2012. "83 Million Facebook Accounts Are Fakes and Dupes." *CNN*. August 2, 2012. http://www.cnn.com/2012/08/02/tech/social-media/facebook-fake-accounts/index .html.

Kerr, D. 2017. "Uber and Lyft Messed with Texas—and Won." *CNET*. June 20, 2017. https://www .cnet.com/news/uber-lyft-toyed-with-texas-to-get-their-ride-hailing-way/.

Kitzie, V. 2018. "'I Pretended to Be a Boy on the Internet': Navigating Affordances and Constraints of Social Networking Sites and Search Engines for LGBTQ+ Identity Work." *First Monday* 23, no. 7. doi:10.5210/fm.v23i7.9264.

King, B. 2018. "Penn Study Links Social Media Use as a Cause of Depression and Loneliness." *Philly Voice*. November 20, 2018. https://www.phillyvoice.com/social-media-use-cause-depression -and-loneliness-penn/.

Komito, L. 2001. "Electronic Communities in an Information Society: Paradise, Mirage, or Malaise?" *Journal of Documentation* 57, no. 1: 115–29.

Kreiss, D. 2016. "Social Media Did Not Give Us Donald Trump and It Is Not Weakening Democracy." *Culture Digitally* (blog). November 9, 2016. http://culturedigitally.org/2016/11/social _media_trump/.

Kulwin, N. 2018. "'We Can Solve Technical Issues, but Can't Pay Our Employees a Fair Wage?': A Conversation with Ellen Pao about the Homogeneity of Internet Pioneers, Reddit's Quest for Growth, and the Inability of Tech Executives to Change." *New York Magazine*. April 16, 2018. http://nymag.com/selectall/2018/04/ellen-pao-reddit-ceo-interview.html.

Lamont, T. 2013. "Napster: The Day Music Was Set Free." *Guardian*. February 24, 2013. https:// www.theguardian.com/music/2013/feb/24/napster-music-free-file-sharing.

Lampel, J., and A. Bhalla. 2007. "The Role of Status Seeking in Online Communities: Giving the Gift of Experience." *Journal of Computer-Mediated Communication* 12, no. 2: 434–55.

Landahl, J. 2006. *Estate Sale Prospecting for Fun and Profit with craigslist® and eBay®*. InfoStrategist .com.

Laner, M. R. 1978. "Media Mating II: 'Personals' Advertisements of Lesbian Women." *Journal of Homosexuality* 4, no. 1: 41–61.

Langlois, G., G. Elmer, F. McKelvey, and Z. Devereaux. 2009. "Networked Publics: The Double Articulation of Code and Politics on Facebook." *Canadian Journal of Communication* 34, no. 3: 415–34.

LaRosa, P., and M. Cramer. 2010. *Seven Days of Rage: The Deadly Crime Spree of the Craigslist Killer*. New York: Pocketstar Books.

Lee, L., T. Slater, and E. K. Wyly, eds. 2010. *The Gentrification Reader*. Vol. 1. London: Routledge.

Lessig, L. 2008. *Remix: Making Art and Commerce Thrive in the Hybrid Economy*. New York: Penguin.

Levy, P. 2018. "An Update on the Constitutional Court Challenge to FOSTA." *Technology and Marketing Law Blog*. August 13, 2018. https://blog.ericgoldman.org/archives/2018/08/an-update-on-the-constitutional-court-challenge-to-fosta-woodhull-freedom-v-us-guest-blog-post.htm.

Light, B. 2014. *Disconnecting with Social Networking Sites*. New York: Springer.

Lindenberger, M. 2010. "Craigslist Comes Clean: No More 'Adult Services,' Ever." *Time*. September 16, 2010. http://content.time.com/time/nation/article/0,8599,2019499,00.html.

Lingel, J. 2017a. *Digital Countercultures and the Struggle for Community*. Cambridge, MA: MIT Press.

Lingel, J. 2017b. "Networked Field Studies: Comparative Inquiry and Online Communities." *Social Media + Society* 3, no. 4: doi: 2056305117743139.

Lingel, J. 2018. "Socio-technical Transformations in Secondary Markets: A Comparison of Craigslist and VarageSale." *Internet Histories* 3, no. 2: 162–79. Published online ahead of print November 2, 2018. doi:10.1080/24701475.2018.1478267.

Lingel, J. 2019. "Notes from the Web that Was: The Platform Politics of craigslist." *Surveillance & Society* 17, no. 1/2: 21–26.

Lingel, J., and A. Golub. 2015. "In Face on Facebook: Brooklyn's Drag Community and Socio-technical Practices of Online Communication." *Journal of Computer-Mediated Communication* 20, no. 5: 536–53.

Linlin, P. 1993. "Matchmaking via the Personal Advertisements in China versus in the United States." *Journal of Popular Culture* 27, no. 1: 163–70.

Lloyd, J. 2009. *Craigslist 4 Everyone*. Indianapolis: Que.

Lorimor, E. S. 1977. "Classified Advertising: A Neglected Medium. *Journal of Advertising* 6, no. 1: 17–25.

Loustalot, V. 2003. "West Siders Get Freaky on Craig's List." *Columbia Spectator*. October 28, 2003. https://www.craigslist.org/about/press/getfreaky.

Lumby, M. E. 1978. "Men Who Advertise for Sex." *Journal of Homosexuality* 4, no. 1: 63–72.

Lund, A. 2017. *Wikipedia, Work, and Capitalism*. New York: Palgrave Macmillan.

Lynn, M., and R. Bolig. 1985. "Personal Advertisements: Sources of Data about Relationships." *Journal of Social and Personal Relationships* 2: 377–83.

Ma, X., J. Hancock, and M. Naaman. 2016. "Anonymity, Intimacy and Self-Disclosure in Social Media." In *Proceedings of the 2016 CHI Conference on Human Factors in Computing Systems*, edited by C. Lampe, D. Morris, and J. P. Hourcade, 3857–69. New York: ACM.

Mapes, D. 2008. "Single Shot: Plenty of Singles Do Wrong in Their Craigslist Ads." *Seattle Post Intelligencer*. November 20, 2008. https://www.seattlepi.com/lifestyle/article/Single-Shot-Plenty-of-singles-do-wrong-in-their-1292115.php.

Markham, A. N. 1998. *Life Online: Researching Real Experience in Virtual Space*. Lanham, MD: Rowman Altamira.

Markham, A. N. 2012. "Fabrication as Ethical Practice: Qualitative Inquiry in Ambiguous Internet Contexts." *Information, Communication and Society* 15, no. 3: 334–53.

Markham, A. N., and P. Bride. 2006. "Ethic as Method, Method as Ethic." *Journal of Information Ethics* 15, no. 2: 37–54.

Markham, A. N., and E. Buchanan. 2012. *Ethical Decision-Making and Internet Research: Recommendations from the AoIR Ethics Working Committee (Version 2.0)*. N.p.: Association of Internet Researchers. http://aoir.org/reports/ethics2.pdf.

Marshall, C. 2009. "No Bull, No Spin: A Comparison of Tags with Other Forms of User Metadata." In *JCDL '09: Proceedings of the 9th ACM/IEEE-CS Joint Conference on Digital Libraries*, edited by F. Heath, 241–50. New York: ACM.

Marvin, C. 1988. *When Old Technologies Were New*. Oxford: Oxford University Press.

Marwick, A. E. 2008. "To Catch a Predator?: The MySpace Moral Panic." *First Monday* 13, no. 6. doi:10.5210/fm.v13i6.2152.

Marwick, A. E. 2015. *Status Update: Celebrity, Publicity and Branding in the Digital Age*. New Haven, CT: Yale University Press.

Masnick, M. 2009. "Attorneys General Ramp Up Misguided Attacks on Craigslist." *Techdirt* (blog). April 28, 2009. https://www.techdirt.com/articles/20090428/0234214676.shtml.

McCarthy, J. 1983. "Reminiscences on the History of Time Sharing." Stanford University Formal Reasoning Group (website). http://www-formal.stanford.edu/jmc/history/timesharing/timesharing.html.

McChesney, R. W. 2013. *Digital Disconnect: How Capitalism Is Turning the Internet against Democracy*. New York: New Press.

McChesney, R. W., and V. W. Pickard. 2011. *Will the Last Reporter Please Turn Out the Lights: The Collapse of Journalism and What Can Be Done to Fix It*. New York: New Press.

McGloin, C. 2018. "The Child Trafficking Film that Forced FOSTA." *Scope*. April 25, 2018. https://www.northeastern.edu/thescope/2018/04/25/fosta-child-sex-trafficking-film-changed-law/.

McGlotten, S. 2013. *Virtual Intimacies: Media, Affect, and Queer Sociality*. Albany, NY: Suny.

McMillian, J. 2011. *Smoking Typewriters: The Sixties Underground Press and the Rise of Alternative Media in America*. New York: Oxford University Press.

Meinrath, S., and V. Pickard. 2008. "Transcending Net Neutrality: Ten Steps Toward an Open Internet." *Education Week Commentary* 12, no. 6: 1–12.

Mendels, P. 1996. "Court's Ruling Expected to Have a Global Impact." *New York Times*. December 7, 1996. https://archive.nytimes.com/www.nytimes.com/library/cyber/week/1207decency.html.

Merskin, D. 1995. "Getting Personal: Daily Newspaper Adoption of Personal Advertisements." *Newspaper Research Journal* 16, no. 3: 75–81.

Millar, L. 2002. "The Death of the Fonds and the Resurrection of Provenance: Archival Context in Space and Time." *Archivaria* 53: 1–15.

Moore, D. J. 2009. "Craigslist Changes Policy on 'Erotic' Ads, but Does It Make a Difference?" *Press Democrat*. May 25, 2009. http://www.pressdemocrat.com/news/2280600-181/craigslist-changes-policy-on-erotic.

Morozov, E. 2013. *To Save Everything, Click Here: The Folly of Technological Solutionism*. New York: Public Affairs.

Mosco, V. 2004. *The Digital Sublime: Myth, Power, and Cyberspace*. Cambridge, MA: MIT Press.

Moskowitz, D. A., and D. W. Seal. 2010. "'GWM Looking for Sex—SERIOUS ONLY': The Interplay of Sexual Ad Placement Frequency and Success on the Sexual Health of 'Men Seeking Men' on Craigslist." *Journal of Gay and Lesbian Social Services* 22, no. 4: 399–412.

Mosthof, M. 2016. "Kinky Nerds Is the Most Popular of OkCupid's New Quickmatch Flavors." *Bustle*. June 3, 2016. https://www.bustle.com/articles/164543-kinky-nerds-is-the-most-popular-of-okcupids-new-quickmatch-flavors.

Nair, R. B. 1992. "Gender, Genre, and Generative Grammar: Deconstructing the Matrimonial Column." In *Language, Text and Context*, edited by M. J. Toolan, 227–54. London: Routledge.

Nakamura, L. 1995. "Race in/for Cyberspace: Identity Tourism and Racial Passing on the Internet." *Works and Days* 13, no. 1–2: 181–93.

Neff, G. 2012. *Venture Labor: Work and the Burden of Risk in Innovative Industries*. Cambridge, MA: MIT Press.

Newitz, A. 2000. "Craigslust." *San Francisco Bay Guardian*. June 14, 2000. https://www.craigslist .org/about/press/craigslust.

Newmark, C. 2004. "Craigslist and eBay." Craig Newmark's official website. Accessed February 28, 2019. http://www.cnewmark.com/archives/000265.html.

Newmark, C. 2017. "Craigslist Founder: Support Military Families, and I'll Match Your Donations to One Group Helping Them." *Fox News*. November 10, 2017. http://www.foxnews .com/opinion/2017/11/10/craigslist-founder-support-military-families-and-ill-match-your -donations-to-one-group-helping-them.html.

Ng, A. 2016. "LGBT Singles Can Now Find Love on Christian Mingle, after Site Settles Discrimination Lawsuit." *NY Daily News*. July 5, 2016. https://www.nydailynews.com/news/national /lgbt-singles-find-love-christian-mingle-article-1.2700019.

Ngai, S. 2015. *Our Aesthetic Categories: Cute Zany Interesting*. Cambridge, MA: Harvard University Press.

Noble, S. U. 2018. *Algorithms of Oppression: How Search Engines Reinforce Racism*. New York: New York University Press.

Nollinger, M. 1995. "America, Online!" *Wired*. September 1, 1995. https://www.wired.com/1995 /09/aol-2/.

Norcie, G., E. De Cristofaro, and V. Bellotti. 2013. "Bootstrapping Trust in Online Dating: Social Verification of Online Dating Profiles." In *Financial Cryptography and Data Security: FC 2013 Workshops, USEC and WAHC 2013, Okinawa, Japan, April 1, 2013, Revised Selected Papers*, edited by A. A. Adams, M. Brenner, and M. Smith, 149–63. Berlin: Springer.

Norris, P. 2001. *Digital Divide: Civic Engagement, Information Poverty, and the Internet Worldwide*. Cambridge: Cambridge University Press.

Nunziato, D. C. 2009. *Virtual Freedom: Net Neutrality and Free Speech in the Internet Age*. Palo Alto, CA: Stanford University Press.

O'Donnell, A. 2019. "How Do I Report Internet Scams/Fraud?" Lifewire. Last updated April 25, 2019. https://www.lifewire.com/how-do-i-report-internet-scams-fraud-2487300.

Oglander, E. 2015. *Mirrors*. Oakland, CA: TBW Books.

OkCupid. 2019. "Photo Rules." OkCupid. July 6, 2019. https://OkCupid.desk.com/customer/en /portal/articles/2953227-photo-rules.

Omens, A. 2018. "Equal Pay for Women: Why the US Needs to Catch Up on Data Disclosure and Transparency." *Forbes*. April 10, 2018. https://www.forbes.com/sites/justcapital/2018/04/10 /equal-pay-for-women-why-the-u-s-needs-to-catch-up-on-data-disclosure-and-transparency /#6a9d30f77c25.

Opsahl, K. 2013. "Craigslist Owns What You Did Last Summer." Electronic Frontier Foundation. April 30, 2013. https://www.eff.org/deeplinks/2013/04/craigslist-owns-what-you -did-last-summer.

O'Reilly, T. 2005. "What Is Web 2.0?" O'Reilly. September 30, 2005. https://www.oreilly.com /pub/a/web2/archive/what-is-web-20.html.

Osucha, E. 2009. "The Whiteness of Privacy: Race, Media, Law." *Camera Obscura: Feminism, Culture, and Media Studies*, 24, no. 1: 67–107.

Papacharissi, Z. 2002. "The Virtual Sphere: The Internet as a Public Sphere." *New Media and Society* 4, no. 1: 9–27.

Papacharissi, Z. 2015. *Affective Publics: Sentiment, Technology, and Politics*. Oxford: Oxford University Press.

Papamarko, S. 2017. "Why Black Women and Asian Men Are at a Disadvantage When It Comes to Online Dating." *Star*. March 21, 2017. https://www.thestar.com/life/2017/03/21/racism-and-matchmaking.html.

Paviour, B. 2015. "Art Show Mines Craigslist Missed Connections." *Mission Local*. July 21, 2015. https://missionlocal.org/2015/07/art-show-mines-craigslist-missed-connections/.

Peiser, J. 2018. "Craigslist Founder Gives $20 Million to CUNY Journalism School." *New York Times*. June 11, 2018. https://www.nytimes.com/2018/06/11/business/media/craigslist-cuny-journalism-school.html.

Persily, N. 2017. "Can Democracy Survive the Internet?" *Journal of Democracy* 28, no. 2: 63–76.

Phillips, K. 2017. "Former Oklahoma State Senator Admits to Child Sex Trafficking while in Office." *Washington Post*. November 20, 2017. https://www.washingtonpost.com/news/post-nation/wp/2017/11/20/former-oklahoma-state-senator-admits-to-child-sex-trafficking-while-in-office/?utm_term=.8afc59e2f5c9.

Picard, R. G. 2008. "Shifts in Newspaper Advertising Expenditures and Their Implications for the Future of Newspapers." *Journalism Studies* 9, no. 5: 704–16.

Pickard, V. 2014. "The Great Evasion: Confronting Market Failure in American Media Policy." *Critical Studies in Media Communication* 31, no. 2: 153–59.

Portwood-Stacer, L. 2013. "Media Refusal and Conspicuous Non-Consumption: The Performative and Political Dimensions of Facebook Abstention." *New Media & Society* 15, no. 7: 1041–57.

Postigo, H. 2016. "The Socio-technical Architecture of Digital Labor: Converting Play into YouTube Money." *New Media and Society* 18, no. 2: 332–49.

Quan, T. 2009. "A Sex Worker's Guide to Craigslist." *Daily Beast*. April 26, 2009. https://www.thedailybeast.com/a-sex-workers-guide-to-craigslist.

Quenqua, D. 2009. "Recklessly Seeking Sex on Craigslist." *Gadsden Times*. April 19, 2009. https://www.gadsdentimes.com/news/20090419/recklessly-seeking-sex-on-craigslist.

Ramsey, D. X. 2015. "The Truth about Black Twitter." *Atlantic*. April 10, 2015. https://www.theatlantic.com/technology/archive/2015/04/the-truth-about-black-twitter/390120/.

Ranganathan, S. R. 1931. *The Five Laws of Library Science*. London: Edward Goldston.

Rao, M. 2008. "eHarmony to Create Same Sex Service, Settling Complaint." *CNN*. November 19, 2008. http://www.cnn.com/2008/LIVING/11/19/eharmony.same.sex.matches/index.html.

Refsal, M. 2012. "I Need to See You Again: Missed Connections Street Art." *Wired*. July 9, 2012. https://www.wired.com/2012/07/missed-connections-street-art/.

Reinan, J. 2014. "How Craigslist Killed the Newspapers' Golden Goose." *MinnPost*. February 3, 2014. https://www.minnpost.com/business/2014/02/how-craigslist-killed-newspapers-golden-goose.

Renninger, B. J. 2015. " 'Where I Can Be Myself . . . Where I Can Speak My Mind': Networked Counterpublics in a Polymedia Environment." *New Media and Society* 17, no. 9: 1513–29.

Reynolds, C. 2015. " 'I Am Super Straight and I Prefer You Be Too': Constructions of Heterosexual Masculinity in Online Personal Ads for 'Straight' Men Seeking Sex with Men." *Journal of Communication Inquiry* 39, no. 3: 213–31.

Reynolds, C. 2017. "Casual Encounters: Constructing Sexual Deviance on Craigslist.org." Unpublished doctoral dissertation, University of Minnesota.

Richtel, M. 2004. "An Online Pioneer Resists the Lure of Cashing In." *New York Times*. September 6, 2004. https://www.nytimes.com/2004/09/06/technology/an-online-pioneer-resists-the-lure-of-cashing-in.html.

Robins, K. 1996. "Cyberspace and the World We Live In." In *Fractal Dreams: New Media in Social Context*, edited by J. Dovey, 1–30. London: Lawrence and Wishard.

Robinson, B. A., and S. Vidal-Ortiz. 2013. "Displacing the Dominant 'Down Low' Discourse: Deviance, Same-Sex Desire, and Craigslist.org." *Deviant Behavior* 34, no. 3: 224–41.

Robinson, D., K. Cosby, G. Gay, and J. Saculles. 2006. *Craigslist Online Community*. Berkeley-Haas Case Series. Berkeley: Regents of University of California.

Rodenbeck, E. 2013. "Mapping Silicon Valley's Gentrification Problem through Corporate Shuttle Routes." *Wired*. September 6, 2013. https://www.wired.com/2013/09/mapping-silicon-valleys-corporate-shuttle-problem/.

Rosenblat, A., and L. Stark. 2016. "Algorithmic Labor and Information Asymmetries: A Case Study of Uber's Drivers." *International Journal of Communication* 10: 3758–84.

Rostow, A. 2005. "The Hottest Spot Online." *Advocate*. August 16, 2005. https://www.questia.com/magazine/1G1-134677455/the-hottest-spot-online-the-explosively-popular.

Rybas, N., and R. Gajjala. 2007. "Developing Cyberethnographic Research Methods for Understanding Digitally Mediated Identities." *Forum: Qualitative Social Research* 8, no. 3. http://www.qualitative-research.net/index.php/fqs/article/view/282.

Salter, L. 2005. "Colonization Tendencies in the Development of the World Wide Web." *New Media and Society* 7, no. 3: 291–309.

Sapnar-Ankerson, M. 2010. "Web Industries, Economies, Aesthetics: Mapping the Look of the Web in the Dot-Com Era." In *Web History*, edited by N. Brügger, 173–93. New York: Peter Lang.

Savage, M., F. Devine, N. Cunningham, M. Taylor, Y. Li, J. Hjellbrekke, and A. Miles. 2013. "A New Model of Social Class?: Findings from the BBC's Great British Class Survey Experiment." *Sociology* 47, no. 2: 219–50.

Savin-Williams, R. 2017. *Mostly Straight: Sexual Fluidity among Men*. Cambridge, MA: Harvard University Press.

Scambler, G. 2007. "Sex Work Stigma: Opportunist Migrants in London." *Sociology* 41, no. 6: 1079–96.

Schulten, K. 2014. "How Sexist Is the Gaming World?" *New York Times*. October 17, 2014. https://learning.blogs.nytimes.com/2014/10/17/how-sexist-is-the-gaming-world/.

Seamans, R., and F. Zhu. 2014. "Responses to Entry in Multi-sided Markets: The Impact of Craigslist on Local Newspapers." *Management Science* 60, no. 2: 476–93.

Serebrin, J. 2015. "VarageSale is the Hottest Canadian Startup No One Has Heard Of." *TechVibes*. January 16, 2015. https://techvibes.com/2015/01/15/varagesale-2015-01-15.

"SF Rooms." n.d. Tumblr. Accessed July 14, 2019. https://sfrooms.tumblr.com/.

Shapiro, A. 2017. "Between Autonomy and Control: Strategies of Arbitrage in the 'On-Demand' Economy." *New Media and Society* 20, no. 8: 2954–71.

Sharma, S. 2013. "Black Twitter?: Racial Hashtags, Networks and Contagion." *New Formations* 7, no. 8: 46–64.

Shifman, L. 2014. *Memes in Digital Culture*. Cambridge, MA: MIT Press.

Sinnreich, A. 2010. *Mashed Up: Music, Technology, and the Rise of Configurable Culture*. Amherst: University of Massachusetts Press.

Sinozich, S., and L. Langton. 2014. *Rape and Sexual Assault Victimization Among College-Age Females, 1995–2013*. Special report NCJ 248471. Washington, DC: Bureau of Justice Statistics. https://www.bjs.gov/content/pub/pdf/rsavcaf9513.pdf.

Sitton, S., and E. T. Rippee. 1986. "Women Still Want Marriage: Sex Differences in Lonely Hearts Advertisements." *Psychological Reports* 58: 257–58.

Smith, C. 2019. "20 Interesting MySpace Statistics and Facts Then and Now (2019)." Digital Media Research. May 10, 2019. https://expandedramblings.com/index.php/myspace-stats-then-now/.

Smith, C. B., M. L. McLaughlin, and K. K. Osborne. 1998. "From Terminal Ineptitude to Virtual Sociopathy: How Conduct Is Regulated on Usenet." In *Network and Netplay*, edited by F. Sudweeks, M. McLaughlin, and S. Rafaeli, 95–112. Cambridge, MA: MIT Press.

Sohn, A. 2003. May 26. "You've Got Tail." *New York Magazine*. May 15, 2003. http://nymag.com /nymetro/nightlife/sex/columns/nakedcity/n_8709/.

Solon, O. 2017. "Airbnb Host Who Canceled Reservation Using Racist Comment Must Pay $5,000." *Guardian*. July 13, 2017. https://www.theguardian.com/technology/2017/jul/13 /airbnb-california-racist-comment-penalty-asian-american.

Spencer, R. D., and G. D. Sesser. 2013. "Provenance: Important, Yes, but Often Incomplete and Often Enough, Wrong." *Artnet News*. June 26, 2013. https://news.artnet.com/market/the -importance-of-provenance-in-determining-authenticity-29953.

Steinmetz, K. 2015. "These Companies Have the Best (and Worst) Privacy Policies." *Time*. August 6, 2015. http://time.com/3986016/google-Facebook-twitter-privacy-policies/.

Stevens, G. E. 1990. "Classified Advertising and the Law." *Newspaper Research Journal* 11, no. 4: 94–104.

Stone, M. 2014. "The Most Extravagant Tech Holiday Parties of the Year." *Business Insider*. December 19, 2014. https://www.businessinsider.com/the-most-extravagant-tech-holiday-parties -of-the-year-2014–12.

Strauss, A., and J. Corbin. 1990. *Basics of Qualitative Research: Grounded Theory Procedures and Techniques*. Thousand Oaks, CA: Sage.

Streeter, T. 1990. "Beyond Freedom of Speech and the Public Interest: The Relevance of Critical Legal Studies to Communications Policy." *Journal of Communication* 40, no. 2: 43–63.

Streeter, T. 2005. "The Moment of Wired." *Critical Inquiry* 31, no. 4: 755–79.

Streitfeld, D. 2018. "How a Villain to Newspapers Is Trying to Save Journalism." *New York Times*. October 18, 2018: B1.

Sundarararjan, A. 2016. *The Sharing Economy: The End of Employment and the Rise of Crowd-Based Capitalism*. Cambridge, MA: MIT Press.

Susman, A. 2017. "Tech Giants' Missteps Highlight Need for More Ad Transparency." *MediaPost*. November 14, 2017. https://www.mediapost.com/publications/article/310225/tech-giants -missteps-highlight-need-for-more-ad-t.html.

Temple, J. 2010. "Craigslist Headquarters Moving to Downtown SF." *SF Gate*. October 31, 2010. https://www.sfgate.com/business/article/craigslist-headquarters-moving-to-downtown-S -F-3247970.php.

Thomas, O. 2009. "Why the Police Pretend to Hate Craigslist's Whoring." *Gawker*. March 5, 2009. http://gawker.com/5164967/why-the-police-pretend-to-hate-craigslists-whoring.

Thoumrungroje, A. 2014. "The Influence of Social Media Intensity and EWOM on Conspicuous Consumption." *Social and Behavioral Sciences* 148: 7–15.

3taps. n.d. "3taps: One-Stop Data Shop for Developers." 3taps Inc. Accessed July 14, 2019. http:// 3taps.com/.

Ticona, J. 2015. "Strategies of Control: Workers' Use of ICTs to Shape Knowledge and Service Work." *Information, Communication and Society* 18, no. 5: 509–523.

Tiidenberg, K. 2016. "Boundaries and Conflict in a NSFW Community on Tumblr: The Meanings and Uses of Selfies." *New Media and Society* 18, no. 8: 1563–78.

Toma, C. L., J. T. Hancock, and N. B. Ellison. 2008. "Separating Fact from Fiction: An Examination of Deceptive Self-Presentation in Online Dating Profiles." *Personality and Social Psychology Bulletin* 34, no. 8: 1023–36.

Trixie the Anonymous Domme. 2010. "A Sex Worker on Life after Craigslist." *Hard for the Money* (blog), *Jezebel*. September 23, 2010. https://jezebel.com/5644988/a-sex-worker-on-life-after -craigslist.

Turner, F. 2010. *From Counterculture to Cyberculture: Stewart Brand, the Whole Earth Network, and the Rise of Digital Utopianism*. Chicago: University of Chicago Press.

Vaidhyanathan, S. 2018. *Antisocial Media: How Facebook Disconnects Us and Undermines Democracy*. Oxford: Oxford University Press.

Van Dijk, J., and K. Hacker. 2003. "The Digital Divide as a Complex and Dynamic Phenomenon." *Information Society* 19, no. 4: 315–26.

Van Doorn, N., and O. Velthuis. 2018. "A Good Hustle: The Moral Economy of Market Competition in Adult Webcam Modeling." *Journal of Cultural Economy* 11, no. 3: 177–92.

Varnelis, K. 2012. *Networked Publics*. Cambridge, MA: MIT Press.

Villas-Boas, A. 2015. "I Tried Using the Internet Anonymously for a Week, but I Caved after a Few Minutes." *Business Insider*. December 29, 2015. https://www.businessinsider.com/anonymous-web-browsing-is-impossible-2015-12.

Wagner, R. P. 2003. "Information Wants to Be Free: Intellectual Property and the Mythologies of Control." *Columbia Law Review* 103: 995–1034.

Walker, J. 2005. "Citizen Journalists: A Threat to Journalism?" *James Walker's Blog*, Press Ethic. December 4, 2005. https://journalism.nyu.edu/publishing/archives/pressethic/node/624.

Waller, A. n.d. "Love Unknown." Angie Waller (website). Accessed February 28, 2019. http://angiewaller.com/love-unknown-2014-ongoing/.

Ward, A. 2018. "4 Main Takeaways from New Reports on Russia's 2016 Election Interference." *Vox*. December 17, 2018. https://www.vox.com/world/2018/12/17/18144523/russia-senate-report-african-american-ira-clinton-instagram.

Ward, J. 2007. "Straight Dude Seeks Same: Mapping the Relationship between Sexual Identities, Practices, and Cultures." In *Sex Matters: The Sexuality and Society Reader*, 2nd ed., edited by M. Stombler, D. M. Baunach, E. O. Burgess, D. Donnelly, and W. Simonds, 31–37. New York: Allyn and Bacon.

Ward, J. 2015. *Not Gay: Sex between Straight White Men*. New York: New York University Press.

Warner, M. 2002. "Publics and Counterpublics." *Public Culture* 14, no. 1: 49–90.

Warschauer, M., and M. Ames. 2010. "Can One Laptop per Child Save the World's Poor?" *Journal of International Affairs* 64, no. 1: 33–51.

Weise, E., and B. Heath. 2017. "*USA Today* Asks FBI to Probe Rise in Fake Facebook Followers." *USA Today*. May 5, 2017. https://www.usatoday.com/story/tech/news/2017/05/05/usa-today-asks-fbi-probe-rise-fake-facebook-followers/101303300/.

Weiss, P. 2006. "A Guy Named Craig." *New York Magazine*. January 6, 2006. http://nymag.com/nymetro/news/media/internet/15500/.

Werde, B. 2003. "Must Sell: Used Sofa, Strokes Tix, My Ass." *Time Out New York*. October 16–23, 2003. https://www.craigslist.org/about/press/mustsell.

Wertz, J. 2009. *I Saw You: Comics Inspired by Real-Life Missed Connections*. New York: Three Rivers.

West, J. 2009. "Craigslist Founder, CEO Accused of $16 Million 'Extortion.'" *NBC San Diego*. December 10, 2009. https://www.nbcsandiego.com/news/tech/craigslist-Founder-CEO-Accused-of-Extortion-by-eBay-Executive-jw-78984292.html.

White, M. 2012. *Buy It Now: Lessons from eBay*. Durham, NC: Duke University Press.

Wildermuth, S. M. 2004. "The Effects of Stigmatizing Discourse on the Quality of On-Line Relationships." *Cyberpsychology and Behavior* 7, no. 1: 73–84.

Williams, R. 1973. "Base and Superstructure in Marxist Cultural Theory." *New Left Review* 82: 3.

Williams, S. 2016. "The Difficulties of Dating with a Disability." *Vice*. November 10, 2016. https://www.vice.com/en_us/article/bn37dz/the-difficulties-of-dating-with-a-disability.

Wired staff. 2009. "Why craigslist Is Such a Mess." *Wired*. August 24, 2009. https://www.wired.com/2009/08/ff-craigslist/.

Wortham, J. 2009. "Missed Connections as Artwork." *Bits* (blog), *New York Times*. September 29, 2009. https://bits.blogs.nytimes.com/2009/09/29/craigslists-missed-connections-as-art/?_r=0.

Wu, T. 2018. *The Curse of Bigness: Antitrust in the New Gilded Age*. New York: Columbia Global Reports.

Zekas, J. 2012. "Why PadMapper Is Worse than Useless for Chicago Renters." *YoChicago*. April 17, 2012. http://yochicago.com/why-padmapper-is-worse-than-useless-for-chicago-renters /26459/.

Zimmer, M. 2010. " 'But the Data Is Already Public': On the Ethics of Research in Facebook." *Ethics and Information Technology* 12, no. 4: 313–25.

Zimmer, M. 2016. "OkCupid Study Reveals the Perils of Big-Data Science." *Wired*. May 14, 2016. https://www.wired.com/2016/05/OkCupid-study-reveals-perils-big-data-science/.

Zukin, S. 1987. "Gentrification: Culture and Capital in the Urban Core." *Annual Review of Sociology* 13, no. 1: 129–47.

Zukin, S. 2009. *Naked City: The Death and Life of Authentic Urban Places*. Oxford: Oxford University Press.

Zyskowski, K., M. R. Morris, J. P. Bigham, M. L. Gray, and S. K. Kane. 2015. "Accessible Crowdwork?: Understanding the Value in and Challenge of Microtask Employment for People with Disabilities." In *Proceedings of the 18th ACM Conference on Computer Supported Cooperative Work and Social Computing*, edited by L. Ciolfi and D. McDonald, 1682–93. New York: ACM.

INDEX

Acker, Amelia, 159
Allow States and Victims to Fight Online Sex Trafficking Act of 2017 (FOSTA), 13, 53, 57–58, 63–64, 114–15, 119–23, 125, 129–30
Amazon: breakup of, advocates for, 156; extravagant parties of, 25; impact in the marketplace of, 2
anonymity: craigslist vs. the mainstream web on, 149–51; by default, double-edged sword of, 143–48; in defense of, 154–56; as a defining feature of craigslist, 143; flagging and, 141–42; litigation relating to, 175n1; online dating and, 123–25; people problems, as a response to, 132, 142–48; physical safety and, 135; politics of, 149–51; safety and, 146–48. *See also* trust
Atamer, Allen, 139–40, 165
Ayres, Jen, 10, 68, 166

bad actors online: anonymity and, 143–48 (*see also* anonymity); assigning blame for bad behavior, 136–37; craigslist's tools for responding to, 132, 138; flagging as a response to, 138–42; potential for, 29, 51; predecessors in classified ads, 44–45; problems of, 132–36; safety and violence, concerns about, 134–35; sexual depravity and financial fraud, moral panics regarding, 49. *See also* scams/scammers; spam
Baekdal, Thomas, 47
Batt, Anthony, 22–25, 165
Bezos, Jeff, 23
bots, 120
boyd, danah, 107, 109, 112
Breyer, Charles, 61–62
Bridges, Andrew, 165
Brisman, Julissa, 55–56
Brown, Matthew Brian, 144

Buckmaster, Jim: blog written by, 10, 169; CEO, longevity as, 3; CEO, selection as, 27; corner office of, 28; on design values, 30, 110; "extortionist," described as a, 173n1; and the fight with eBay, 34–36; Newmark and, 27; on personal ads, 55; platform politics, commitment to a vision of, 154; print-media journalists, criticisms of, 48–49; as shareholder, 34
buying and selling. *See* classified ads; secondary market, the

California Ideology, 20–21, 37
capitalism: the secondary market as critique of, 67, 73–75, 80–81; the secondary market as part of, 80
Cardona, Rich, 169
CDA. *See* Communications Decency Act
Chandler, William, III, 35–36
Chun, Wendy, 6, 149–50, 159
class: craigslist and, 90–91, 103–6, 110–12; gentrification and, 109–10; methodological issues regarding, 174n3; Myspace vs. Facebook and, 106–9
classified ads, 39–40, 49–50; anonymity as a feature of, 143; bad actors and, 44–45; counterpublics and, 41–44; legal liability for publishers of, 45; marketing ads and, distinctions between, 40–41; as a media form, 40–45; personal ads (*see* personal ads); revenue, as a source of, 43, 45–48
Cocks, H. G., 40–44
Communications Decency Act (CDA), 52–54, 57, 63, 153
community moderation: flagging as, 138–42; paradox of, 149
Cooper, Steve, 155
Cox Enterprises, 48
Craig Newmark Philanthropies, 32, 48

A NOTE ON THE TYPE

This book has been composed in Adobe Text and Gotham. Adobe Text, designed by Robert Slimbach for Adobe, bridges the gap between fifteenth- and sixteenth-century calligraphic and eighteenth-century Modern styles. Gotham, inspired by New York street signs, was designed by Tobias Frere-Jones for Hoefler & Co.